UNNECESSARY ROUGHNESS

UNNECESSARY ROUGHNESS

ROUGHNESS

INSIDE THE TRIAL AND FINAL DAYS OF
AARON HERNANDEZ

JOSE BAEZ

WITH GEORGE WILLIS

hachette
BOOKS

NEW YORK   BOSTON

Hachette Books
Hachette Book Group
1290 Avenue of the Americas, New York, NY 10104
hachettebooks.com
twitter.com/hachettebooks

First Edition: August 2018
Hachette Books is a division of Hachette Book Group, Inc.
The Hachette Books name and logo are trademarks of Hachette Book Group, Inc.

The publisher is not responsible for websites (or their content)
that are not owned by the publisher.

The Hachette Speakers Bureau provides a wide range of authors for speaking events.
To find out more, go to www.hachettespeakersbureau.com or call (866) 376-6591.

Editorial production by Christine Marra, Marrathon Production Services.
www.marrathoneditorial.org

Book design by Jane Raese
Set in 12-point Chaparral

LCCN 2018945257

ISBN 978-1-60286-607-2 (hardcover); ISBN 978-1-60286-606-5 (ebook)

Printed in the United States of America

LSC-H

10 9 8 7 6 5 4 3 2 1

DEDICATION

When Aaron Hernandez and I sat down for two days straight as he told me his entire life story, I could not believe the incredible life he had lived in such a short time. I thought the story was the most interesting I had ever heard, but I also felt it would never see the light of day.

It wasn't until after his trial was over and we awaited the verdict that we discussed the idea that I could be the one to tell his story. His interest in the project was not a forecast of his intentions to commit suicide as much as an acknowledgment that he was tired of people who didn't know him telling lies or spinning the truth. Ethically I could not tell his story without his informed consent, so I gave him time to think about it. A couple of days later he told me, *"I want you to tell it, Jose, and don't hold back. Tell the good, the bad, and the ugly."* I told him I would think about it, and I really had no intention of revisiting the subject until after his death.

Aaron's death has affected me in ways I cannot begin to describe. You're not taught in law school how to deal with situations and scenarios like the ones I encountered with Aaron. I could not sit idly by as people who didn't even know him came out of the woodwork, telling outrageous stories about Aaron. He was dead, but many people were not content until they could dance on his grave.

This story is filled with tragedy and victims: Daniel De Abreu, Safiro Furtado, Odin Llyod, Aaron Hernandez, their families, and the countless football players who carry inside them the silent killer of CTE—including the children who play this game, idolizing their heroes on the gridiron. It is for this reason that I dedicate this book to a number of children. First to two very special children in my heart: to Avielle Hernandez, may you take the gift that God and your parents have given you and live life to the fullest and remember that your father had so many wonderful qualities and touched many people in many special ways. His truth will always lie in your heart, as you are the living proof of the good in him. He loved you beyond words and will always be by your side.

To my own son, Jose Baez Jr., who will never play tackle football, so don't even think about it! What many people don't know is during the trial I was also going through a divorce and my family was adjusting to a new way of life. It was you, my son, who inspired me then and still do, along with your sister, Christina, to hope that one day you will be proud of your daddy. I am already proud of you and love you with all my heart and soul.

To all of the children whose parents might read this book and realize that a game is not worth the risk of a future: this brain disease is real, and I pray for your parents' wisdom. God bless you all.

CONTENTS

Foreword by Shayanna Jenkins-Hernandez · · · · · · · · · · · · ix

1. The Beginning or the End · 1

2. Fuck Yeah! · 8

3. Blood in Boston · 16

4. Magical Monday and the Luck of the Irish · · · · · · · · · · 26

5. The Not So Anonymous Call · · · · · · · · · · · · · · · · · · · 34

6. A Video Game Called *Motive* · · · · · · · · · · · · · · · · · · 46

7. Making of a Murder Weapon · · · · · · · · · · · · · · · · · · · 56

8. *Weekend at Bernie's* · 67

9. Eye Phone · 77

10. Sharrod the Shooter · 90

11. Trapping a Rat · 106

12. Patriot Games · 114

13. Who Shot Odin Lloyd? · 127

14. Prison Life · 137

15. Family Matters · 146

16. Would You Please Convict If There's No Evidence? · · · · · 160

CONTENTS

17. Independent and Not So Independent Witnesses   170

18. The Street Sweeper   180

19. Marinating the Jury   190

20. Desperate Measures   206

21. Tears behind the Glass   213

22. WTF?   227

23. The Battle for the Brain   235

24. Chronic Traumatic Encephalopathy   244

Acknowledgments   259

Index   261

FOREWORD

Shayanna Jenkins-Hernandez

When I signed the papers giving Aaron's brain to the Boston University Chronic Traumatic Encephalopathy (CTE) Center it was a decision I made as his fiancée, along with Aaron's defense team. If I could potentially help someone else, why not do it? Also, I wanted answers. I wanted to know why my fiancé died just when there was hope he might someday come home. There's still a ton of answers I want. But this is a start.

This may sound weird to say about someone you love, but I feel like CTE researchers hit the jackpot when they got Aaron's brain. Of course the news that he had Stage 3 CTE, how severe it was, and that he had the brain of someone so much older was devastating for us to hear. But if examining the condition of his brain can help others, especially football players, Aaron would be pleased. It's like he's back on a team again.

I have loved Aaron Hernandez since we were in high school. I will love him until the day I die. I miss his smile every day and I miss seeing him being a father to our daughter. My prayer is that he is finally at peace. Free of chains, bars, courtrooms, and judgment. I cried when Jose Baez and his law partner Ron Sullivan told me the news that Aaron had suffered such a severe case of CTE. After all we had been through—his arrest, his trials, and his death—it was still devastating news. I cried because I realized I had tried to help him for so long, but there was nothing I could have done. I cried because there was a battle going on within his brain and he didn't even know it. None of us did.

We met in grade school, became friends in middle school, and were sweethearts at Bristol Central High School. I ran track. He was a football player. He was very popular, and I was just trying to get through school and get good grades. He had girls vying for his attention, and I had a strict mom at home, who was a single parent. But even though we were raised differently, we got along. We talked; we became close.

When he left for the University of Florida, I went to community college and let him do his own thing. He was a baby. I wanted him to grow up and experience all he needed to experience. Our relationship was on and off until he showed up at my work one day, not long after he was drafted by the Patriots.

I was working three jobs, but soon moved into his apartment in Plainview, Massachusetts. Then I became pregnant with Avielle. He proposed at my baby shower in front of almost fifty people, and in what seems like a blink, Avielle was born on Aaron's birth date. We moved into our dream home and everything was going the way it was supposed to. Life wasn't perfect by any means, but it was close.

Then on June 26, 2013, he was arrested and charged with shooting Odin Lloyd, and our lives were never the same. My sympathies go out to all the victims. Murder can never be condoned. But Aaron never got a fair trial—in the media or in court. He listened to people he thought would give him the best legal advice and although they tried, I don't think they tried hard enough, which makes me extremely upset. We could have avoided so much, and maybe he would still be alive. When I heard the guilty verdict, it kicked in that he wasn't coming home. I was going to have to raise our child all by myself and lose the love of my life, all in one fell swoop.

I cried even more when in 2017 he was found innocent of an earlier crime, the 2012 Boston double murders of Daniel de Abreu and Safiro Furtado, because I knew there was victory ahead. He was finally acquitted. We (Jose and his team were his defense attorneys) knew our fighting wasn't going to waste. That's why I believe Aaron cried so much when they said "not guilty." We had waited so long and fought so hard. We realized we were moving in the right direction.

When someone from the prison informed me by telephone that Aaron had died, I cried the tears that come with tragedy. I first called my lawyers to try to figure out whether it was a hoax, because people had been very cruel. After the victory he had, and having spoken to him the day before, I couldn't imagine him committing suicide.

A few calls later I learned it was true. Aaron was dead. I thought, What do I do now? I raced to the hospital, but the doctors wouldn't let me be with him. His death was still under investigation, they said. Someone told me he wasn't even at the hospital, but that was a lie because I saw him being wheeled into a room. He had died alone. I didn't want him to be alone any longer. I wanted to see him while all of him was still intact. I wanted to hold him.

Instead of being with my fiancé, I was told I had to wait. I didn't see him until days later when he was already embalmed and prepared for his funeral. It was beyond awful.

There has been much speculation about Aaron's sexuality since his death. I can say this: Aaron was very much a man to me. I saw no indication that he was gay or homosexual. I wish I had known how he felt, just so we could have talked about it. I wouldn't have disowned him. I would have been supportive. I can't fault him if he was feeling that way. When you love someone so much you just want to be there to support them. The fact that he felt he couldn't come out to me or he couldn't tell me these things hurts, because we had that bond. I've accepted that he may have been the way he was said to be, or that it may not be true. Regardless, I won't know.

The alarming part is we'll never know exactly what was going through Aaron's mind during those final days, months, and years, and what impact CTE had. Things I never picked up on, now I sit back and question. What was the real reason for this outburst or that outburst or him forgetting to do this, that, and a hundred different things? It's hard to imagine how many people have CTE and their families have no idea.

I haven't figured out how to tell my daughter about everything that happened. Avielle is healthy, and I'm breathing. She's very smart and asks a bunch of questions, especially about Daddy. When the time is right and she really wants to understand, I think she'll be all right. She's smart for her age, and that's important considering what she may face in the future.

In his last note, written moments before he died, Aaron asked me to tell his story. I also know he had a similar conversation with Jose, because he felt he had a fighter in Jose: a big brother who would defend him to the end. Aaron and Jose grew extremely close during Aaron's final year on earth. Jose never judged him. He was only there to help; that help extended to me and Avielle. Even after Aaron's passing, Jose is still here willing to keep fighting for Aaron and his legacy.

The easiest thing for Jose to do is to take his incredible legal victory, which was achieved against all odds, and move on, but that is not Jose. I hope all those who read this book see what we went through and understand the importance of having someone in your corner. While that was my role in Aaron's heart, Jose maintained that role in the courtroom.

I also want to recognize that Jose was not alone. He put together the greatest legal team, which included Harvard professor Ronald Sullivan, Linda Kenney-Baden, George Leontire, and Michelle Medina. They became and to this day remain family, to not only Aaron but to Avielle and myself. I'm glad Jose is telling Aaron's story. This is an insider's story written by the man who knew him best at a time of triumph and tragedy. I'm glad the truth will finally be told.

1.

THE BEGINNING
OR THE END

This was the part Aaron Hernandez hated most: having to say goodbye. The telephone calls with his high school sweetheart and devoted fiancée, Shayanna, were never long enough. Their talks were his chance to escape the confines of prison and connect to a life outside the walls that kept closing in on him. "Babe, they're locking up now," Aaron said after a guard gave him that nod to end his call.

Shayanna Jenkins-Hernandez also hated this part. Outwardly, she was free to live her life. But she was in bondage too. The telephone calls to her fiancé were their only communication now, until she and her daughter, Avielle, could make their next visit. Each phone call had meaning; a couple sharing their day like any other couple would.

"I love you," Shayanna whispered.

"I love you too," Aaron said. "I'll call you tomorrow."

Shayanna would later speak of how their talk had been a good one. They dared to dream about a day when Aaron would be out of prison and free to be the father and husband he hoped he could be. He had been acquitted of double murder charges five days earlier, and now his previous conviction for the death of Odin Lloyd in 2013 would be appealed.

Home to Aaron for now was Souza-Baranowski Correctional Center in Lancaster, Massachusetts, located about an hour's drive west of Boston. The maximum-security prison is where he was inmate W106228 serving, in what seems like a hopeless existence, life without parole. He would be there for two years. Handcuffed and dressed in the white and red wardrobe for prisoners, Aaron would be escorted back to his cell as he always was. Any guard, in a test of strength, would be no match for the younger, stronger, former Pro Bowl tight end. But as Aaron liked to say, "Those days are over."

As they reached the second floor of the G2 housing unit the guard yelled, "Open cell 57." Those heavy metal doors separate slowly, often squeaking like a pig in pain.

This was the kind of night Aaron often told Shayanna about. The nights when his trademark smile is gone and it's back to his reality: the loneliness, the solitude, and the bright light through the window.

Aaron would often describe how he'd sit down on his bunk and rub his temples. His friends knew of his frequent migraines that began with a dull ache in his head. They had become more frequent of late. He would lie down and throw a T-shirt over his eyes to block the light shining through the small, barred window about eighteen inches wide and three feet long.

"My head is going to explode" is how he once described it to Shayanna.

The migraines came with hot flashes. That's what he called them. He would then strip off his T-shirt and jailhouse pants until his six-foot-two tattooed body was naked. He had mentioned doing this a lot in recent days, going from hot to cold, cold to hot. He would pace, holding his head.

Aaron said it took three steps to pace from one end of the cell to the other. Back and forth he would pace, trying to concentrate on the steps to help keep his mind off his pain.

He would think all kinds of things. If you knew Aaron, there was only one thing that brought him comfort in times like this: a picture of his four-year-old daughter, Avielle. She always made him smile. She always made him feel better. Avielle, born on Aaron's birth date of November 6, looks just like Shayanna; she has brown cocoa skin and gorgeous hazel eyes just like her mother. To Aaron his daughter and her mother are symbols of strength, beauty, love, and better times.

"How is it possible to love someone so much," Aaron would say. "Did I fuck it up?"

Prison is scary quiet at night except for the sounds of an occasional cough, or a scream. No one really knows what Aaron was thinking on this night, or even if he was in his right mind. No one knows what kind of pain he felt.

When did Aaron decide this would be his last night on earth? Maybe the disease CTE knows. He was upbeat when he talked to me on the telephone earlier in the day. "I'm so happy," he said. "I can't remember the last time I was this happy."

One moment he is lost in love and thankfulness, looking forward to a future as a free man again. Then the depression and the pain must have come back.

Prison was his reality; the reality behind the smile. The past, the present, the pain, the paranoia had taken Aaron from the highest high to the lowest low; from playing in front of thousands of cheering fans to being alone in a prison cell.

Aaron became religious in prison. He had learned from his college coach Urban Meyer that the Bible was the word of God, and those who believed would have everlasting life; an everlasting life free from judgment, free from pain, and free from depression.

Aaron reached for the Bible on his final night. Perhaps he was searching for a promise. At some point he turned to the New Testament, John 3:16: "For God so loved the world that He gave his only begotten Son that whosoever believes in Him should not perish but have everlasting life."

Prison had been a constant battle: fighting the justice system, fighting inmates, fighting officers, and fighting the depression caused by his choices. A drop of blood falls on the scripture and John 3:16 would be scribbled in blood on Aaron's forehead. Somewhere during this time, Aaron must have decided that life was no longer worth living.

VARIOUS CORRECTIONAL and law enforcement reports detail a timeline account of the final hours of Aaron Hernandez's life. He deserved a better ending than this. Here's what's believed to have happened.

It's 3:00 A.M. on April 19, 2017. Corrections Officer Gerard Breau is making his normal rounds at the G2 housing unit at Souza-Baranowski Correctional Center. He is working the 11:00 P.M. to 7:00 A.M. shift. As he slowly walks the unit's second floor, Breau looks into inmates' door windows to make sure they're where they're supposed to be. It's normally a boring routine.

Breau reaches cell 57 and stops. There is a cloth or curtain of some sort blocking the window, preventing him from seeing into the cell. A lifelong Patriots fan, Breau knows it's a private cell for Aaron Hernandez, the former football star. Breau knocks on the door. There's no response. He knocks again with more force. Again, there is no response.

Breau, bald and stocky, looks up to see part of what appears to be a curtain sticking through the top of the door. It's not uncommon for an inmate to do that. It's their way of having some fun with the guards. Breau reaches up, grabs the cloth, and slides it to the side, allowing him to look into the cell. His eyes grow wide with shock.

Aaron Hernandez is naked, his tattoo-covered body dangling lifeless from a white bedsheet wrapped tightly around his neck. The bedsheet is attached to a bar in a back window, located a few feet higher than his six-foot-two, 240-pound frame.

"Oh shit. Oh fuck," Breau says.

With adrenaline flooding his body, Breau reaches for his radio and clicks it on. "Code 99. Repeat, Code 99 . . . Inmate hanging, G2 cell 57," he yells. "Repeat, Code 99. It's Aaron!"

Regulations for officer safety prevent Breau from entering without a supervisor's approval. He begins to pace nervously as he waits for a response team to arrive. Seconds seem like minutes.

Breau wonders whether he missed something during his rounds earlier that night. At this point he realizes the screwup. He did not make his rounds in the last hour, contrary to policy making it mandatory to check on inmates every hour. There will be hell to pay for this.

At 3:05 A.M. Corrections Officers Shawnn Gyles, Mathew Way, and Nicholas Lawton arrive and give the okay to enter the cell. Breau hurriedly unlocks the door and tries to push it open. There's resistance. It barely budges.

"Help me," Breau says. "It won't open."

It takes the strength of three grown men—Gyles, Way, and Breau—to push the door open. Once inside they see that it had been blocked by various paper materials, including a piece of cardboard from the back of a notepad. They also quickly notice that the floor of the small cell is covered with a soapy substance, perhaps shampoo. It's hard to keep their balance.

The corrections officers' instincts are to save Aaron's life. Breau rushes to grab Aaron's nude body by the legs while Gyles follows regulations by handcuffing the inmate's wrists. It seems like a useless exercise but it follows regulations. Gyles then helps Breau lift

Aaron's lifeless body upward to relieve the pressure from around his neck.

Officer Way, who is built like a power lifter, grabs a pair of shears brought into the cell and tries to cut through the bedsheet wrapped around Aaron's neck. The sheet is tighter than wet rope.

Officers and medical personnel throughout the prison have been alerted. The whole prison is abuzz. Soon the cell has more people than it can hold. Sergeant David Lambert is next to arrive and begins assisting Breau and Gyles to hold up Aaron in case there is some chance for a miracle.

All are struggling with maintaining their leverage on the slippery floor. Way meanwhile is still having trouble cutting through the fabric. The shears are dull and the bedsheet is wound with knots meticulously tied in different locations.

"It's just not cutting," Way says in frustration.

Corrections Officers Tyler Courtney and Edmond Pavia, along with a medical team consisting of nurses Kelly Ryder and Coleen Narvaez, arrive at the cell. As Way struggles to cut through the sheet, Courtney stands on the bed and helps lift Aaron's cold body by pushing under his arm, creating more slack in the bedsheet.

It takes nearly two minutes of frantic cutting before the dull shears finally slice through the bedsheet. It seems like it took forever. Once the material is cut, Aaron is lowered to the floor and Courtney loosens and then removes the noose from around his neck.

Is he still alive? Is he breathing? Ryder checks for a pulse. There is none. Aaron isn't breathing. Breau, Gyles, and Lawton immediately begin CPR. There is still no response.

Ryder looks closer at Aaron's body and sees he has defecated on himself. His body is cyanotic. He is cold to the touch and his ears and lips are blue: all signs of death.

As CPR continues, Ryder radios for a life support ambulance that will bring advanced life-saving equipment and an experienced paramedic.

Ten minutes after Aaron is first discovered, a stretcher arrives at his cell. Other inmates are straining through their small door windows to see what's going on. Aaron's body is placed on a stretcher, his hands still in restraints, and carried by corrections officers to a downstairs holding room where he is placed on a gurney where Courtney continues CPR at a rate of one hundred compressions per minute.

At 3:25 A.M. the ambulance arrives. Paramedics take over medical care and hook Aaron to a heart monitor. They also stick an intravenous line into his leg. Everyone is moving quickly. Time is of the essence. No one is ready to give up.

As Aaron is being placed in the ambulance, the gurney somehow gets stuck halfway in. This can't be happening. Courtney continues CPR while an EMT officer struggles to unhinge the gurney. "Push," he tells his team. After a hard shove, the gurney slides into the ambulance. The door closes. Aaron is leaving prison, but not the way he imagined.

He is transported to UMass Memorial-HealthAlliance Hospital in nearby Leominster, Massachusetts, where he is placed in emergency room one. Hospital personnel greet the ambulance and resume life-saving measures.

Among those working on Aaron is Dr. Evan Swayze, an emergency medicine doctor with seventeen years of experience. He knows it is hopeless. Aaron's body, still in restraints, has shown no sign of life since it was discovered an hour earlier. Swayze takes a step back and pronounces time of death at 4:07 A.M.

Aaron Hernandez, the former high school standout, college All-American, and NFL football star, was pronounced dead while naked and in restraints. He was twenty-seven years old.

2.

FUCK YEAH!

The letter arrived on May 15, 2016.

Jose,

I have heard a lot about you from Kristina and I'm very intrigued. I am not sure where to start but I really just want to touch base with you on everything on my end, where I'm at in my thoughts going forward. I, also, want to know about your mindset on appeals and your experience with them. I have heard that your resume is very impressive, the reason I'm reaching out to you. Hopefully, this may lead to something positive in my future.

As you, most likely, know, I am currently serving a life sentence for a crime I didn't do. Yes, all convicts say their [sic] innocent, or most, but there are actually many that truly are as I'm sure you know being in this profession dealing with this corrupt system. My trial was definitely not a fair trial; I was convicted before I went to trial; it was all over the media, evidence allowed in court as well as evidence not admissible.

That's only the beginning of it, but all in all, theres [sic] so much to talk of if we go forward in the future. It all depends on if your [sic] interested, if could truly help, and where you head is at with this. I'm just trying to fight for my life and not do life for some something I didn't do. My CO-D, one of them just beat his case and was only convicted of accessory after the fact, sentenced to a 4½ to 7 year bid. The other hasn't went to trial yet. I truly believe there's a ton of things to attack in this trial, or at least I hope but time will tell. I have two lawyers currently working on my appeal—court appointed. I'm not sure your views on everything but going forward if you could truly help we will figure a way to make it happen in this battle marathon to get my freedom back.

I am going to trial soon for another murder trial which I should win but who knows with this system. I just hope I receive a fair trial. There is a lot going on and I just wanted to touch base with you hoping something positive can come from it. So if you have a second, I would truly appreciate you getting back to me letting me know your mindset on whatever comes to mind. I hope you're interested for I feel that something can be done to take steps closer to my freedom.

I am going to let you go. I hope to hear from you soon. I hope all your loved ones are doing well. As well as yourself. I will be in touch!

Sent with respect,
Aaron Hernandez
W106228
P.O. Box 8000
Shirley, MA 01464

I'd known of Aaron Hernandez long before that letter arrived. I went to Florida State University (FSU) in the early 1990s and was a big college football fan. I have to admit that when I first saw Aaron playing tight end for the University of Florida, the main in-state rival school of FSU, I didn't like him. After seeing him destroy my Seminoles on the football field, I was sure I hated him.

Still, I followed him when he got drafted by the Patriots in 2010 and as he emerged as a young star in the NFL. He reached the Super Bowl in 2011 and I remembered he had signed a $40 million contract. I admired him for being one of the few Hispanic players in the NFL to make it.

I immediately took notice when he was named as the number one suspect in the murder of Odin Lloyd, who had been dating Shayanna's sister. I thought there was a good chance I might be on the short list of lawyers he was considering hiring for his case. We shared a Puerto Rican heritage and had ties to the state of Florida. I even asked around to see if anyone had heard my name being mentioned. I got mixed feedback. A reporter called me and told me he had heard I was being mentioned by sources close to Aaron, but that turned out to not be true. I didn't get the call. When elite athletes get themselves in trouble, they go to their agents and managers.

You look at guys like Aaron and Mike Tyson, the former heavyweight champion convicted of rape. They follow their handlers' advice, and their handlers base their judgments on their relationships, not necessarily who is the best person for the job.

So Aaron ended up with a lead attorney in his first case named Michael K. Fee, who worked for a large national law firm. Those lawyers do not try murder cases. Usually their cases are white-collar crimes, if they do any criminal work at all. Trust me when I tell you there is a *huge* difference between the worlds of murder and white-collar-crime cases. I would be surprised if he had ever represented a defendant in a murder case. The truth is I don't know. Aaron had millions of dollars and could have put up a defense that most accused citizens could only dream of, but that was the case. His dream team failed him. He was convicted for murdering Lloyd and sentenced to life without parole.

At this point I was reluctant to defend him on charges of killing two men during a shooting at a downtown traffic light in Boston in

July 2012. It's difficult to defend someone in a murder case—and even more difficult when they've already been convicted of murder and have a reputation as a thug, gangbanger, and reckless athlete who had blown a prosperous career in the NFL. I also questioned whether he had the financial resources to build a proper defense. Hiring a defense team and investigators takes money. Aaron had signed a $40 million contract extension with the New England Patriots in August of 2012, with part of the $12.5 million signing bonus deferred. When he was arrested in June 2013, the Patriots released him from the team and refused to pay the remaining $3.2 million of his signing bonus.

I figured I would at least meet Aaron and hear what he had to say. A week after he contacted me, I met him for the first time in the visiting room at Souza-Baranowski. I asked my good friend and colleague Ronald S. Sullivan Jr. to come with me. "Sully," as we call him, is a Harvard law professor, and I figured if I ended up taking the case it would be good to have someone I trusted nearby to help out.

The first thing I noticed was that Aaron was bigger than I expected. He was listed as six foot two, but believe me, Aaron was much bigger. He looked more like six four, 250 pounds. I had represented football players before, and Aaron looked the part and then some. Although he was heavily tattooed and in prison, his smile and handshake were warm and friendly.

We met in a part of the prison that looked like a large cafeteria, but wasn't. It was where inmates had their contact visits with their families. As lawyers we were allowed to go into a private room and speak to Aaron with plenty of privacy, while a guard stood outside the door. Aaron was gracious and complimentary when we met. He extended his hand and we gave each other a firm handshake. "Man, I have heard so much about you," he said. "Thank you so much for coming to see me. I really appreciate it."

We sat down and began by discussing the appeal of his conviction in the Odin Lloyd case. He was very concerned with the fact that he felt he did not get a fair trial. He explained how before he set foot in a real courtroom, the court of public opinion had already convicted him.

"Welcome to my world," I chimed in. Absolutely every person accused in a high-profile case feels convicted before the trial begins. Our laws do not protect the constitutional presumption of innocence the way they protect the constitutionally based freedom of the press. Unless the defense lawyer knows exactly how to address this in each and every phase of the trial, they will likely lose. Unfortunately, 99 percent of the lawyers out there have never handled a national high-profile case before, or do not invest the time in the minute details required to truly combat media-induced bias in the courtroom. As I was explaining this to Aaron, I could see that he was following every word and asking serious, insightful questions.

Like, "So you take the approach of attempting to insert reasonable doubt not only during jury selection but in all phases of the trial, including but not limited to cross-examination?"

This is no stupid jock, I thought to myself.

Our conversation shifted to the Boston double-murder trial he was set to start in a couple of months. His initial thoughts were to hire me for the appeal and continue working with his current lawyers on the trial in Boston. He liked his current lawyers; he thought they were capable and had genuine feelings of affection for them.

"I think if you like your lawyers you should stay with them, and let's talk again after your double-murder trial because if you lose that one, the Odin Lloyd appeal is almost meaningless." He quickly followed the logic and asked, "How would you feel about representing me in the Boston case?"

"Well, let's talk about it. Tell me what happened," I said.

"I didn't do it," Aaron told me, his eyes piercing.

"Okay," I said. "Tell me what you know."

"It was my boy Sharrod. He had some beef with those dudes. I still don't know why he did that shit. But my dumb ass just kept hanging around him like an idiot. It was almost as if we had one of those toxic relationships where you really care about someone but you just know they are no good for you. Do you know what I mean?"

He said this in a way that expressed real affection for this Sharrod guy; not in a homosexual way, but like a brother. I asked him, "But, Aaron, you had so much. Why would you risk it all for someone like that?"

He dipped his head, stared down at his hands on the table, and said, "I know. I can't explain it. Sometimes I have extreme difficulty with impulse control. It's like I can't control it and I constantly go back and question why the fuck do I hang out with these people? And why don't I just say no."

He literally used the words "extreme difficulty with impulse control."

Then he continued. "Jose, believe me. I am innocent. I have never killed anyone. Anyone, period," he said emphatically. "I just do some really stupid shit, and I can never understand why."

We then discussed the Boston case at length. Sharrod, whose real name was Alexander Bradley, had testified before a grand jury and Aaron had received a copy of the transcript from his lawyers. Aaron had it committed to memory and could almost recite Bradley's testimony verbatim. But as we talked more, I noticed Aaron sometimes had an amazing memory and sometimes a horrible one. He couldn't even give me the name of some of his lawyers. Or of people who handled his money.

It was odd. One minute I felt I was talking to an incredibly intelligent and sophisticated man; another minute I felt like I was speaking to a child. Aaron seemed more frustrated by the lapses than I was. I could see he really disliked that part of himself.

One thing I noticed right away and throughout the entire time I knew him was his heart. It was genuine. He wasn't a fake. He owned his flaws and never made excuses for them. He also had a sense of humor, which I could tell was going to make this case interesting, to say the least.

There was an immediate bond. We were both of Puerto Rican descent, and we had some similarities in our personalities. He always understood what I meant and how I meant it. Most lawyers like to speak in legalese and always keep a certain distance from their clients. It's like they feel that some of their dirt or criminality is going to rub off on them. I am not that way. I like to understand my clients. I try to speak to them on a level that's real. I believe if you truly understand the person you're representing, you can convey that to a jury, and in many ways the jury can see them through you as you fight for their cause. People always ask me, "What's your secret to winning cases?" I don't know. I wish I could bottle it up and sell it. But I know this much. Understanding your client and remembering that you are not only fighting for them, but also for the family who wants them back home is key to showing the jury a level of sincerity that wins trials. Many lawyers simply do not understand or want to understand their clients, and are "just doing their job."

I wanted Aaron to immediately understand what I was trying to do. So I looked him in the eye and told him: "I'm Jose, nice to meet you. I'm your new best friend, your priest, your father, your brother, everything. People have to see you through me. When I try your case, I want people to look at me and believe as I'm defending you that I'm you, or at least that we're relatable."

That was the beginning of my relationship with an Aaron Hernandez that probably no one else really knew. An Aaron Hernandez who died way too young, for reasons no one understands.

We met for more than eight hours that day. I looked at the case from his perspective as we talked, and saw the state's case had more holes in it than Swiss cheese; but it was being held together by Aaron's bad-boy gangster image. Usually when the media hype is keeping a case together and not the evidence, my eyes light up and

I can feel the hair on the back of my neck stand up, because I can see something is just not right. At the end of our meeting that day, I said to him: "Aaron, get ready, 'cause we are about to start some shit up!" I could see Aaron's mood light up like a rising phoenix as he slapped my extended hand and with a smile said, "Fuck yeah!"

3.

BLOOD IN BOSTON

Aquilino Freire was catching up on some much needed rest and never heard his cell phone ring when his friends Gerson Lopes and Raychides Gomes Sanches called from Providence. It was Sunday morning, July 15, 2012. After getting no answer, Lopes, twenty-four, and Sanches, thirty, decided to take Lopes's car and make the hour's drive to Freire's home and ring his doorbell. That's when Freire woke up.

"Yo, wake up," his friends shouted as he opened the door.

Freire, twenty-six, had arrived from Cape Verde, a small island off the coast of West Africa, four years earlier and had since lived in the Dorchester section of Boston, where there is a large concentration of African Americans and foreign-born immigrants from the Caribbean, West Africa, and Asia.

Freire, known as "Delmar" to those close to him, invited his friends in. He wasn't at all surprised they were there. This was a weekend ritual of sorts. Going out and having a good time was all part of the American dream. It was time to decide on their plans for the day and into the evening.

"My baby mama is having a cookout at her house," Freire said. "It's my baby mama's brother's birthday. Do you want to go?"

All agreed it would be a good way to start the day. Some food, a few drinks, and whatever else might happen was intriguing enough to go to the nearby cookout before getting on with the rest of the day's activities.

Freire took a shower while Lopes and Sanches waited. Within an hour they were at the cookout on Elm Street. Another friend, Safiro Furtado, was already there. Furtado, twenty-eight, lived across the street from Delmar's baby mama's house and was a frequent visitor to the home, where there often were parties, whether planned or impromptu.

Furtado had tight, light-brown skin and a slim body conditioned from playing countless hours of soccer. He had been a tour guide in Cape Verde and gone to school through the eleventh grade. He arrived in America in December of 2011 to visit his mother and sister who lived in Dorchester, and planned to return to Cape Verde in August. To make money while in Boston, he worked with his cousin cleaning business offices and schools overnight, usually working from 10:00 P.M. to 2:00 A.M.

As the four friends began to settle in at the cookout, Freire's cell phone rang again. It was Daniel de Abreu calling. "Where you guys at?" Abreu said. "I'm about to get off work. What we doing tonight?"

Abreu, twenty-nine, was one of twelve children that included nine sisters. He was also from Cape Verde and had spent nearly three years in the Cape Verde military after high school. After leaving the military, he served as an officer for the Cape Verde national police for five years before coming to the United States in August of 2008.

Like many immigrants, he came to the States to visit family members in Boston. He too worked in the cleaning business, in the overnight shift. Sundays were his days to relax and have some fun.

Freire told Abreu about the cookout and to meet the group there. Abreu said he would ask his sister Neusa if he could borrow her BMW, and later called her to make arrangements to meet her when she got home from work. They met at their mother's house, where Abreu took the car keys. It was about seven thirty in the evening. "I'm just going to go out and have some fun," he told his sister. "I'll see you in the morning."

"Make sure you bring it back in the morning," his sister told him.

"I've never let you down," Abreu said.

When Abreu arrived at the party, he pulled his sister's silver four-door 2003 BMW 325xi into Furtado's driveway.

The group of five mingled at the cookout for a couple of hours, but as night closed in they decided to plot their next move. Someone suggested going to a liquor store and getting something to drink before heading to a nightclub. They had already had Coronas at the cookout, but Freire wanted something that would give him a stronger buzz.

The young men said their goodbyes to the backyard party, then stopped by a liquor store on Dudley Street to buy a bottle of vodka and some cranberry juice. Drinks in a club could be expensive. It was better to consume as much as possible before arriving.

The men piled into the silver BMW and headed back to Delmar's house to change into their nightclub clothes. They decided to go to Cure Lounge in Boston's theater district. The group went out at least every other Sunday night to a party or nightclub where they would have a few drinks, dance, and try to talk with girls despite their thick Cape Verdean accents. Cure was a popular spot on Sundays, because Latin and hip-hop were the primary music played on those nights.

Furtado initially didn't want to go back out. He didn't want to drink and feel sluggish the next day. "I have to play soccer tomorrow," he said as the others changed. "You guys go."

After being promised the group would not stay out long, Furtado eventually agreed to join them. All were in good spirits as they headed to downtown Boston excited about the evening ahead. It was eleven o'clock.

Abreu was the only one who had to been to Cure Lounge, a trendy spot where locals mingled with celebrities. After parking the car in the garage at Tufts Medical Center, a covered garage that also serviced the public, the five friends walked up Tremont Street to the club entrance.

Sunday was industry night, designed to attract people who worked in the club industry. Most were off on Sundays and it offered an attraction for what otherwise would be a slow night. All five worked their way through the velvet ropes, waiting to enter the club. It was like waiting for a ride at Disneyworld.

As they waited, two extremely tall and muscular men began to cross Tremont Street right near the club line. One would later be revealed to have been Alexander Bradley, the other NFL football star Aaron Hernandez. As Bradley and Hernandez walked past the line, Abreu immediately turned to his left and as a result avoided any eye contact with the two men.

Bradley and Hernandez, meanwhile, lingered on the corner of Stuart and Tremont while finishing a bottle of water, waiting for the line to clear. Bradley then gestured toward the line in the direction of Abreu and said something unintelligible. Both men decided to head toward the Cure waiting line. The football star started shaking hands with all the club security employees as he walked down the line, greeting them as if they were old friends from the neighborhood.

Freire, Abreu, Furtado, Sanches, and Lopes each paid the $25 cover charge, a price they thought well worth the evening's entertainment. As they were paying the cover charge Jeffrey London, the club's VIP promoter, greeted Hernandez and immediately ushered him into the nightclub bypassing the cashier, and as fate would have it, directly behind the five Cape Verdean men.

To anyone who might be paying attention, including bouncer Jamie Furtado, all seven men looked like they were entering the club together. It stood out on what would be a slow night.

While he is not a football fan, Furtado notices Aaron Hernandez's size and watches him closely as Hernandez says a couple of words to someone in the group of seven, then casually walks to the main bar and orders a drink.

Abreu pays for the first round of drinks for his group: five Coronas. Once the beer is gone, Freire sips on a shot of Hennessy as he watches the crowd and then gets Safiro Furtado to buy him another shot once the first was finished.

Abreu then spots an attractive blond girl by the name of Paige Aiello and decides to strike up a conversation. His friends watch him as he tries to be pleasant and make small talk. Eventually, he is persuasive enough for Aiello to agree to dance with him for a bit. Aiello, a frequent clubgoer, would later testify that she had seen Aaron Hernandez at Cure many times before but did not see him on that evening.

Sanches's luck isn't as good. He tries to talk to a tall white-skinned woman who wants no part of his attention. When Sanches persists, she finds a bouncer and tells him Sanches is bothering her. The bouncer gives Sanches a mild warning and tells him to leave the girl alone. Sanches backs off and spends the rest of the evening with his group.

"She's a racist," he mumbles under his breath.

When last call is announced just before the 2:00 A.M. closing, the five friends head for the exit happy with their evening. They had danced with a few girls, enjoyed their drinks, and people watched. They had no confrontations, no fights, nothing out of the ordinary. A "normal" night, Freire would call it. "No problems."

Once in the night air, they linger for about thirty minutes for what is called the "let out." Since all clubs close at the same time, there is no shortage of intoxicated people on the sidewalks looking for one last encounter to see who might get lucky. Abreu is trying the hardest. He begins to kiss and hug Aiello, who seems willing at times and other moments, not so much.

As the streets die down Freire, Abreu, and Furtado slowly make their way up the stairs to get the BMW parked in the garage, while Lopes and Sanches wait to be picked up on the sidewalk. Lopes and Sanches begin laughing at two gay men kissing as the couple walks by.

It isn't long before the silver BMW stops abruptly in front of them. A smiling Abreu is in the driver's seat, still thinking about the beautiful woman he talked to. Furtado is in the front passenger seat. Freire winds up in the middle as Sanches, on the passenger side, and Lopes, behind the driver, join him in the back seat. It's 2:20 A.M.

Hungry after their night of drinking, they decide to go to Boston's Chinatown. Abreu turns on the car's air conditioner, rolls up the windows, and steps on the accelerator. The silver BMW begins heading south on Tremont Street, which turns into Shawmut Avenue just up the road on the other side of Oak Street. As the car crosses the overpass that covers the always busy Massachusetts Turnpike, the BMW reaches the intersection of Shawmut Avenue and Herald Street. The traffic light turns from yellow to red. Abreu presses the brakes and flicks on his turn signal to make a left turn from the left lane.

The five immigrants are conversing about the night as they listen to a CD Sanches, an amateur rapper, produced. He plans to make it big one day.

One block behind them Donald Gobin, forty-nine, and Brian Quon, forty-eight, are heading home after working security at the Underbar, a nightclub close to Cure. Gobin notices how quiet things are as the co-workers walk up the left-hand side of Tremont Street and work their way toward a silver Saturn parked near Oak Street.

Once they reach the car, Gobin opens the door and slips into the driver's seat. He turns on the ignition and drives the car forward before stopping at a red light on Marginal Road. As the security guards are stopped at the light, an SUV pulls up about an arm's length next to them.

Quon, sitting in the passenger seat, looks to his right and sees a dark-skinned male driving the SUV and feels him staring at him. Gobin questions himself as to why the SUV is so close and follows his instinctive habit. He inches his SUV forward just a bit, breaking direct line of sight with the opposite car. It's a tactic he often employs late at night, just to be safe and avoid any kind of potential road rage with drunken drivers.

As Quon turns back toward Gobin, the driver of the SUV next to them suddenly guns it and runs the red light. Gobin, who has a thing about recognizing state license plates, notes that the SUV's tags are from Rhode Island where both he and Quon are from.

"Where's this loser going in such a hurry?" Gobin says with a laugh.

The SUV speeds over the overpass to the next traffic light and quickly pulls up in the right lane next to the BMW waiting at Herald Street. Freire and his four passengers think nothing of it until someone in the SUV yells, "What's up now, niggas?"

Then at least five shots ring out in rapid succession.

Pow—pow—pow—pow—pow.

Bullet after bullet after bullet, a seemingly endless stream of deadly destruction blends with the sound of cars racing along the Mass Pike under the overpass. The shots finally end and the SUV speeds away with wheels squealing.

Still waiting for the light at Marginal Road, Quon turns to Gobin. His face expresses disbelief. "I think that was gunshots."

Gobin is unsure. "Where?" he asks.

Quon points toward the traffic light ahead of them. A car is stopped in the left lane.

The light at Marginal Road turns green and Gobin slowly presses the accelerator of his Saturn, unsure whether he should rush to the scene of gunshots. As they drive closer they see the silver BMW surrounded by shattered glass.

"I think that car got shot up," Gobin says.

"What makes you think so?" Quon asks.

"See the glass on the road," Gobin says.

Quon replies, "Oh yeah, that's true."

As Gobin and Quon roll closer to the BMW, suddenly the back doors swing open on both sides. Gobin stops his vehicle.

Lopes rolls out of the left side of the BMW. He stands and checks the white T-shirt he is wearing, looking for wounds. He then checks his dark-colored pants. He sees no injuries. Sanches pops out from the right side of the car. He looks at his maroon shirt; there's blood, but his legs are fine. He can run.

Gobin slowly steps on the gas and inches his Saturn alongside the BMW. He and Quon look into the front seat of the bullet-riddled car. Two men sit motionless in the front seats. Quon thinks whoever is in the passenger seat is dead. His face is covered in blood.

The driver, Abreu, is gasping desperately for his last breaths. His eyes are open. They show fear and desperation. Blood is pouring out from a hole in his chest. It's a gruesome scene.

Gobin and Quon have trouble comprehending what has happened. They roll past the BMW and pull over to the curb, unsure what to do next.

A terrified Freire is on the floor of the back seat with his arms covering his head. Slowly, he looks out to see if the carnage has ended. He checks himself and sees his shirt is covered in blood. He has been grazed by bullets in the right and left forearms.

Freire looks next to him. Sanches and Lopes have exited the car. His friends in the front seat, Abreu and Furtado, are motionless. Furtado's face is a ball of red. There is a hole above his right eye.

Scared and in a state of shock, Sanches's first instinct is to run. He is afraid the shooter will return. He starts walking away from the car, leaving his friends behind. He spends the next two hours walking around downtown Boston, his shirt soaked in so much blood that passing taxi cabs refuse to pick him up and take him to

Brockton. He will not get home for several hours. A panic-stricken Lopes deserts the scene as well, leaving Freire, the only coherent victim left, to find help on his own.

A day that began with a friendly cookout has turned into a tragedy. This was not the American dream the five immigrants from Cape Verde envisioned.

Freire climbs out of the back seat and begins franticly waving his arms. He sees a car ahead and starts walking toward it. It's Gobin's Saturn.

"Help us. Help us," Freire pleads as he approaches the car.

As a bloody Freire gets closer, Quon fears he might have a weapon and tells Gobin: "Go around the corner."

Gobin drives just far enough from the commotion to feel safe and calls 911. He is connected to the Massachusetts State Police and quickly transferred to the Boston Police Department dispatcher. Gobin reports the shooting and the possibility of at least one death. He gives the location and is told police are on their way.

Gobin hangs up and looks at Quon. They discuss going back to the scene, then decide a killer is still on the loose and perhaps they would be safer at home. They head toward Highway 93 and drive back to Rhode Island.

At 2:34 A.M. on July 16, 2012, Boston police officer Luciano Cirino is flagged down by a frantic taxi cab driver alerting him that shots have been fired on Shawmut Avenue. Cirino, a member of the Boston police force since 2006, immediately notifies dispatch and speeds to the scene.

Once he arrives, Cirino sees the bullet-riddled BMW stationary in the street with the two rear doors open and glass on the road. Freire is on a nearby sidewalk screaming frantically for help. "These are my best friends. Help me, please!"

Cirino then sees two black males in the driver and front passenger seats of a BMW. They're not moving.

The officer calls in his location and requests additional units as well as emergency medical services (EMS). Officer Thomas

O'Donnell of the Boston Police Department arrives and sees a street sweeper slowly pass through the crime scene and thinks, How is that happening?

Within minutes EMS arrives on the scene and pronounces Abreu and Furtado dead from their wounds. Boston EMS paramedic David Cioffi makes a decision to cover the victims with sheets to "preserve dignity."

An autopsy conducted on July 17, 2012, would later show Abreu died from a gunshot wound to the right side of his chest. He also had a bullet wound under his right arm.

Furtado had gunshot wounds just above his right eye, which lodged in his head. He also had another wound to the right side of his head and his right shoulder.

Freire had a gunshot wound to his right forearm and a graze wound to his left forearm. Two days after the shooting, he could not offer police a description of who pulled the trigger.

Within minutes the scene is crawling with police, and crime scene tape is in place blocking access to both sides of Shawmut Avenue. A law enforcement official would leak to the media that the victims were from a Cape Verdean gang based in Dorchester. The official requested anonymity because he was not authorized to speak about the case.

It was Boston's twenty-fifth and twenty-sixth homicides that year. Exactly one month later Aaron Hernandez signed a $40 million contract extension with the New England Patriots. He would later tell reporters: "Now that it happened, it's definitely a blessing. I'm excited to go on with my life."

4.

MAGICAL MONDAY AND THE LUCK OF THE IRISH

Aaron Hernandez didn't become a suspect until nearly a year after the killings of Daniel de Abreu and Safiro Furtado. Up to then the case had gone stale and was largely forgotten after Boston homicide detectives failed to come up with a credible suspect. Two black immigrants shot dead in their car on Boston's South End wasn't exactly big news in New England where anything about the Red Sox, Celtics, and Patriots dominated the daily headlines.

Boston was also still recovering physically and emotionally from the April 15, 2013, bombing at the finish line of the Boston Marathon. The act of terrorism had killed three people and injured hundreds of others. But the cold case heated up on Wednesday, June 19, 2013.

Marc Sullivan, a very unusually tanned, Irish fortysomething-year-old sergeant detective with the Boston police homicide unit, was watching the news and saw that Aaron was a suspect in the death of Odin Lloyd, who was dating Shayanna's sister Shaneah, a resident of Dorchester. Detective Sullivan's interest was piqued because he remembered the video footage he had seen of Hernandez entering Cure Lounge at the same time as the Cape Verdeans on the night of the Boston shootings on July 16, 2012. Sullivan, a twenty-year veteran of the Boston Police Department, was still the squad supervisor investigating the case and hadn't forgotten the details.

When he got to work, the first thing he did was to hold a meeting with his entire squad and inform them they were going to begin tracing the whereabouts of Aaron Hernandez on that night. And just like that Aaron Hernandez became the lead suspect in the deaths of Daniel de Abreu and Safiro Furtado. This was an unusual way to start an investigation, to say the least. Police don't usually decide on a probable suspect and start looking for a way to connect him to a crime. They usually follow the evidence and see who it leads them to, not the other way around. What was truly stunning was just how quickly their case developed and how "lucky" they would get.

Sullivan ordered a detailed analysis of video footage taken in and around Cure Lounge on the morning of July 16, 2012, with the primary focus on tracking Hernandez's movements that night. Detective Joshua Cummings was assigned the task and observed video surveillance footage showing Hernandez pulling into the Tufts parking garage at about 12:04 A.M., driving a silver 2006 Toyota 4Runner with Rhode Island license plate 635035. Hernandez is seen wearing a gray baseball hat with a red or orange brim and a gray T-shirt with a red, green, and white design on the front. He is with a then-unknown dark-skinned Hispanic male or light-skinned black male, later identified as Alexander Bradley. The two men are seen entering the club immediately after the five men from Cape Verde: Furtado, Abreu, Sanches, Freire, and Lopes.

Hernandez and Bradley go downstairs into Cure where there are no operable cameras. They appear again and exit about nine minutes later, after Hernandez consumes two drinks and takes a photo with a fan.

After hanging around outside for several minutes and crossing the street at 1:10 A.M., Hernandez is seen leaving the garage, approximately one hour before the shootings, driving the silver 4Runner with Bradley in the front passenger seat. Detective Cummings then looked at other street cameras and saw an SUV similar in color and shape appear to be "looping the block" on Tremont Street and Stuart Street, in the area of Cure.

About an hour later at 2:10 A.M., the Cape Verdean group is seen leaving Cure Lounge. As Lopes and Sanches wait on the sidewalk while Abreu, Furtado, and Freire go to get the BMW in the garage, the silver 4Runner is seen traveling at a slow rate of speed on Tremont Street cruising past Lopes and Sanches. The silver 4Runner then disappears from camera view around the block just minutes before the shootings, which was never caught on camera.

The very next day, on Thursday, June 20, 2013, Detective Sullivan reached out to the Massachusetts State Police handling the Odin Lloyd investigation and began what would become a cooperative effort.

Three days later, on what I liked to call "Magical Monday"—June 24, 2013—investigators would hit the jackpot with several major developments. After speaking with Sullivan, the State Police followed up by calling the Boston detectives that day with information about an anonymous caller who had contacted the North Attleboro police saying there was a connection between the Lloyd murder and the Boston shootings. The caller was later identified as Sherif Hashem, a manager at Cure and other nearby nightclubs. Hashem said he came across information that led him to believe Aaron Hernandez was involved in both cases. He said a frequent clubgoer told him he saw Hernandez get into a silver SUV with Rhode Island plates, which matched the description of the car involved in the Boston shootings.

Hashem's information wasn't exactly conclusive. But now with the anonymous call and the fact they knew Aaron was at Cure that night in a car similar to that of the murderer, the call was just enough to put them over the threshold of having enough probable cause to start issuing search warrants and subpoenas, and issue them they did.

The first thing the police did was ask First Assistant District Attorney Patrick Haggan, who was already assigned to the case and would be my main adversary throughout, to preserve all of Aaron's cell phone records, a task that might help police track his movements that night. Haggan also obtained records from the Enterprise car rental company showing that Aaron had rented a car on Monday, July 16, 2012, hours after the murders.

The police ran the license plates of the 4Runner Aaron was seen in while exiting the Tufts garage and found out it was registered to Jana Leasing and Rental Corporation of Providence, Rhode Island. It was a demo model given to Hernandez in 2012 for his use, in exchange for promotional work for Fox Toyota. The owner of the dealership said he had not seen the vehicle since May 2012. Needless to say, things were piling on fast for Aaron.

Now all the police needed was a murder weapon, and Magical Monday would not disappoint. Detective Sullivan put out a notice to all police agencies in the tristate area, comprising Massachusetts, Rhode Island, and Connecticut, that they were looking for a gun used in a double homicide in Boston. Based on the bullets recovered at the scene, forensics were able to narrow down the possibility of the gun caliber being a 9 mm, a .38, or a .357.

The luck of the Irish would smile upon Detective Sullivan once more on Magical Monday, as on that very day Massachusetts State Police responded to a red 2012 Toyota Camry involved in an accident on I-91 in Longmeadow, Massachusetts. When the vehicle was towed and examined, an unloaded Smith & Wesson .38-caliber-special revolver along with three rounds of ammunition were located in an unlocked briefcase in the trunk of the car.

Boston police took a sharper interest when they learned that the driver of the car, nineteen-year-old Jailene Diaz-Ramos, was from Bristol, Connecticut, the same hometown as Aaron. She initially told police that she gave a ride to a friend of hers and some amateur "football players." Her friend, who went by the name "Chicago," had left the case in her car without her knowledge after she gave him and some of his buddies a ride. The gun was soon transferred to the Boston Police Firearms Analysis Unit and examined by Detective Camper, who would issue a report stating that the gun recovered from Bristol resident Jailene Diaz-Ramos was in fact the same gun used to kill Safiro Furtado and Daniel de Abreu.

With the investigation now in high gear, two days later on June 26, 2013, a search warrant was executed for 114 Lake Avenue in Bristol, Connecticut. During a search of the property, a silver Toyota 4Runner with Rhode Island license plate 635035 was found in a locked garage. It was covered in dust and cobwebs and the battery was dead. This house would become extremely significant because police would later identify Chicago as John Alcorn, a childhood friend of Diaz-Ramos. Alcorn had once listed this house as his mailing address because his cousin Thaddeus Singleton lived there. Thaddeus, also known as T. L. Singleton, was the husband of Tanya Cummings-Singleton, the cousin of Aaron Hernandez.

Diaz-Ramos would later change her story to say that she purchased the gun from a person named "Flaco" in Springfield, Massachusetts; but that didn't matter much to police. They preferred her original story.

Two days later, Boston police returned to take possession of the car. Detective Sullivan was joined by Detective Peter Dauphinais of the Bristol Police Department. Dauphinais was familiar with Hernandez's family and the friends he hung out with. Sullivan showed Dauphinais photographs from the video taken of Hernandez and Bradley during the night at Cure.

"I know that guy," Dauphinais said. The detective had immediately recognized Bradley, who sometimes went by his middle name Sharrod. Bradley, who was thirty at the time of the Boston shootings, was a native of Hartford, Connecticut, and the father of three children by different women, and also known by police to be involved in drugs and guns. Getting Bradley's name was a huge break for the police, especially after Bradley agreed to speak with them under a proffer agreement, which allows individuals under criminal investigation to give their knowledge of crimes with the supposed assurance that their words will not be used against them in any later proceedings. He was later given full immunity.

Bradley appeared to be gold for investigators and the prosecution. His detailed account of the morning of July 16, 2012, fingered Aaron Hernandez as the trigger man for the Boston shootings. During interviews and testimony before a grand jury, Bradley said Hernandez came to his apartment in Manchester, Connecticut, to pick him up with plans of going to a nightclub in Boston. Bradley said that as they were about to get into a silver Toyota 4Runner Hernandez raised the hood and put a gun somewhere in the engine.

After arriving at Cure Lounge, Bradley said he and Hernandez were standing at the bar when an unknown male bumped into the football player, causing him to spill his drink on Hernandez. Bradley described the unknown male as five ten, light skinned with long braids, basically describing Daniel de Abreu. Hernandez allegedly became angry, saying, "I hate when people try me."

After Bradley and Hernandez left the club, Bradley said they stopped at another bar before going back to the garage where the 4Runner was parked. He told police that two men matching the description of Abreu and Sanches followed them to the other bar and were staring them down, laughing at them. Bradley told police that this infuriated Hernandez to the point that they had to leave the bar because Hernandez felt they were "trying him."

After exiting the club Bradley said they got the 4Runner and left the garage. But it wasn't long before Hernandez, who was driving, pulled over to the curb, jumped out of the SUV, opened the hood, and retrieved the gun from the engine compartment and put it in the glove compartment inside the car. Hernandez told Bradley to drive.

In the 4Runner, they circled the area for a bit then pulled over and got out to try and pick up girls during the let out. A few minutes later Hernandez said, "There they go, right there, let's go, let's go!" Bradley said he saw a BMW and assumed that was where Hernandez wanted to go. They both jumped in the 4Runner, Bradley pressing the accelerator to the floorboard. Bradley said he ran a red light before pulling up to the passenger side of the BMW, which was stopped at the intersection of Herald Street and Shawmut Avenue.

According to Bradley, Hernandez took the gun out of the glove box and told him: "Watch out" and "Sit back." Hernandez then leaned across Bradley's body and extended his arm out the driver's window. Bradley stated Hernandez said, "Yo, what's up now, niggas" and started shooting, firing six shots and emptying the chamber; he could hear the clicking of the gun after all the bullets were used. When the attack ended, Bradley said he was told to drive away from the scene while Hernandez checked the GPS on his cell phone for directions.

"Did you see that? I got one of them in the head and one in the chest," Hernandez bragged, according to Bradley.

Several minutes later, while on the Massachusetts Turnpike, Bradley said he told Hernandez that he needed to get rid of the gun. So Hernandez opened the chamber on the revolver and dropped the casings from the gun out of the window. Bradley then said that Aaron took his shirt off to wipe down the gun. Bradley said that while driving down the turnpike, Hernandez later threw the gun out of the window into a heavily wooded area.

The two wound up in Hartford, Connecticut, at the home of Brooke Wilcox, Bradley's girlfriend at the time. It was there, Bradley said, that Hernandez used a laptop to search the internet for news of a double homicide in Boston and also placed a phone call to Tanya Cummings-Singleton. No one in the Hernandez extended family had been more loyal to Aaron than Tanya. He considered her his best friend and confidant.

Bradley said Hernandez's cousin arrived at Wilcox's home in a white Nissan Maxima. After speaking with Hernandez, Tanya left the Nissan Maxima and took the Toyota 4Runner. Bradley said Hernandez told him that Singleton took the car to clean and hide it.

Bradley admitted his relationship with Hernandez soured after that to the point where he accused his former friend of shooting him in the face seven months later in February 2013. The Boston shootings were now solved. All cops and prosecutors had to do was wait their turn as Bristol County prosecutors tried and convicted Aaron for the murder of Odin Lloyd. With all of the video evidence, murder weapon, and Bradley's testimony, the case against Hernandez for the Boston shootings was a slam-dunk conviction and Boston police would have nabbed themselves a fallen Patriot.

5.

THE NOT SO ANONYMOUS CALL

Early on in the case we had a team meeting in Boston. We brought the entire trial team together for the first time so I could bring everyone up to date on the facts of the case, give an overview, and explain to each team member what the defense strategy would be based on what we knew at that time.

I had put together what I believe could very well be the best defense team ever assembled. They say O. J. Simpson had a dream team, but Aaron's legal team was built for speed and precision. As an attorney and student of the game, I love working with great lawyers. They make me step up my game, my skill set improves, and I always walk away a better lawyer. This time I would be working with an attorney I had been waiting five years to partner up with: Harvard law professor Ronald S. Sullivan Jr.

Sully is the dean of faculty at Harvard Law School and runs the Harvard Law School Criminal Justice Initiative. I met Ron when he invited me to teach at Harvard's Trial Advocacy Workshop, or "TAW" as it's known at the law school. TAW is a hands-on course in which second- and third-year law students take a fictional case and try it from its inception to its closing, with the help of professors and faculty pulled together from throughout the country. The mock trial is an enriching experience not only for the students, but for the faculty as well. The faculty gets together and exchanges ideas, and you get to see other styles. It's an important part of my year; I always enjoy getting away, going to Cambridge, and focusing on trial advocacy for a week or two in an environment that lives and breathes trials.

Sully is a constitutional scholar and an expert in criminal law. He's a rare breed of lawyer not only well versed in the law but also street smart, which proves a deadly combination. I was eager to work with someone like that. As a team, I always felt we would complement each other well.

As third chair I brought in Linda Kenney Baden, with whom I had consulted on the Casey Anthony trial (a mother accused of killing her two-year-old daughter). While Linda did not try Casey's case with us, I was extremely impressed with her knowledge of forensics. Linda has for many years served as a mentor to me, teaching me various skills, and she's always on top of the latest in forensic science. She's now a friend; I call her "Mom." Linda suggested that we bring in a local lawyer, George Leontire. I had met George and his partner several years earlier at a birthday party for Linda's husband, the preeminent forensic pathologist Dr. Michael Baden, whose HBO show *Autopsy* was a favorite of mine. I had never worked with George and was very hesitant, having been burned in the past by bringing in people I didn't know to other high-profile cases. Lesson number one is *be careful who you bring in!* But I trusted Linda. So after much prodding and suggesting by my trial mother, George Leontire joined the team and I am glad he did. George was a tremendous asset; we never would have pulled it off without him. We would also have numerous lawyers and law students assisting us. Early on I knew this team would be epic.

The first thing I do whenever I look at a case is to start reading the police reports, because the prosecutor's case always aligns with the investigation. I don't know how other lawyers do it, but that's what I do. I find that prosecutors employ very little creativity when they prepare their strategy because the cops, from the inception of the investigation, develop a case in one direction, letting one clue lead to the next, and the prosecutor always follows. If a prosecutor comes up with an alternate theory of the crime, then the police ultimately become defense witnesses and can be easily impeached.

As I began to review the police reports on my computer, I was eager to see how Aaron's case developed, and one of the things that really jump-started the investigation was that anonymous call. The call was of considerable concern to me because it meant that either Aaron confessed to someone, despite having told me he was innocent, or there was a witness to the crime somewhere out there. Typically, anonymous calls come in when someone sees something, is personally involved, or overheard something. Long story short, we needed to find this guy.

This case had over thirty thousand pages of *discovery*, which means police reports, witness statements, and forensic findings. I hadn't finished reading all of it when I noticed the police had begun to identify Sherif Hashem, an employee of Cure Lounge, as the anonymous caller. The reports never pointed out how they knew it was him. Reports just said, "The caller was later identified as Sherif Hashem."

After our first team meeting, getting more information about Hashem was on everyone's mind. As a defense attorney I like to get out in the field. I want to see where everything happened; I like to see, feel, and touch the case and its important places of interest. So I suggested to Sully that we go out to Cure that night; it was a Saturday night. "Trial lawyers need fun too," I said. Sully and I decided to meet there and bring along one of our investigators just in case we needed to document something.

I was coming from Dartmouth, about forty-five minutes outside of Boston, so I was about twenty minutes behind Sully. When Sully arrived, he decided to wait outside until I got there. Suddenly he heard a voice calling out to him, "Professor!" He ignored it, then it got louder: "Professor!" Great, now I am going to have to explain to one of my students what the hell I'm doing at a nightclub on a Saturday night, thought Sully, who is a married man and father of two.

As he turned around to acknowledge the voice, he saw a familiar face, but he just couldn't place it. He knew the man was from Harvard, but how did they know each other? Then it hit him: this was the IT guy from the law school. His name was none other than Sherif Hashem.

Sully is no dummy, so he struck up a conversation with him, and while he's speaking to him he texts me and tells me that he's outside speaking to Sherif, and this is when my foot hits the gas. I arrive minutes later to not only find Sully speaking to Sherif, but he's also speaking to another man, a short, stocky black man in his late fifties who I recognize as a Cure employee from the surveillance tapes we were given during discovery. He clearly stood out because of his weight, age, and the distinct hat he wore. It was one of those fedoras, the kind detectives in the fifties used to wear, like Dick Tracy. I was surprised to hear him introduced to me as Miller Thomas, Cure's director of security.

My adrenaline began to kick into high gear. I remember thinking, Wow, this is amazing that they are willing to speak to us so freely. Usually witnesses are extremely reluctant to talk to defense lawyers, especially when a business like Cure is involved. People have this incredible fear of defense lawyers, like we are going to sue them or something if they step out of line and say something they shouldn't. Yet the truth is the truth, it takes no sides, and the truth is never actionable. Put simply, just tell us what happened, and there's not a damn thing anybody can do to you.

Moments after I arrived, Miller Thomas walked away to take care of some of his duties. Sully then asked Sherif to share with me what he had told him. His was a jaw-dropping tale, to say the least. He told us that on June 21, 2013, detectives Hall-Brewster and Craig

Jones, both from the Boston Police Department, were at Cure serving a subpoena and began to speak with Hashem. Hashem was well known to Boston police: he was the go-to-guy when they needed information on criminal activity involving nightclubs and liquor establishments in the area. They often asked Hashem to provide video footage or customer and employee information when such crimes occurred.

While Hashem was speaking to the detectives, someone known to Hashem as simply either "B" or "G" walked up and told him there was a connection between the Odin Lloyd murder and the Boston shootings, and implicated Aaron Hernandez.

Hashem described the conversation this way: "He said something to the sense of, 'Well, it's not his first time,'" referring to the Odin Lloyd case.

"What do you mean by that?" Hashem asked.

"Well, you know he probably did it because he got away with murder before."

"What are you talking about?" Hashem asked.

"Remember the incident where two people got shot up in a car, two Cape Verdean kids, got shot up in a car by Cure last summer?"

Hashem said, "Yes, I remember hearing about that incident."

"Well, I was outside getting into my car and I saw [Hernandez] get into a silver SUV with Rhode Island plates and after that they said that was the car involved in the shooting, and I also heard both shootings are connected."

After this B or G guy left, Hashem said he turned to Detective Jones and asked him what he thought of that. Hashem then told us that Jones just stared and didn't say a word. That might sound plausible on the surface, but it really doesn't make sense. Two homicide detectives are talking to Hashem, and this B or G guy is going to interrupt them and all of a sudden have this conversation? The detectives get a lead in the highest profile case in the state and potentially have a lead to solve a double murder and they don't say a word to this B or G guy? Or interrupt B or G and start to ask him any questions, like his name? What else does he know? Instead of doing a report or following up on the lead, they just tell Hashem: "You may want to call that in."

Hashem didn't really know this B or G guy. He described him as about five foot seven, about 170 pounds, clean cut, dark skinned, and probably of Cape Verdean, Haitian, or Dominican descent. "He's not a person that I have firsthand knowledge of, but he's an unusually nice person that just comes to the club and I talk to him on the way in and I talk to him on the way out," Hashem explained. "He's not there every week, but maybe I see him once a month, once every other month."

The next day, June 22, 2013, Hashem got a call from a supervising detective, Michael Talbot, telling him that he should tell the homicide detectives what he heard. Hashem assumed Detective Jones must have told Talbot about the conversation with B or G and that's why Talbot called. So Hashem dutifully made his anonymous call to the tip line and linked Aaron Hernandez to the Boston shootings.

In order to understand the significance of the not so anonymous call, you have to remember that up to this point all the cops had was that Aaron was at Cure that night and he drove a similar silver SUV. That meant nothing. There's a boatload of those in Boston, Rhode Island, and Connecticut. It's a very common car. None of it means Aaron was involved in any way, shape, or form.

What the cops needed was a connection to the murder, and to establish that they needed more evidence. What they needed was to get several search warrants to investigate Aaron's home, examine his cars, and seize his telephone records. But before police can do that they need to convince a judge they have probable cause. The law provides that "the right of the people to be secure in their persons, houses, papers, and effects, against unreasonable searches and seizures, shall not be violated, and no warrants shall issue, but upon probable cause, supported by Oath or affirmation, and particularly describing the place to be searched, and the persons or things to be seized." Oh yes, that pesky little thing called the Constitution and law enforcement's archenemy, the Fourth Amendment. So for a judge to sign a warrant allowing them to search Aaron's house and cell phone records they had to show he had opportunity, that he was there, and that he was driving a car similar to what the witnesses said they saw near the shooting. But even that wasn't enough to get a warrant. Many people were at Cure that night and I am sure a few of them or people near the area drove similar vehicles. What they needed was a connection to the shooting: something that pointed the finger squarely at Aaron Hernandez. What they needed was B or G.

As outrageous as it sounds, I believe the cops staged this whole encounter with B or G for Sherif Hashem. They knew Sherif was a gullible, cop-friendly kind of guy. So they staged this conversation in order to get him to make the anonymous call and give them the missing link they needed to obtain warrants and get the ball rolling in the investigation.

Of course once Aaron was indicted, the police never found this B or G guy who knew so much about everything that happened. After his innocuous conversation with Sherif, he was never seen again at Cure, or anywhere else for that matter.

This tells me one of two things: he's either a cop working undercover at the club about once a month to see if there are any drugs being bought or sold there; or he's a confidential informant cops know was frequenting the club, and the cops have him in their pocket to the point where they can say, "We want to leak that Aaron Hernandez was involved in the shooting" and he goes and does it. My money is B or G is a cop. But we will never know.

What's also telling is the way Hashem sounded when he made his anonymous call, a year after the shootings in Boston:

ANONYMOUS: How you doing, sir?
DISPATCH: Good

ANONYMOUS: I was wondering if I could leave you an anonymous tip that might help you with an ongoing investigation.

DISPATCH: Okay

ANONYMOUS: Okay . . . on July 15, I think, of 2012

DISPATCH: Okay

ANONYMOUS: Yeah, that was . . . I believe a Sunday night into a Monday morning

DISPATCH: Okay

ANONYMOUS: Yeah, it was the 15th

DISPATCH: July 16, 2012 you're saying, right?

ANONYMOUS: July 15 sir

DISPATCH: 15th okay

ANONYMOUS: Oh, yeah so yeah . . . it would be the 16th because it was around 2:30 A.M.

DISPATCH: Okay

ANONYMOUS: Yeah, there was a shooting in Boston that killed two people.

DISPATCH: Okay

ANONYMOUS: Yeah, um . . . two people died. Near the south end . . . near the bridge by the Turnpike from 2:30 in the morning

DISPATCH: Okay

ANONYMOUS: Yeah. and um. I believe the people were just talking about an SUV with Rhode Island plates

DISPATCH: Okay

ANONYMOUS: Yeah, and I believe that this might be related to the ongoing investigation in Northern Attleboro right now [the Odin Lloyd murder]

DISPATCH: Okay, alright just because of the description of the vehicle or do you believe it as something to do with the um person of interest [it was widely reported Aaron was the person of interest in the killing of Odin Lloyd] or whatever is going on?

ANONYMOUS: Both

DISPATCH: Both?

ANONYMOUS: Yes

DISPATCH: Both . . . okay. Alright . . . now without giving your name, do you know anyone who's an acquaintance type of thing that knows or heard something said about it?

ANONYMOUS: Um . . . I also don't like to get more involved . . . I think it's the right thing to do by giving you that information.

DISPATCH: Okay, no, I understand, obviously I'll pass it down to them to look into it but I just wanted to know if there was more of a background stuff, you know . . . to differentiate anything behind it . . . like if you heard from various group of people or certain, without giving me your name.

ANONYMOUS: Yeah, it's exactly.

DISPATCH: Okay

ANONYMOUS: I think somebody might have accidentally spilled the beans in front of me.

DISPATCH: Okay

ANONYMOUS: You know . . . as a society we can't have three homicides.

DISPATCH: No!

ANONYMOUS: And you know . . . not do anything about it.

DISPATCH: Okay . . . alright . . . so that was July 15th into the 16th

ANONYMOUS: Yeah

DISPATCH: About 2:30 A.M. in south Boston

ANONYMOUS: No, south end

DISPATCH: South end near the Turnpike, right?

ANONYMOUS: Yeah, you know where the bridge is?

DISPATCH: Yup

ANONYMOUS: It's like where area one in Boston ends and district four begins.

DISPATCH: Okay

ANONYMOUS: By that tower over there.

DISPATCH: Okay

ANONYMOUS: Yeah

DISPATCH: Alright so . . .

ANONYMOUS: So it's like you remember the . . . I don't know if you
remember that probably because

DISPATCH: Uh . . . a lot of the stuff unfortunately the news [referring
to Aaron Hernandez in the news], every night there's something
on there so . . . um . . . but I will definitely pass that on.

ANONYMOUS: Yup.

DISPATCH: And hopefully they will look into it and go from there.

ANONYMOUS: You know, I wish you guys all the best, and good luck.

DISPATCH: Alright, thank you very much

ANONYMOUS: Thank you very much for all that you guys do sir.

DISPATCH: Bye, bye.

ANONYMOUS: Bye

The three things that stand out to me when I look at this call
transcript are first, that he remembered the exact date over a year
later. I think it's fair to say that a lot happened to Hashem in that
year and to remember the exact date of the shootings is an odd
coincidence. Second, that he says he thinks "somebody accidentally
spilled the beans in front of" him. This is clearly puzzling because
the way Sherif describes it, nobody accidently spilled anything. He
had an open, direct conversation with B or G. He didn't happen to
overhear another private conversation. This part makes me question Sherif's version of events. Third, he describes the location of
the shootings as "where Area One in Boston ends and District Four
begins." He's referring to police districts. Even with all of the contact Hashem has with law enforcement, I seriously doubt that any
security guard or systems analyst has any clue where the lines between different police districts are. The detail regarding the police
district location could have come only from a police officer; one trying to ensure the anonymous call would be forwarded to the right
department as soon as possible.

Sherif was an interesting character. I could never figure him
out, because he was so open with us that I felt he was telling the
truth. Yet some of his story didn't make any sense. What I really

think is that probably the bulk of what he told us was the truth, but he was also trying to protect the cops in his strange misguided way, at the same time. Deep down he just kind of wanted to be helpful—to everyone. The other notably peculiar behavior was how he handed us off to Miller Thomas, the director of security, without giving him any caution whatsoever.

Shortly after Sherif was done telling us his fantastic tale, and as soon as I was done picking my jaw off the ground, Thomas walked back over to us and Sherif told him to show us around. Now remember I arrived a little late, so I had no idea what Sully had discussed with them before I arrived, and I didn't have an opportunity to ask Sully when I got there. So Miller Thomas then escorted us into the club, bypassing all of the lines, like Aaron did on that fateful night. He then began what I can only describe as a boring VIP tour of Cure. He began to show us every inch of the club, as if we were going to buy the place. He showed us the bathrooms, the exits, behind the bar, and so on. I was particularly interested in the back room, where I had read Aaron had gone that night to take a picture with a fan, so he showed us that area as well. He also began pointing out all of the cameras.

I could not have been more impressed with Miller Thomas. I was amazed that Thomas, a retired homicide detective and the former president of the detectives' union, had taken on this private gig working for a club, where perhaps something happened in the biggest murder case in Boston since Lizzy Borden, and he had no qualms about showing us, Aaron's lawyers, around every inch of the place and answering all our questions like it was nothing. I was under the impression that Sherif had told Thomas who we were, so I asked a simple question: "Are all of these cameras in the same place as the day of the incident?"

"What incident?" Thomas asked. That was when my heart began to race and I realized he had no clue who we were. I guess Thomas thought we were either some kind of VIPs Sherif knew, or friends of Sherif's or the owners. Thomas's demeanor changed instantly after Sully chimed in and told him we were Aaron's lawyers.

Thomas immediately walked away, but he didn't go far. He literally stood ten feet from us for the rest of the night. We decided to stay and have a drink to discuss what we had just found out while Thomas stood nearby staring at us like a jealous boyfriend. Sully and I could not get over how awkward it was with him standing there staring at us.

"This is weird," I told Sully. "Tell me about it," he responded. I looked over at Thomas and met his gaze and quipped: "Do you think he'll leave if we start dancing?" Sully and I had a good laugh and decided we had seen enough. As we walked outside and stopped on the sidewalk near the entrance, we noticed Miller Thomas follow us out wearing his Dick Tracy hat and trench coat. I looked at Sully and said, "I swear you can't make this shit up."

Right then and there I knew we were going to have to keep digging and rattle some cages, because Thomas was extremely nervous, and it really shouldn't have been easy to rattle this experienced retired homicide detective. What was he hiding? Was he covering something up for the club? His cop buddies? Little did I know that we would get at least some of those questions answered . . . and a hell of a lot more.

6.

A VIDEO GAME CALLED *MOTIVE*

Before I got involved with the case, I remember seeing in the news that the double murder in Boston began with a spilled drink. The motive fell perfectly within the story line. This hothead jock Aaron Hernandez became enraged when Daniel de Abreu spilled a drink on him. He was so angry he retaliated by unloading a gun on him and his friends, killing Abreu and Safiro Furtado and injuring Aquilino Freire. I think if you were to poll everyone who knows anything about this case, that is exactly what they would tell you. All this happened over a spilled drink.

Never mind the fact that a spilled drink causing murder seems absurd, and the fact that Aaron would have been risking millions and his perfect life. You still have Aaron, at a hulking six foot two, 265 pounds, against Daniel de Abreu who was five foot seven and 170 pounds soaking wet. Aaron would have destroyed Abreu with his bare hands. He didn't have to lie in wait for two and a half hours and then gun him down on a street corner. You can't ignore common sense like that. Even if Aaron were the hottest of hotheads, the fact is he would have pounced on him then and there. Aaron was never shy about getting into fights before this incident and even after. This motive just did not make any sense. Where did the story originate?

That distinct honor would be attributed to the common-wealth's star witness and informant, Alexander Bradley. Once he mentioned the spilled drink motive to prosecutors in court during a pretrial hearing it stuck, and now everyone refers to the double-murder case in Boston as the "spilled drink case." So naturally the first thing I wanted to see when joining the case was the video. After all, isn't that everyone's instinctive reaction when trying to understand things? The why?

Having a client caught in the act on video is every defense lawyer's worst nightmare. Video evidence is the only thing a good lawyer cannot overcome. There is very little a lawyer can say at that point, except to deliver the famous Groucho Marx line "Who are you going to believe, me or your lying eyes?"

The Boston case against Aaron Hernandez was always described as a video case, yet it was anything but. True, the video of Cure Lounge on the night of the shootings a year earlier was the thing that reminded Detective Sullivan that Aaron was in Cure. But how police got that video and what was actually on it was a different story altogether.

Cops and prosecutors had one *big*, glaring problem. This so-called spilled drink incident was not on any video. It was missing! One had to ask, did it even exist? Prosecutors were saying the police could only obtain outdoor video of the club that night. The only interior video they had was of the front door, and a video ID scanner the club used to capture the ID of everyone who walked through the door. So to convince a jury that a spilled drink was enough to spark Aaron Hernandez into a murderous rage, prose-cutors were going to have to rely on the word of their drug-dealing snitch Alexander Bradley, because no one else saw it.

I needed to take a close look at what video evidence they ac-tually did have in order to understand why they didn't have the biggest missing link to the case so far. Whenever any kind of video evidence exists, the first thing I like to do is look at the chain of custody. Let me explain chain of custody and how that all works. *Chain of custody* is an evidentiary requirement for court. You may notice if you watch trials that sometimes prosecutors put on an incredibly boring series of witnesses before they finally open an evidence bag and show what's inside. All of that testimony helps them trace the chain of custody for that item. Basically, a prosecutor must be able to account for the whereabouts of a piece of evidence from the moment it is collected all the way through to the trial. That way the defense can't argue that the evidence was tampered with and/or that it's not in the same condition it was in on the night of the crime.

You may recall that during the O. J. Simpson murder trial, OJ's blood was everywhere and the DNA results were damning. Barry Scheck, one of Simpson's lawyers, did not challenge the validity of the DNA results. What he did was challenge the collection of the evidence and its weaknesses in the chain of custody. Everyone knows the saying "a chain is only as strong as its weakest link." Well, the same theory and approach apply here. So I went looking to answer the basic question, which was where did this video come from? Is there more?

The first place I looked was in the evidence log to see when the video was logged into evidence, along with other items of evidence collected in the case. To my surprise, not a single piece of video evidence was ever logged into evidence. I remember mumbling to myself aloud in front of my computer when I discovered this. "OMG! They don't have chain of custody." Now I was the one carrying an ace up my sleeve. The question was, when was I going to use it? At trial? Let them think they were going to introduce the video then object under chain of custody grounds? No, the problem with that approach was there was no guarantee the judge would follow the law; he might give them a break in the proceedings in order to try and prove it up.

The other option was to file a pretrial motion and get the judge to rule in advance on whether he would exclude any video because the prosecutor couldn't verify chain of custody. The problem with that approach was I was dealing with a police department that I already knew had probably created an anonymous call. How hard would it be to create chain of custody for the videos? No, I decided the best option was to keep digging and see what other nuggets I could find.

Later on while reading through the more recent police reports, I found a gem written by the ever-interesting Detective Talbot.

What's important to remember is that until now I had been looking at the earliest records on file, because all of the collection of evidence was done in the summer of 2012. Back then there was very little discussion of the video or its chain of custody. But on October 1, 2013, months after Magic Monday, and after Aaron Hernandez was implicated in the double murder in Boston, Detective Talbot penned his first report on the case against Aaron Hernandez, and he thoroughly explained his actions in collecting the video evidence.

On July 17, 2012, the day after Daniel de Abreu and Safiro Furtado were gunned down, Sergeant Detective Marc Sullivan began issuing assignments to various detectives in his squad. One of those assignments required getting the video from Cure Lounge. That duty fell upon Detective Talbot, the same detective who would press Sherif Hashem to make the not so anonymous call. The problem was Detective Talbot's name was not mentioned in any of the early reports describing how the video was obtained. In fact, the video was barely mentioned at all, other than it was picked up approximately a week after the shootings. His new report describing his activities, which was penned over a year and three months later, was shocking.

Talbot wrote that upon being given this assignment by Sullivan, he immediately called his old friend Sherif Hashem. Yep, the same Sherif Hashem who made the anonymous call to the police. Since 2008, Hashem had worked with law enforcement and detectives in that division numerous times delivering video surveillance for them. Talbot also knew that Hashem was a computer expert who managed all the video systems for Cure and its sister clubs. Talbot even knew Hashem was employed by Harvard University as a programming supervisor.

Detective Talbot wrote that "on July 16, 2012, I did contact Sherif Hashem and requested any and all video (interior and exterior) from Cure Night Club. Sherif stated that he would handle it and call me back when the video was obtained. Sherif Hashem called me back and advised that he was still working on it and would get back to me the following day. I inquired if the video system was working properly and he advised it was working and a copy would be made." Talbot then goes on to write that two days later he got a call from none other than Dick Tracy himself, Miller Thomas. He states that Thomas called him on his cell, which he found odd because he never gave Thomas his cell number. He then goes on to write: "This call was unusual because since he became the manager of record for Cure Lounge I try to limit my interaction with him. I personally know Miller Thomas because he was a Boston Police Homicide Detective and former President of the Detectives' Union. Due to his prior employment, I have always tried to avoid dealing with him professionally at Cure Lounge to avoid any allegations of favoritism."

Immediately my antennae went up. Police deal with security guards and private investigators all the time. An overwhelming number of them are former law enforcement. I could not understand for the life of me why Talbot would avoid dealing with one of his own: someone he could trust. As I continued reading Talbot's report it appeared to me that maybe he didn't trust Miller Thomas as much as I thought he did.

Talbot then writes that Thomas began to question him about the relevance of any video and began to ask Talbot about the underlying homicide investigation. Talbot says he advised Thomas to direct his questions to Detective Sullivan. Okay, so now I know there's definitely some beef here between Talbot and Thomas because this is way too much information to include in a report, and at the time this was not a high-profile case. What would have been the harm in giving a former colleague some information that might better assist him in helping him? It made no sense. They didn't have any suspects, so sharing information would not have helped anyone flee or get away with anything. In fact, all the cops knew at this time was that the victims were in the club partying before the shooting, and Talbot could have easily said, "We just want to see what they were doing in the club and see if they had any fights or disagreements with anyone." Where's the harm in saying that? You don't have to be a rocket scientist to figure that out. There's more to it than that, I kept thinking to myself.

Then Thomas writes to Talbot requesting a letter from law enforcement with an explanation as to why they need the video and a receipt to prove that Cure complied and gave them the video. Talbot informed Thomas this was an odd request and that out of the hundreds of prior requests, when detectives had gotten video from Cure they never had to write a letter explaining why they needed the video. It was at this point that Talbot told Thomas to call Detective Sullivan.

The next day, Talbot received a call from Detective Sullivan telling him the video was ready to be picked up. Talbot, along with Detective Arthur Hall-Brewster, the same detective present when Sherif spoke to B or G from the not so anonymous call, and another detective went to retrieve the video. Now here is where I start to get really paranoid. *It takes three detectives to go and retrieve a video? And then this video never gets logged into evidence? What the hell is going on here?*

Talbot says it is only then that Miller Thomas tells him the club only had video from the exterior cameras and that the interior cameras were not working. When Talbot confronts Thomas with the fact that Sherif Hashem had previously told him, when he initially made the request, that *all* cameras were working, Thomas responds by telling him Sherif was mistaken.

The three detectives leave Cure allegedly with footage of only the exterior cameras. Talbot concludes his report by saying one last peculiar thing in probably the most peculiar police report I have ever read by saying, "I did direct Detective Hall-Brewster to give the video to Sgt. Det. Sullivan. At no time did any of the Area A-1 personnel view the contents of the video."

There is only one reason Talbot would write that fact in there, and that was to distance himself or his detectives from this video debacle. None of them saw the video. The three detectives were simply errand boys.

The first thing we decided to do was to start asking for more information on the video. We asked for the receipt Talbot gave Miller for the video. Wouldn't you know that neither the police nor Cure could produce a copy of the receipt? It was as if it never happened.

Next we asked to inspect the video equipment to get a better understanding of how the system worked. The day before we were to go and inspect the system at Cure, the prosecutor, Pat Haggan, called me with some interesting information. Apparently Cure was now changing its story. They were claiming the police initially requested only the exterior cameras, not the interior cameras, and by the time the police made the second request the DVRs had already recorded over what had been previously recorded. Now I knew we were onto something big. When people start changing their stories midstream, something's up.

This prompted another field trip to meet with Sherif, so Sully and I set up a meeting with him at a Starbucks across the street from Harvard Law School. We asked Sherif point blank: "What exactly did Talbot request?" Sherif told us Talbot requested "the usual," which he took to mean *all* cameras, including the interior. He had absolutely no recollection of Talbot asking only for the exterior footage and said he would have found it odd, because everyone, including the bouncers who drove up to the scene immediately after, knew the victims in the BMW had been inside Cure moments earlier.

The police stood by the assertion that they had requested *all* cameras, not just the exterior cameras. That did not surprise me one bit, because once the police put something in a report, it would take an act of Congress to get them to change it.

So what really happened to the interior video footage of that night? There are really only two possibilities. Just have a look at each party's motive—not Aaron's motive, which the video allegedly depicted, but these two dueling parties, the cops and Cure. What is Cure's motive for this video to disappear? Well, drug dealing is prevalent in nightclubs; it is a major problem. Alexander Bradley is a drug dealer, so was Bradley or someone else dealing drugs inside Cure that night? If drug dealing were discovered, then Miller Thomas's job would not only be at risk, but the club would undoubtedly get shut down in a minute and it could say goodbye to its liquor license forever. So clearly if the video showed drug dealing, Cure had a motive to bury it.

What's the cops' motive to lie? That's a simple one. If the video does not show Aaron interacting with Daniel de Abreu, their whole motive goes bye-bye. So does their case, because the absence of a spilled drink would prove unequivocally that Bradley was lying. It would have been devastating to the commonwealth's case.

What evidence is there the cops would bury the video? The lack of a chain of custody is a big indicator. Then there is the timing of Talbot's report. The date on his report is October 1, 2013. That's a year and a half after the shooting. It was also the week that Bradley turned state's evidence against Aaron. Were cops tossing evidence that didn't mesh with what Bradley was saying?

To my mind, the most suspicious thing cops did was something they didn't do. With the exception of Paige Aiello, the blond woman who was talking to Daniel de Abreu that night, the police did not speak to a single patron present at Cure that night. Now, I was not surprised that at the beginning of the investigation they didn't go out of their way to question the people present. In 2012, this was just a case about two dead black immigrants on the side of the road. No one was going to be putting up any roadblocks or some great manhunt here. This kind of apathetic investigation is common throughout the United States when victims of crime are people of color. Cops do next to nothing to investigate their cases. The moment an NFL football player was suspected of being involved, however, the Commonwealth of Massachusetts spared no expense in its prosecution and law enforcement investigation. Detectives flew all the way across the country multiple times to talk to certain witnesses and deliver subpoenas they would never use.

Before Aaron was a suspect, the initial investigation yielded approximately 670 pages of police reports, and most of those were transcripts from interviews and the grand jury proceedings. After Aaron was accused, the number would jump to more than thirty-four thousand documents and several hundred hours of audio and video. To say the investigation got a steroid shot in the arm would be a gross understatement. I would estimate the investigation and prosecution of Aaron Hernandez cost the commonwealth somewhere in the $3 million range. The point being that considering all the time and money invested as the police scrambled to find anything to corroborate Alexander Bradley's story, you would think they would have gone looking for as many people as possible who were there that night and asked if anyone saw an altercation between Daniel de Abreu and Aaron Hernandez, a clearly recognizable figure.

The omission is even more glaring when you consider the statements of Cure security guard Jaime Furtado, who saw all seven men enter the club around the same time. He told police that moments later, a Patriots fan walked up and asked if he could have access to the back room so he could take a photo with Aaron Hernandez. The man had immediately spotted Hernandez and requested a photo, which Aaron politely declined; but then the guy told him it was his birthday. Aaron relented and said, "Fine, but let's do it in the back area. I don't want anyone else asking for one."

Jaime Furtado told the police that the fan and Aaron were escorted to the back area where Furtado took a picture with the man's cell phone. Not long after that, Furtado saw Aaron leaving Cure.

This lead was huge, but the cops never asked for any details about the Patriots fan. The photo on his phone could have shown whether Aaron had a spilled drink on his clothing. The time stamp on the photograph could have also given them a time frame for Aaron's movements. Police already knew Aaron was only in the club for nine minutes; the photo would have taken a good chunk of that time, and in the absence of video evidence could have given law enforcement a critical understanding of what occurred that night.

Another important fact not to be overlooked is that it should not have been hard for them to find this man. The police had the video of all people entering Cure that night and the time they arrived. Even better, they had the video of the ID scanner, which showed the driver's license or ID of everyone who entered the club.

The fan photo may have been missing at that point, but its existence told us a lot, and the cops did not want to go looking for anyone who could tell them what happened inside Cure during those nine minutes.

This loose end was going to come back to haunt them. The spilled drink incident never happened. The day would come when we would be able to prove it.

7.

MAKING OF A
MURDER WEAPON

There are people who become extremely angry when my clients are acquitted. Their frustration is unlike anything else I've ever seen. They may not even have known the alleged victims, but media coverage makes them feel like they did, so they dedicate untold time and energy to venting their frustration. But no one expresses the same frustration over the suffering of the innocent man: a man who has been beaten, sodomized, and incarcerated, possibly held for years on death row, for a crime he did not commit. No one weeps for him. No one demands accountability from those responsible for his wrongful incarceration, and no one seeks out the real killer. That's why as a defense attorney, tracking every point of evidence and connecting the who, how, and why of a case is vital.

Locating a murder weapon and linking it to a suspect is gold for homicide detectives. It answers the element of *how* in a murder case. If there are fingerprints and DNA on a gun that match a suspect, and ballistics show the bullets in the shooting came from the same gun, the chances of a conviction skyrocket. Without a murder weapon that directly ties to a suspect, police have to rely on eyewitnesses and circumstantial evidence to make their case. It's why the Boston police were desperate to link Aaron to a murder weapon once his name surfaced through the not so anonymous call about the Boston shootings. How they tried to do that is a lesson in how easy it is to convict someone through either faulty science or police misconduct.

Consider the timeline. First Aaron is linked to the Odin Lloyd shooting, which causes Detective Sullivan to remember seeing Aaron on the video at Cure Lounge on the night of the Boston shootings. Then Sherif Hashem makes his call to the tip line naming Aaron as a suspect in the Boston shootings. Then this: four days after Sherif's call, Trooper Joshua Winters from the Massachusetts Police Department responds to a multiple-vehicle crash on Interstate 91 near the Longmeadow, Massachusetts, exit. Jailene Diaz-Ramos, a five-foot-tall, nineteen-year-old Puerto Rican girl with dyed red hair, had crashed her 2012 red Toyota Camry while on the way to Six Flags to spend the day with her sister and her nieces and nephews.

As a precaution, she was transported to a nearby medical center. Meanwhile, her car was towed after Trooper Winters determined there was no licensed driver to drive the car away. While Winters investigated the crash, Troopers Paul Aten and Derek Cormier assisted in doing an inventory of the vehicle, during which the troopers located and unlocked a black briefcase found in the trunk of the car. It contained an unloaded silver-colored Smith & Wesson .38 revolver along with three loose rounds of ammunition. Trooper Aten then transported the gun back to the barracks where initial reports said it was logged into evidence, though that turned out not to be true. Jailene was then arrested for failure to produce a firearm ID card.

Boston police became aware of the traffic accident and the discovery of the gun, and were especially intrigued when they learned

Jailene was from Bristol and had graduated from the same high school as Aaron Hernandez. Jailene, who was very active on social media, often posted pictures of herself and her friends. Not only did her hometown grab the attention of Boston police, but she was also a Facebook friend of Aaron's brother D. J. Hernandez.

A week following the crash, Boston police received custody of the firearm and the three bullets. On August 1, 2013, firearms expert Tyrone Camper conducted an examination of the gun and did a test firing. His report came back saying there was a "reasonable degree" of certainty the gun matched the weapon used in the Boston shootings.

Jailene initially told police she had given a ride to a friend named "Chicago" and his "buddies," a group of semipro football players, who put their belongings in the trunk of the car. She believed one of Chicago's friends must have left the case containing the gun in her car without her knowledge.

Later, after getting an immunity agreement that indicated nothing she said could be used against her, she changed her story. She told the detectives during an interview in her attorney's office that she had purchased the gun in March of 2013 from a Puerto Rican named "Flaco" in Springfield, Massachusetts, for $300. She said she bought the gun after being robbed and needed it for protection.

The Boston cops didn't like the updated version, even though I believe it was the truth. They preferred the story that the gun belonged to Chicago, a nickname for John Alcorn, also of Bristol. Alcorn's home address was the same as T. L. Singleton's, the husband of Tanya Cummings-Singleton, who happened to be a cousin of Aaron Hernandez.

When we contacted Alcorn to hear his side of the story, he was pissed for being dragged into it. Alcorn, twenty-one at the time of the Boston shootings, grew up in Illinois and moved to Bristol when he was fourteen. He said he considered Jailene to be "like a sister" after meeting her in eighth grade. Alcorn, a semipro football player, admitted he had been in Jailene's car the day of the crash while getting a ride to work out at LA Fitness. She then drove him to work at a landscaping company. At no time did he have a gun or have knowledge of a gun, he insisted. He also said Jailene had become afraid for her safety after an ex-boyfriend kicked in the door of her home, and may have had the gun for protection. Despite the convoluted story, the police version of the "way of the gun," as we called it, went like this: the trail started with Jailene and led to Alcorn to T. L Singleton to Tanya Singleton to Aaron Hernandez.

Just like that, the Boston police, who had nothing linking Aaron Hernandez to the Boston shootings less than a week earlier, had found not only an anonymous caller linking Aaron to the crime, but also the potential murder weapon—all in a case that had been stone cold for nearly a year.

On the surface, the police had made several viable connections to Aaron. One would think that Boston's finest got extremely lucky, or possibly this is simply the way stupid criminals get caught all the time. But when someone's life is in your hands, it's hard to just accept what's on the surface. We really have to go where people are not willing to go to get the real answers. Most of the time things are exactly as the police say they are, but more often than you might think, they are not.

It is terrifyingly easy for someone to be nearly convicted on what appears to be solid evidence, and then the evidence turns out to be just a house of cards waiting to be blown away.

I decided to back up and deconstruct the "solid evidence" of the murder weapon one step at a time, and quickly it became clear that this was definitely not the right gun. Let's start with the original ballistics report conducted *before* Aaron was listed as a suspect. One spent bullet and one bullet fragment were recovered from Safiro Furtado's head during his autopsy. Another spent bullet was recovered from Aquilino Freire's forearm. Other ammunition was gathered at the crime scene the day after the shootings. A week after the shootings, Boston police conducted an analysis of the casings found at the crime scene, and the initial ballistics report came back showing some of the bullets could have been fired by a .357 magnum, a .40-caliber semiautomatic, or a .38 special.

Now think about this for a second. As soon as Aaron becomes a suspect, Detective Sullivan puts out a notice to all police departments in the Massachusetts, Connecticut, and Rhode Island tri-state area that they are looking for either a .357-, .40-, or .38-caliber gun. Just think of how many individual .357 guns there are in those three states, then add that to all of the .40-caliber guns in those three states, then add that to all of the .38 specials as well as .38-caliber guns in those three states as well. Can you imagine the astronomical odds of finding the one gun that matches the bullets fired into the BMW that night? Add these two little facts for good measure: it was the only gun confiscated and tested by the Boston Police Department; and it was found three days after naming Aaron Hernandez a suspect for a double murder that occurred a year earlier. These cops should not be working the beat. They should be playing Lotto!

What's unclear is how Detective Sullivan found the gun to begin with. In Florida, we have depositions in criminal cases, which give us the opportunity to ask officers under oath how they came about certain information. This is not the case in most states, Massachusetts included. Consider this. When a detective is looking for a particular gun, he enters the information he has into a statewide system and gets a list of all guns found on the streets, either at crime scenes or through arrests. Without a deposition, we don't know when Detective Sullivan entered his request, but by all indications it was after Aaron became a suspect.

On Magic Monday, a gun suddenly appears and it was the only gun ever flagged. I still don't know when the Massachusetts State Police recovered this gun. How did they know to call Detective Sullivan? These were questions I intended to ask him on the stand but oddly, prosecutors never called Detective Sullivan, the lead supervisor and detective in the case. Curiously enough they called two detectives from his squad about other less important matters.

It was the only gun ever recovered that was turned over to the Boston Police Department and the only gun ever tested by the Boston Firearms Analysis Unit. What's even crazier is that not a single witness ever identified the gun. Alexander Bradley, the commonwealth's star witness, after being granted immunity, told the police he bought the murder weapon for Aaron and that it was a .357 Magnum. Bradley would later testify he had been dealing drugs for over a decade, was very familiar with guns, and owned a vast arsenal. As Bradley had been the one to buy this gun, logic would tell you that he knew the difference between a .357 Magnum and a .38 six-shooter. He also told police that after the Daniel de Abreu and Safiro Furtado shootings, he and Aaron sped away in the Toyota 4Runner, and while driving down the turnpike on their way home, Bradley told Aaron: "You better get rid of that gun." According to Bradley, Aaron then took his shirt off, wiped the gun down, and threw it out the window into a wooded area. This occurred just outside of Boston, but somehow the gun miraculously made its way back to Aaron Hernandez's hometown of Bristol, Connecticut. Boston detectives also showed Bradley a picture of the gun found in Jailene's car and he said, "That's not the gun." Bradley was again asked to identify the gun in front of a grand jury. After asking the prosecutor to turn it around he said unequivocally: "That is not the gun."

Why was Bradley so certain? Perhaps because the gun that prosecutors claimed as the murder weapon was unusual: it was an antique. It was made in 1913. It looked like one of those six-shooters from a western. It was worn with scratches in several areas, and had greenish yellow stains.

There's no way a twenty-one-year-old NFL baller making millions of dollars is going to go around town carrying an antique gun. The idea is just beyond stupid. Our investigators tracked the history of the six-shot revolver and learned it was stolen from a hardware store in Kentucky in 1927, two years before the Great Depression. It had been on the streets ever since. I know my opinion on this is not scientifically based, but I just can't see Aaron carrying this old gun around in his glove compartment. It didn't make any sense.

The murder weapon story continued to evolve until it was just plain bizarre. After being granted full immunity, Jailene was given a photo lineup of five guns and asked to pick which gun was hers. She picked the wrong gun.

Jailene also informed detectives that the gun she owned had the serial number scratched out. The antique gun logged into evidence and used in the trial of Aaron Hernandez had a clearly visible serial number. Was the gun switched by Boston detectives when they picked it up from the Massachusetts State Police? I can't say that. I wish I had evidence to support that. While I'd be the first person to call out a shady cop, I simply do not have enough to reach that conclusion without speculating.

The Boston police made a big deal out of Jailene having gone to the same high school as Aaron Hernandez. But the fact is there are only two high schools in Bristol, and Aaron was older and off playing football at the University of Florida by the time she attended Bristol Central. While that connection to Aaron may have been a tenuous one, a clever prosecutor could connect the dots and make a jury accept that a connection existed, especially considering our next hurdle: the forensic expert's findings. Juries like forensics, and they were going to believe this gun was in fact the gun that killed these two men, regardless of how bizarre the circumstances surrounding the gun were.

Right off the bat, I wanted to know if any of these Bristol people were connected to Alexander Bradley. I figured that while the prosecutor was trying to connect the gun to Aaron, I could just as easily trace any connections to Bradley, and thereby create reasonable doubt.

While the prosecutor would argue there were only six degrees of separation between the gun and Aaron, we would soon find there were even fewer degrees of separation between the gun and Bradley.

One of our investigators, former New York City homicide detective Jerry Lyons, dove into this task and immediately established a relationship with Jailene's mother, Marilyn Ramos. He learned, for example, that Jailene was a serious pothead. We knew that Bradley was a marijuana trafficker, so naturally we wanted to see who Jailene's weed connection was.

He was a guy named Jamar, who happened to be Bradley's right-hand man. Jamar was named in a police report we uncovered involving a shooting in Bristol of a rival marijuana dealer's home.

We also found out her child's father, Ljune Smart, not only knew Bradley but had actually introduced Jailene to Bradley on several occasions. Given these connections, it was not surprising that Jailene kept a gun in her car.

The only one saying the antique six-shooter was the murder weapon was Detective Tyrone Camper of the Boston Police Department's Firearms Analysis Unit. We got our first look at Detective Camper during pretrial hearings, when we tried to exclude the testimony that the gun was a match for the bullets that killed Abreu and Furtado. He came across as a genuine witness, so I knew we would do very well taking a friendly but professional approach in attacking the science. He was not going to deny criticism of what are falsely called "ballistics" (technically the correct term is *tool mark evidence* because the markings made by a firearm are studied and compared to the bullets, not the other way around).

Many people watch TV programs like *CSI* and really believe that when prosecutors call "forensic experts" to the stand they are going to talk about sound forensic science based on proven scientific principles. Generally, believe it or not, the science is not always so cut and dried. To understand the problem you have to understand the criminal justice system. It's a system where an overwhelming majority of accused defendants are people of color and/or impoverished. So a majority of the people are represented by overworked and underpaid public defenders who neither have the time nor the resources to challenge forensic evidence by hiring their own experts. Those who have the money to pay for a private lawyer rarely have funds left over to pay costs for forensic experts and investigators. Think about it. If you were ever accused of a serious crime, how much money could you and your family pool together to not only pay for a good lawyer but also the costs of litigation? Prosecutors have an entire police force and crime labs at their disposal, and tax payers to cover the bill.

This unbalanced system got a real kick in the ass when two idealistic, hard-working defense lawyers started a small nonprofit organization called the Innocence Project out of the Cardozo School of Law at Yeshiva University in New York. The Innocence Project began retrying cases of inmates throughout the nation, using DNA evidence to overturn wrongful convictions. They made the system look at itself by utilizing the very science used to convict the guilty, and employing it to exonerate the innocent.

These two lawyers, Barry Scheck and Peter Neufeld, who first earned national attention by representing O. J. Simpson, created a movement that has rocked our criminal justice system and continues to teach lawyers across the country that this broken system of ours can be fixed.

The ripple effect from the innocence movement has prompted several governmental agencies to conduct studies on the validity of certain forensic sciences. In 2009, the National Academy of Sciences wrote a scathing report blasting almost every type of forensic science with the exception of nuclear DNA testing. The scientific community fought the findings and still fights to this day rather than accept there are flaws in the way we assess evidence, and try to fix them. Firearms comparison is a case in point.

Firearms comparison is not definitive the way DNA evidence is. DNA evidence protocol was developed through rigorous scientific study and is applied in carefully controlled laboratories. Firearms comparisons are usually done by cops with no scientific background. The police will have the gun they suspect is the gun involved in a crime, so they fire a bullet from it. They then try to

match all the striations created by the gun on the bullet to the striations on a bullet taken from a crime scene. Basically they're taking
a microscope and eyeballing two bullets side by side, and saying
the markings look the same. Now in Aaron's case, don't think for
a second that Detective Camper did not feel pressure when he received the .38, knowing it was a high-profile case and the suspect
was Aaron Hernandez. He knew that detectives were trying to tie
this gun to Hernandez; or at the very least there was some prede-
cisional bias.

A few years back the Massachusetts supreme court ruled that
firearms comparison evidence was faulty and should not be vali-
dated by a police officer testifying by using the word "science." This
is because many federal government-based reports from 2008 and
on found there was essentially no science behind this area of forensic testimony.

The only witness called to testify about the gun for the prosecution in Aaron's case was Sergeant Tyrone Camper.

We had learned from our discovery that Camper had taken a
number of courses in which he was taught there was a lack of scientific foundation for the category of forensics he practiced. We
focused our cross-examination of him on that fact, knowing he
would have to concede that very prestigious organizations such as
the National Research Council, the National Academy of Sciences,
and the President's Council of Advisors on Science and Technol-
ogy found that what he would be testifying to would not have the
validation of the scientific community behind it. We would also be
pressing the issue of bias, and the fact that he knew when he tested
the 104-year-old Smith & Wesson that the Commonwealth of Massachusetts was trying to connect it to Aaron Hernandez.

Finally, we confronted Sergeant Camper with a photograph he
had taken of a bullet he believed matched the Smith & Wesson. He
had to agree that it clearly had more differences than similarities,
even though he held firm to his opinion that in his judgment the
bullet came from the Smith & Wesson. Aside from the flaws in the

science was the damning fact that both the gun and the bullets re-covered were tested multiple times for fingerprints and DNA and *all* experts agreed that neither Aaron Hernandez's fingerprints nor his DNA were on the 104-year-old six-shooter. After two days on the stand, the final nail in the coffin for Camper came when my co-counsel Linda Kenney Baden asked him if he had found any-thing in his years of testing (related to the case) that connected Aaron Hernandez to any of the objects or the gun he had tested. His answer was no.

8.

WEEKEND AT BERNIE'S

Going into the Boston murder trial of Aaron Hernandez, many thought the crime scene would have little to no significance. At least I'm sure that's what the prosecutors and the media were thinking. Most people thought this was going to be about Alexander Bradley and his story. Most people could guess what the defense was going to argue: that Bradley was in fact the shooter. So who cares what happened at the crime scene if it wasn't Aaron Hernandez who did the shooting?

A crime scene, however, reveals so much more than just what might have happened. The scene can tell you a lot about how the investigation itself was handled, the culture of the police agency, and the thought process of the investigators early on in the case. Never was the Boston Police Department more on display than when it processed the murder scene of Daniel de Abreu and Safiro Furtado.

The crime occurred on an overpass, a bridge of sorts such as one would wait on before getting on the Massachusetts Turnpike, on the corner of Shawmut Avenue and Herald Street, very close to the theater district in the South End of Boston. It's a very upscale neighborhood, and Shawmut turns into Tremont Street, an artery of downtown Boston.

The first thing I noticed when examining this scene was the time it was cleared, which was just before six o'clock on a Monday morning. The shootings occurred at approximately two thirty in the morning, so in three and a half hours Boston PD came upon the scene; notified EMS; tended to the victims; blocked off the scene; called in detectives and crime scene personnel; cleared the area; then photographed and documented everything visible in the dark including all glass, blood patterns, and blood trails. They also had to find and speak to any relevant witnesses and then tow the BMW to the forensic bay for further processing. I don't care if there were ten police departments assisting that night; there is no way they could have processed that scene properly that quickly.

Immediately, I knew there were going to be a slew of concerns about how the crime scene was handled. Breaking down crime scenes is something I have a great deal of experience in. Almost all the cases my firm handles are homicides, and I have been blessed to work with some of the best forensic experts in the world, so spotting the issue comes fairly easily to me. My experience is an asset, but the fact is that processing crime scenes is really quite straightforward once you know what to look for.

Everything begins with the first officer on the scene. This is usually a patrol officer, and while they are trained in crime scene protocol, rarely do they follow it. I don't know if it's adrenaline or lack of experience, but 90 percent of first responders do a terrible job of preserving a crime scene. Their one and only job, after safeguarding any victims, is to secure the location so others can document and process evidence, because you never get a second chance to preserve a crime scene.

The first cop on the scene that July night was Officer Luciano Cirino. His priority when arriving at a scene like this is the preservation of life, so Officer Cirino's first order of business was to see if he could save the life of either Daniel de Abreu or Safiro Furtado. His report says that neither one showed any signs of life, so after he called EMS his focus should have shifted to keeping others out of the area. Boston PD crime scene regulations state that officers must place crime scene tape approximately a hundred feet around the scene in all directions. This is pretty standard across many police departments. When I cross-examined Cirino, he had no clue how far he was supposed to put the crime scene tape. Based on the pictures I saw, I would estimate the tape was placed approximately thirty feet in each direction. Why is this important? It's a shooting, and cops will be looking for projectiles and possibly shell casings that have traveled outside the immediate area. You don't want bystanders stepping on, kicking, or destroying any potential evidence that could make a difference in the case.

One of the biggest issues in the Aaron Hernandez trial would be how many shots were fired and the direction of the bullets. We contended there were six shots fired and the prosecution wanted to argue there were only five. Because they only recovered five, Bradley would later change his story to match that of the prosecution; so it then became a point of contention as to Bradley's credibility. But for the purposes of the crime scene, the distance of the tape was important.

After an officer puts up the tape he needs to start a crime scene log. Again, this is not rocket science. You want to know and identify all members of law enforcement coming and going from the crime scene in case something goes missing or an issue occurs at the scene and you need to know who was there. No crime scene log was ever created for the Daniel de Abreu and Safiro Furtado crime scene.

As more officers began to arrive, their job was to assist in maintaining the perimeter and to look for potential witnesses. Usually they park their cars to block off access for other cars and pedestrians, not to mention the media. Instead of containing the area, however, the scene of the Boston shootings had police cars so close they were potentially on top of bullet projectiles and blood trails. You see how this is unfolding?

Once EMS arrives the officers are to escort them into the scene, watch what they disturb and take note of it, and remain with them. They also are to inform them they are not to disturb any other portion of the scene. None of this was done. EMS arrived and went straight to the bodies without an escort and weren't told to not disturb the scene. Had they been told, they might not have done what they did, which was to place sheets on top of the bodies of Daniel de Abreu and Safiro Furtado, thereby destroying any potential blood pattern evidence that could have assisted law enforcement in determining how all of this occurred.

If DNA had been an issue, placing sheets would clearly have contaminated the bodies, as the sheets were taken from an ambulance where they could easily have had some prior contact with either other patients or nonsterile areas. Then the EMS officer went further, and took it upon himself to cover the front windshield of the vehicle to prevent the media from taking pictures from a distance of thirty feet of the bodies and scene. All these actions fell outside the purview of EMS, whose only function at a crime scene is the preservation of life.

There is no need to put sheets up to block a windshield. Crime scene investigators have *scene screens*, mobile screens that block bystanders' view. In addition to extending the perimeter, a police officer can also instruct anyone, including the media, to back up a safe distance to allow police to do their work. During the trial, after several police officers insisted there was nothing else they could have done besides contaminate the scene with sheets, I did a Google search to show what a scene screen looks like, and I happened to find one with BOSTON POLICE DEPARTMENT in big, bold letters across it. The police officers didn't have an answer to that.

One of the first things I noticed when going through the police reports on the crime scene was just how many were there. I found it very peculiar that the same police department that didn't even set up a crime scene log had almost each and every officer who arrived at the scene fill out a report.

I couldn't help but think, They're hiding something. Many of the filled-out reports had nothing important to say and were unusually mundane. When police officers do this it's usually to distance themselves from something they know happened but do not want to say they witnessed. I kept looking and struck gold.

One of the officers, Officer Thomas O'Donnell, mentioned that before he arrived on the scene he saw a street sweeper go by the area. I couldn't believe my eyes. I had never seen anything remotely close to an actual street sweeper going through a crime scene. That's just unheard of. This officer's report downplayed the fact by saying the street sweeper came by on the side street where the silver SUV had been, not the BMW. Therefore the street sweeper was irrelevant. *What a crock of shit.* If anyone in the BMW fired off shots toward the SUV, those projectiles would have landed on the far side of the street and been swept away. This made me take a closer look at these five Cape Verdeans in the BMW to see if that was a possibility, and things just started to fall into place.

The first thing that stood out was that two of the three guys, Raychides Sanches and Gerson Lopes, fled the scene after the shootings. *What?* Two of their good friends lie dead in the front seats of the car, another one is shot in the arm and bleeding, and while one of them stays to get medical attention for his arm, the other two who are unharmed take off? Something's just not right here. Raychides Sanches would later tell police he actually did not run but stayed around at the scene dripping in blood and that one of the officers even took his name. (There's no such mention in any report.) Then he said he got tired of waiting around and left. He testified that no cab drivers would pick up a black guy covered in blood, so he had to go to an ATM, then clean up a bit before catching a cab home. When police asked him to produce the clothes he was wearing that night to perhaps see if there was any gunshot residue on them, Sanches informed them, as he would later testify, that in the morning he gathered the clothes he was wearing that night and burned them.

Police also asked him for his cell phone. We were also interested in it. His cell phone records could have given us an idea of his movements, what kind of stuff this guy was into, etc. Sanches, a dark-skinned man with short hair and thin beard, testified that he didn't own a cell phone. Yet we went on his social media and saw numerous selfies taken with a cell phone in his hand around the time of the shootings. Sanches's response was that he had a phone but no cell service. He just used the phone for selfies.

Gerson Lopes was much more cryptic about his actions after the shootings. He told police that after exiting the car unharmed, he waited around with Aquilino Freire until EMS started working on him, and then he just walked away. As critical as I have been of Boston PD, I have a hard time believing they would miss Gerson Lopes and Raychides Sanches, especially if they were talking to Freire in an ambulance. Police reports from the early responding officers all say they knew there were five guys in the BMW and two of them fled before police arrived on the scene. But what if anything did they take with them? That kept popping into my head. Was this a drug deal? Was it gang related? Did the Cape Verdeans fire shots at the SUV? Apparently, I wasn't the only one thinking along these lines: a Boston police detective speaking to the media under anonymity told the *Boston Herald* the shootings were gang related.

Aquilino Freire was rushed to a nearby hospital that night. Upon reviewing his medical records Linda Kenney Baden noticed that when asked by the emergency room nurse what happened to him, Freire responded that "he and his friends had been in a gunfight." Emergency room personnel are especially trained to note all statements made by individuals with gunshot wounds. Add the fact that Freire told the nurse he was in "a gunfight," which implies an exchange of fire, not just a one-sided attack, and it seriously

brought into question what these guys were up to. Were they innocent victims?

The police were interested in knowing this too. Although they
didn't expend much effort trying to figure things out, they did do
something that would knock me off my chair, and knock the street
sweeper off the top of my list as the most outrageous thing I had
ever seen done at a crime scene. After EMS finished putting sheets
over the bodies and the windshield, crime scene investigators were
called to photograph and document the evidence. Crime scene personnel took long-range photos of the scene and close-ups of various blood trails and then took photos of the BMW. When it finally
came to photos of the bodies, I noticed the lighting was much better. Then I realized the photos had been taken in a forensic bay
garage. How did the bodies get to the police forensic bay all the
way across town in Roxbury? They literally towed the car with the
bodies in it!

I could not believe what I was seeing. Imagine this if you will.
You're driving to work on a Monday morning and you're at a stop
light next to a tow truck. You look to your left and see a BMW on
top of a flatbed with bullet holes, blood, broken glass, and two dead
bodies covered in sheets. That is Boston's finest. I cannot begin to
tell you the number of reasons for crime scene preservation why
you would *not* do that. Just simply keep in mind that the goal of
the crime scene investigator was to document the deceased at the
scene as it was that night. Not after the car was propped up on a
flatbed tow truck, driven across town, then lowered and pulled into
the forensic bay.

The scenario was so ludicrous I was reminded of a 1989 comedy
movie called *Weekend at Bernie's* in which two guys find their boss
dead and decide to throw parties at his house while propping up
his dead body and pretending he's still alive. I cannot imagine the
indignity of seeing these bodies bounce around in a car as they're
being transported across downtown Boston at rush hour. I didn't
know Daniel de Abreu or Safiro Furtado. I don't know if they were

good men or not. But I met their families. They were all good, decent people who loved them dearly. They did not deserve to have their loved ones' bodies treated that way. I know the families were not fans of mine because I was defending the man they thought killed their sons. But they were always respectful. We interacted numerous times each day for almost two months. They would greet me with a somber "good morning" and hold the door open for me if they were walking into the courtroom. I had taken an oath to defend my client, but still my heart went out to them.

What many don't understand is that victims never receive justice unless the defendant gets a fair trial, and the most important part of a fair trial is a vigorous defense. Justice means fairness, not punishment, and what many people don't realize is that the accused is the one on trial, and the consequences and punishment are his or hers alone. If an accused does not get a fair trial and is found guilty the case will come back on appeal, or reappear via many other types of post-conviction motions. The families will never receive closure, and will have to relive the pain of another trial years later.

I was most interested in justice, which would also bring finality. Not only was Aaron Hernandez innocent of this crime, but the real killer was not being held responsible. The Boston police, through their own ineptitude, hadn't truly focused on the case until Detective Sullivan saw Aaron Hernandez on the news. Before that these were just two dead black guys on the side of the road. I'm not describing the attitude of just one or two officers. I'm describing a culture within the department that reared its ugly head throughout this case.

You may be wondering, why did police tow the BMW with the bodies still in the car if it would hurt their murder case and destroy evidence? Detective Paul MacIsaac, one of the three main detectives assigned to the case, would testify that the reason they towed the car with the bodies was that they needed a search warrant to get in the car to photograph the bodies. I cannot begin to tell you how much of a crock this excuse is. While it is true that the Fourth Amendment protects our citizens against unreasonable searches and seizures, there are a plethora of exceptions that enable law enforcement to do its job. One of the exceptions is known as *exigent circumstances*, which basically says police can enter an area if they either believe someone might be in danger or that evidence might get lost or destroyed. That is the most common reason used by law enforcement when entering a place without a warrant.

There are other exceptions that would allow police to enter a vehicle to photograph a body. Even more compelling is the legal principle called *standing*. Standing means that a person must have a reason to challenge an illegal search; in this case someone would have to argue that they had a reasonable expectation of privacy in the BMW and therefore police entry was illegal. However, in this case the windows were either down or shattered by bullets, and the inside of the BMW was clearly in *plain view*, as it is called. Nobody can claim a reasonable expectation of privacy to something that everyone can see.

What was not in plain view was the trunk of the BMW, which the police searched after receiving the warrant. The only person who could challenge the search of the trunk was the owner of the car, Daniel de Abreu's sister (unknown at the time), or the five guys in the BMW, two of whom were dead. That left only three surviving guys from the BMW who could challenge the search. Two of them fled the scene, while the other was in the hospital telling people he was in a gunfight.

The ugly truth is the cops were faced with a decision that night. Should we process this scene correctly in hopes of finding the murderer of these two men, if in fact it was murder and not self-defense? Or should we roll the dice and see what's behind door number three, the trunk? Maybe we find guns, drugs, or even better, money. As I said earlier, these were two black guys on the side of the road. These circumstances tell me one thing and one thing only, and that is that Boston PD was clearly more interested in making a drug or gang bust than they were in catching the killer of Daniel de Abreu and Safiro Furtado.

When I questioned multiple police officers on the stand about the yellow crime scene tape, standing true to the blue code of silence each police officer answered: "We never entered the BMW." But the truth is that the cops were all up in that car even before getting a warrant, and we were able to prove it.

When I first read that their excuse for moving the BMW with the bodies in it was that they were waiting on a warrant, I started to scour the internet for photographs from the media and crime scene photos to see if I could prove they went in the car anyway. I hit the jackpot when I found a photo of the back seat of the BMW taken at the crime scene. I began to zoom in and I could see a clear image of yellow crime scene tape stuffed in the middle of the back seat of the BMW. To this day I have no idea how the hell it got there or for what earthly reason it was put there. But imagine the look on each officer's face as I showed him that some idiot at the crime scene had stuffed a piece of yellow crime scene tape in the back seat. As it turned out, there was nothing of interest found in the trunk of the BMW. But evidence that could have helped them in their investigation of the shooting was lost forever.

9.

EYE PHONE

Seven months after that fateful night in Boston, the relationship between Aaron and Bradley had cooled. Aaron had just signed a new contract with the Patriots and was busy rearranging and prioritizing his new life. In October 2012, he got engaged to his lifetime love Shayanna, pregnant with Avielle, who would be born a month later, on Aaron's birthday. Things were slowing down, but in a good way. Aaron also began to realize the long-term lifestyle a professional football career could provide. Football and family were starting to become his priorities.

Aaron knew Bradley could be trouble and began to distance himself slightly from him, but not so much as to raise suspicion. The last thing Aaron wanted was for Bradley to feel he couldn't trust Aaron anymore. He told me how dangerous Bradley could be if he felt crossed. Aaron knew only too well that Bradley was feared and respected in Bristol as a notorious drug dealer, and had seen him gun down two people in cold blood. He knew his propensity for violence, and that would have been a dangerous thing. Aaron had no intention of jeopardizing his family. Shayanna, or "Shay," as friends call her, allowed Aaron to be Aaron. He was still just twenty-two years old and if he wanted to play video games, she let him. If he wanted to go out with his friends, she let him. If that included a weekend getaway, she was not going to stand in his way. After all, Aaron was still being responsible, meeting all his professional responsibilities, being where he needed to be and when he needed to be there. While it wasn't the ideal family situation, Shay felt comfortable in her own skin, her place with Aaron, and their future. Hopefully, he would mature as he grew older and became a father.

For now it was okay for him to enjoy his success. Shayanna was busy with Avielle, born on November 6 in the midst of what proved to be an up and down 2012 season for Aaron, who would miss six games because of injuries to his ankle and shoulder. He needed to rehab, get healthy, and come back with a monster 2013 season. That was the plan.

In early February 2013, Aaron was in New Orleans to watch Super Bowl XLVII between the Baltimore Ravens and the San Francisco 49ers at the Superdome. That's the game during which there was a power outage in the third quarter, stopping play for thirty-four minutes. Conspiracy theorists suggest someone pulled the plug to keep the Ravens from gaining momentum. "You're a zillion-dollar company and your lights go out?" offered Ray Lewis, the Ravens legendary linebacker who retired after the game. I guess we'll never know.

While Aaron was there he ran into Deonte Thompson, an old college teammate and a rookie wide receiver for the Ravens. The Ravens won the game 34-31 and became Super Bowl champions. Thompson was not only excited to be a champion, he was also excited to see Aaron and catch up on their old college days. There was going to be a celebration in a couple of weeks in Thompson's hometown of Belle Glade, Florida, or "the Muck," as it is known locally due to its unique swampy soil used to grow sugar cane. The Muck, or Muck City, is a small town in Palm Beach County just minutes from the beaches, golf courses, polo grounds, and multimillion-dollar homes owned by Donald Trump, the Kennedy family, and many others. While it may be close to all that wealth, it's worlds apart in its realities.

With a little more than four thousand residents, Belle Glade is the breeding ground for more NFL football players per capita than any town in the country. Deonte Thompson, a product of the Muck, invited Aaron to the Super Bowl party he was throwing with his teammate Pernell McPhee, who was also from the Muck and played linebacker for the Ravens.

Aaron really wanted to go, but did not want to go alone. He asked Bradley to go with him. They were only going to be there for five days, then Aaron had to go to Arizona for a promotional photo shoot for Muscle Milk, with which he had an endorsement deal. Aaron told me Bradley initially did not want to go, so in order to entice him Aaron said he would introduce him to contacts who would supply him with any cocaine purchases he wanted to make.

While Aaron didn't know anyone personally who was selling cocaine, he knew enough people there who would introduce Bradley to those who did. Aaron assured Bradley: "Don't worry, these are my boys. They will definitely not fuck you." That one assurance would set off a chain of events that would affect the lives of several people forever, including Aaron's.

Aaron and Bradley landed at Palm Beach International Airport on February 10, 2013. Once they landed, Aaron used his cell phone to make a call. Not long afterward two men arrived, Deonte Thompson and a man named Tyrone Crawford, who Aaron was meeting for the first time. Bradley, all business and ever alert, began introducing himself to everyone as "Rock." Drug dealers almost always use aliases when conducting business, especially with people they don't know. This way no one knows their real name and if there's a snitch in the house it's never getting back to him, especially all the way back to Connecticut.

The group then drove a rented white Porsche to Springfield Suites off I-95 in West Palm Beach where a number of people in town to attend the party were staying. After a few hours of getting acquainted, the group headed to the Super Bowl celebration held in Belle Glade, about a thirty-minute drive from West Palm Beach. The party took place at a hip-hop bar called Club 21 and was attended by a large number of friends and other locals from the area. It was essentially a neighborhood get-together that Deonte Thompson was excited to host. He was proud of where he was raised and this was a way for the graduate of Glades Central High School to share his Super Bowl success with his hometown.

At Aaron's suggestion, one of Thompson's friends began introducing Rock to the "right people." It wasn't long before Rock and this individual I will call "X" began talking, a conversation that extended throughout the party and after.

Aaron, Bradley, Thompson, Crawford, and another man named Je'rrelle Pierre and X, also of Belle Glade, were together at least two more nights in South Florida, spending much of their time in clubs in Miami and South Beach. Bradley and X were essentially tied at the hip while the others partied like rock stars, or ballers I should say. Thompson's birthday was also February 14, adding more reason to celebrate.

Bradley and Aaron tell completely different stories about what happened during the last twenty-four hours of their trip. The following is Bradley's version.

During one of those nights, Bradley and Aaron were still in South Florida at a club where they worked their way to the VIP section. It was there, according to Bradley, that Aaron noticed two white guys with low haircuts standing on the other side of the club. Aaron whispered to Bradley that they might be undercover police officers.

"If they are it's because of the stupid shit you did in Boston," Bradley said abruptly.

That comment allegedly upset Aaron. "I knew he didn't like what I said," Bradley testified. "He turned away and it wasn't really mentioned anymore . . . He seemed to be mad and angry."

Aaron and Bradley were still in West Palm Beach on the night of February 13, 2013, when they decided to make a return trip to Tootsie's Cabaret, a well-known strip club located at NW 183 Street in Miami Gardens near the stadium where the Miami Dolphins play football. They had been there the previous night. It was their after-party spot when they were tired of regular nightclubs.

Tootsie's is normally a lively establishment where well-endowed women dance fully nude for tips. The club, which features private suites and private skyboxes, is open seven days a week from noon to six in the morning and caters to a varied clientele that includes college kids, laborers, businessmen, and celebrities.

Aaron, Bradley, and a group of men, including Crawford, arrived at about three in the morning. The group went upstairs to a private room and settled in for some personal attention. Private tables aren't cheap. They include bottle service, a personal waitress, and more intimate access to the dancers. Aaron put his credit card down to open a tab.

At some point, Bradley says he told the woman providing the bottle service that his cell phone was about to die and asked whether she could charge the battery for him. He said the woman initially came back with a charger for an iPhone 4 that didn't fit into Bradley's iPhone 5. The woman said, according to Bradley, that she would take the phone and charge it at the back bar.

For the next two hours, the group continued to party like ballers and had numerous dances with the naked girls as a steady stream of liquor was consumed. Eventually, as the club prepared for closing, the bill arrived. It was in excess of $10,000.

At this point, Bradley testified that Aaron demanded Bradley pay half the bill. Bradley balked at the idea. "I was telling him it's not fair," Bradley would say. "There's no way. These are your friends. I don't know these guys."

Bradley said Aaron got upset at that response, but Bradley persisted. "If it was going to be split, then these guys shouldn't have been with us if it was going to be a tab that was split."

Bradley said a brief verbal argument ensued until the group was asked to leave. Bradley then said five men got into an SUV to leave Tootsie's with Pierre in the driver's seat, Aaron in the passenger seat, Crawford in the back seat behind the driver, a friend of Pierre's called X in the middle seat, and Bradley in the back seat behind the front passenger seat.

About five minutes into the trip back to West Palm Beach, Bradley said he realized he had forgotten his cell phone at Tootsie's. Bradley says he asked the driver if he could drive back to the club so he could retrieve his phone. The driver looked at Aaron as if to seek his approval. "No, don't turn around," Aaron said, according to Bradley.

Another argument ensued. "What do you mean? I need my phone," Bradley said. "There's important stuff in there. I have my kids' pictures in there."

"Oh, don't worry about it. I'll buy you one," Aaron said.

"Why would you want to buy me a new phone?" Bradley said. "The phone's right here. We could just turn around and get it."

Bradley says he pleaded with the driver: "Why are you listening to this guy like he's your boss or something? He's not the boss. I'm an adult. Turn around so I can get my phone."

As Aaron turned the music up in the car, Bradley turned to one of the passengers in the back seat and tried to make his case. "Can you believe this? This is crazy. What's up with your brother?" Bradley said, referring to the driver.

Bradley said he finally gave up and fell asleep from the long night of drinking and partying as the SUV continued north toward West Palm Beach. Bradley's account was that he was awakened when the car stopped moving. He opened his eyes to see "a gun in my face."

In his grand jury testimony, Bradley said the gun came from someone who "was from the front" seat. When asked then if he could tell who was holding the gun, he said, "I think it was Aaron Hernandez."

Bradley said he put up his right hand to shield his face just as a shot was fired.

"It was a loud, ringing noise," Bradley said.

The bullet pierced Bradley's right hand and entered his head between his eyebrows, traveling through his right eye.

The car was in an alley in an industrial area about seventy miles north of Miami. Bradley said he was then pushed out of the car by the passenger next to him in the back seat. Bradley said he rolled over and grabbed on to a fence and tried to pull himself up as blood streamed down his face.

Though his right eye was badly damaged, Bradley said that's when he saw Aaron's leg hanging out of the passenger door. "He was the only light-skinned guy in the car," Bradley said, and believed Aaron had helped push him out of the car before it sped off. Bradley said he walked almost to the end of the alley where an African American man arrived and called for help.

Bradley said he woke up a day later in a hospital after undergoing three surgeries. His right eye was so severely damaged it had to be removed.

Law enforcement officials soon arrived to question Bradley about the shooting, but all he would offer was that his attackers were two unidentified African American males. He told EMS and police at the scene that he didn't know who shot him. Bradley would later say he didn't tell police he was with Aaron Hernandez because "he wanted revenge."

"I almost didn't want to believe what was happening," Bradley told the grand jury. "I mean this guy was my best friend for so long prior to that. It was a shock to me that he wasn't the first person I saw when I woke up. I wanted to get in touch with him and see what was going on."

Once the police left, Bradley said he used a hospital phone to call Aaron and offered this account of their ensuing conversations.

"Where you at?" Bradley asked when Aaron answered.

"Who's this?" Aaron said.

"It's your friend. You don't miss me? Why are you not here?"

Bradley said Aaron seemed shocked to learn he was still alive and offered a few "huhs" before hanging up.

Bradley said he called right back. "Why are you hanging up on me? What are you scared of? What are you worried about? Why are you not here?"

Bradley said Aaron hung up again without responding. Bradley called back a third time.

"Look, I don't know why you keep hanging up the phone. This is not like some recorded call. There's not law enforcement in my room. They all just left, so I don't know what you're so scared of."

Aaron mostly listened as Bradley's tone became threatening.

"You know what's gonna happen when I see you? When I get home, you know what time it is."

A couple of days later, a cousin who had flown down from New England bought Bradley a temporary cell phone that he used to call Aaron again and continue his threats of retaliation. "I told him I would kill him," Bradley said to the grand jury. "I told him I can't wait to see him. I told him I was going to sue him, then kill him."

Bradley said Aaron tried to explain by saying, "The guy that shot you down there wasn't your boy. This is your boy talking to you. That guy was out of his mind."

The words sounded to Bradley as if Aaron was saying he wasn't in his right mind when the shooting occurred. "That's the way I took it," Bradley said.

Interestingly, amid his threats, Bradley said there was no mention of the Boston shootings in 2012, even though that was presumably the cause of their initial conflict.

Palm Beach homicide detectives visited with Bradley at the hospital, but he offered no details of the shooting. "I didn't want to cooperate. That's not the route I wanted to go," Bradley would testify at trial. "I didn't want to cooperate with the police. I wanted Mr. Hernandez's life."

AARON'S VERSION was far different than the story Bradley told police. Aaron told me the plan was that Bradley was going to make a "buy" from X and that if all went as planned Bradley was going to rent a car and drive back to Connecticut with the drugs. It's worth noting that Bradley only had a one-way ticket to Florida. His return flight or a flight going with Aaron to Arizona was never purchased. That alone told me something was up. Why would Bradley not have a return flight home? He didn't live in Florida and didn't really know too many people there.

Aaron said the plan, hatched as they left Tootsie's and went their separate ways, was to meet back at the hotel in a couple of hours so Bradley could get his things out of the hotel room before Aaron left for the airport.

The next thing he knew, Bradley called him from the hospital threatening to kill him. But he wasn't angry about Aaron shooting him. He was angry because Aaron had vouched for "these crazy Florida niggas." Bradley was livid about being shot, and somebody was going to pay for it. That somebody was Aaron, who he felt had put him in that position to begin with. He even accused Aaron of setting him up so his Florida boys could steal his money.

When I asked Aaron about this interaction, Aaron told me: "Bradley was pissed. He wanted to kill me."

I asked him: "Why didn't you try to tell him you had nothing to do with it?"

"Convincing him had nothing to do with it. Once you vouch for a nigga, that's it! You're responsible if anything goes wrong. That's the way of the streets."

He was right. I knew better, and so did he for vouching for anyone. Aaron had gotten out of the hood but the hood hadn't gotten out of him. Aaron had no business being involved in Bradley's business. Aaron was twenty-two, rich, educated in nothing but the streets. As we discussed these things, I could see his eyes water with regret.

IN ORDER TO ATTACK Bradley's version of events, all I had to do was look at the crime scene. Ignore the fact that Bradley is a drug dealer. Ignore the fact that South Florida is a haven for drug trafficking. And ignore the fact that Bradley had no return ticket. While all of that is circumstantial evidence suggesting Bradley was down there buying drugs, by themselves those facts prove nothing. To convince the jury Bradley was lying about this I was going to have to show them cold, hard facts. Therefore we began at the crime scene and that is where we found the proof.

The first thing we did was to hire a blood pattern analysis expert to examine the evidence at the scene. We set up an appointment with Palm Beach County detectives to inspect the clothes Bradley was wearing that night to see if we could determine if the shooting occurred the way Bradley said it occurred. To our surprise, Palm Beach police in all of their wisdom gave Bradley back his belongings after he refused to cooperate. This is extremely disturbing to me. I realize Bradley was not cooperating with them during their investigation, but that was no reason to do nothing at all and destroy evidence of a crime that had been committed against him. What if Bradley wasn't the only victim? What if Bradley also had a gun? So what if Bradley didn't want to cooperate; they might have found other evidence to put together a case.

Instead of considering other factors, they literally threw in the towel and destroyed what little evidence they had. This was ultimately to Aaron's detriment because now we couldn't inspect the evidence that would disprove Bradley's claims. Fortunately, there were photographs taken at the scene that completely contradicted Bradley's testimony.

Bradley testified he was shot by Aaron in the car with a semiautomatic pistol. We were able to inspect the photographs of where Bradley actually hit the ground, in a grassy area near a chain-link fence. Next to the fence was a red baseball cap Bradley says he was wearing. The cap had high-velocity blood spatter on it, which told us he was wearing the cap when he got shot. It had fallen off his head outside the car, not inside. The chain-link fence was in a location where a car could not fit. Clearly Bradley was outside the car when he was shot, not inside as he testified.

Confirming this were two other important pieces of evidence: the blood pattern on the other side of the fence also had high-velocity blood spatter, which again showed he was shot outside; and the shell casing from a .40-caliber semiautomatic bullet was found right next to the baseball cap, near the chain-link fence. This is the exact caliber of bullet shot into Bradley's eye. If Aaron had shot him from the front passenger side inside the SUV, the shell casing would have ended up inside the SUV, not twenty feet away near a chain-link fence.

Also significantly damaging to Bradley's account was the testimony of two independent witnesses who worked at the warehouse next to where the shooting occurred. Mingle Blake Jr. testified that after he heard the gunshot he ran outside and saw a dark SUV fleeing the area. He ran back and encountered his colleague Kevin Riddle. Together they looked down the alley where they heard the gunshot but saw nothing. Then Mingle, fifty-nine at the time, got in his truck and began driving down the same alley, where he eventually saw Bradley walking approximately thirty yards from the chain-link fence, where he had been shot. Where was he from the time Mingle first heard the shot and searched the alley until he was discovered walking in the alley? Bradley literally disappeared for five minutes after being shot.

Mingle, an African American, and Riddle, a Caucasian, testified that Bradley was surprisingly alert. The first officer on the scene would also testify that Bradley was very alert, and told him two black guys shot him, not NFL football star Aaron Hernandez. Where did Bradley go for those five minutes? Was he alert enough to hide a gun? Was there another car parked around the corner? Did he hide his cell phone so it wouldn't be searched by cops? These are all questions I posed to the jury.

Another huge problem for Bradley's story would be the VIP manager at Tootsie's who would testify on behalf of the defense.

He testified there were not four people with Aaron's party that night, but a number closer to fifteen. A big party like that stood out on both nights that Aaron was there. It's also much easier for a group of fifteen people to run up a $10,000 tab than a five-person group. The manager at Tootsie's knew Aaron not only from football but also from Aaron's visits to the club on two prior occasions. He also recalled that his waitress was charging an iPhone and that the iPhone was returned to Bradley, thereby debunking Bradley's story of arguing about the iPhone in the car.

Now, the iPhone is significant because cell phones can be tracked. Bradley never gave police any information about his phone number. He gave police his aunt's number in Connecticut, not his cell phone number, of which he had two. With the number of the cell phone he had in Florida police could have obtained cell tower information and perhaps tracked his movements on those five days, only two of which Bradley could account for. Neither police nor prosecutors ever obtained cell tower data from any of Bradley's phones.

Nothing would have been more damning to Aaron's case than if his movements had matched Bradley's on that night. But Aaron's cell phone data showed that he was at the hotel at the time of the shooting. His call history also showed multiple calls to Bradley as Aaron was leaving for the airport. The data confirmed Aaron was trying to get hold of Bradley all the way from West Palm Beach to Miami International Airport, where Aaron flew out to go to Arizona. Aaron's cell phone records also show that Bradley had two phones with him in Florida, and he made calls from those phones to Aaron both before and after being shot in the eye.

Aaron told me he had been pacing back and forth inside the hotel room, waiting for Bradley to return. He knew something had gone wrong; he feared the worst. These were "crazy niggas" as Bradley would later say.

"I was in such a panic I started driving in the wrong direction to the airport," Aaron told me. "I finally woke up and went the right way."

Aaron's worlds were in conflict again: his professional athletic career pulling him to the airport and the lucrative world of endorsements; his history with the missing drug dealer pulling him back to the streets. Aaron may have headed to Arizona that day, but this was the moment when the two worlds could no longer coexist, and eventually his ties to his past would bring everything crashing down.

10.

SHARROD THE SHOOTER

While the case against Aaron came together quickly for prose-cutors, they knew it needed more punch. The evidence they had connecting Aaron to the crime lacked substance. The prosecution needed something else, or rather someone else. The person they would build their entire case around was the man with Aaron on the night of the shootings: Alexander Sharrod Bradley. Prosecutors were handed their golden ticket when Detective Peter Dauphinais of the Bristol Police Department immediately identified Bradley from the video footage of him and Aaron entering Cure Lounge at the same time as the Cape Verdean five. "Oh, that's Sharrod," the detective said without hesitation.

ON MY FIRST COURT DATE I got to meet my counterpart on this case, First Assistant State Attorney Patrick Haggan. He was the first assistant to the district attorney in Boston, which meant he was the top lawyer in that office. The district attorney is technically the top lawyer, but in practice he's a politician who just happens to be a lawyer. This is the case in 90 percent of the offices across the country; the first assistant is usually the star of the office. He or she is usually paid better than any other attorney in the office, and they usually have full autonomy and all the resources they need. That's why there is not much turnover among first assistants.

I was eager to size him up and right away could see this was an exceptional lawyer. Not only was he sharp but he was likable. He also knew the law and I could tell juries really liked him. Hell, I liked him, and I was by definition his enemy. Pat, as we called him, had an aw-shucks type of demeanor combined with urban street smarts that made him fit in on all occasions. He was not a tall guy; he and I were twin towers at about five foot eight. He was not completely bald but getting there, and wore gray and blue suits off the rack that gave him the look of a dedicated selfless warrior for the commonwealth. His was a kind of very unassuming look that charms jurors and gives them the impression he's trustworthy. His appearance says, I'm a fighter for the people, for the victims who can't speak for themselves because of this piece of shit monster defendant sitting right over here.

However, Pat was so much more than that; he was genuine. The fact that I liked him bothered me tremendously. I do better when I hate the opposition; my game goes up another level. Generally speaking, defense attorneys and prosecutors think differently. We have different objectives. Prosecutors are trying to put people in jail; defense attorneys are trying to keep people out of jail. I thrive off the competition, the challenge to pick apart a prosecution's case, so it helps when I dislike the opponent. But that was not the case with Pat, and I cannot overstate how worried that made me. The jury is going to love him, I thought to myself. His likability would be one of my biggest concerns throughout the case.

I may have been friendly with Pat, but a zebra of course cannot change its stripes. One of the first things I like to do with prosecutors is to bait them with a common question that, believe it or not, always gets them talking about their strategy. It's like they can't help themselves.

While chatting with Pat one day, I said, "Where the hell is your evidence? There's reasonable doubt all over the place." Sure enough he took the bait and answered: "You know, there's no point in hiding it. This case is going to boil down to Bradley, and whether or not the jury believe him." That was their case in a nutshell. They were going to ride Bradley all the way to the finish line.

Bradley was well known to the police in Bristol, and for good reason. He was a major drug dealer in the city, the kind police knew was capable of just about any criminal activity possible. Bradley grew up in Hartford, Connecticut, graduated from East Hartford High School, and spent two years at community college trying to major in computer science. He did various kinds of work that never amounted to much, spending time at Home Depot, Dunkin' Donuts, and other kinds of jobs he would describe as "warehouse stuff." His only source of income was selling drugs, marijuana, and crack cocaine.

Our investigator Jerry Lyons went digging deep into his past. I wanted a clear picture of who we were dealing with, and I wanted Bradley front and center. Not because we planned on focusing on him, but because we knew the prosecutors were going to do it and we needed to be ready to respond. Jerry went to both Hartford and Bristol and was told the following. After quitting community college Bradley tried to be a major gangster in Hartford, a city of about 125,000 people known for its rough streets and abundance of drugs and other illegal activity. Drug dealers and drug users aren't the most reliable people, so when Bradley, who stood about six foot two, about 265 pounds, didn't get his way he tried to use force to get people to do what he wanted.

Bradley was not only tough, he was also very smart. He couldn't stay in one place too long; violence always catches up to you unless you keep moving. When the heat started to build from the competition and the cops in Hartford, in 2007 Bradley decided to move his operation to Bristol. His excuse was that he was moving in with the mother of one of his three children, a woman named Kelly Kay. As soon as he got to Bristol he began selling marijuana, sometimes up to thirty pounds a month. When you're moving that much weed, you're running a serious business.

The clientele was much softer in Bristol and his strong-arm tactics were more successful there. It was a small town with small-town attitudes. If people had a beef with you they tended to discuss things. They wouldn't shoot up your neighborhood or your house. Bradley brought a Hartford attitude to Bristol. People in Bristol became afraid of him, and Bradley liked people being afraid of him.

We came across a police report from Bristol detailing a disagreement Bradley and Jamar, who was also Jailene's weed connection, got into with a rival drug dealer; in broad daylight both Jamar and Sharrod (as Bradley was called) were seen by multiple people in the neighborhood walking up to a house and riddling it with bullets. Then they walked away as if nothing had happened, not knowing if there were children inside or where each bullet went. The police went around talking to people, and some clearly identified Sharrod because everybody knew Sharrod, or "Sharrod the Shooter," as he quickly became known on the streets of Bristol.

What shocked me about this police report was that after Bradley became their suspect, police just called him on the phone to question him. Police never call up suspects to confront them or question them about a shooting. They go and find the person. They never know what the suspect might be doing at the time—they may walk into a drug deal in progress; the suspect may give them permission to search his house; he may blurt out something incriminating and they may decide to arrest him on the spot. But not here in Bristol County. Detectives just called Bradley on the telephone. He spoke with them briefly and that was the end of it. That detail showed me that not only the people of Bristol were afraid of Bradley; the cops were too. Bradley liked doing business there. He became a big fish in a small pond.

Inevitably, Bradley met Aaron Hernandez through a mutual friend named DaQuan Brooks, a basketball player who had attended Bristol Eastern High School and was now at Western Connecticut State. Brooks briefly lived with Bradley; they had become friends while playing hoops together.

Bradley and Aaron met right around the time Aaron was getting ready for the 2010 NFL Draft. They were casual friends initially. "He was a cool dude," Aaron would tell me. "He never wanted anything from me. He didn't need anything. The guy was rolling in cash. At that time in my life everyone was asking me for money, houses, cars, tickets, jerseys, and I hadn't even gotten drafted yet. Preparing for the draft was a lot of hard work. I had to go to California, wake up at the crack of dawn and work out all day, do drills, and prepare in the classroom for the interviews.

"It wasn't a slam dunk for me. Teams were afraid of drafting me. I just wanted cool people around me that weren't around me for money and fame; people I could relate to that accepted me for me."

The NFL offers programs for rookies to teach them to stay away from people like Bradley. But it was too late. Bradley was in Aaron's life and from all appearances he wasn't going anywhere.

Bradley said their relationship started out as a business relationship and grew from there. They played video games and occasionally gambled at one of the Connecticut casinos, Foxwoods or Mohegan Sun. Their real common bond was weed. Aaron was a notorious pot smoker, a habit that grew while he was attending college at the University of Florida in Gainesville.

At one point during his sophomore year at Florida his coach Urban Meyer wanted to throw him off the team just when Aaron was beginning to emerge as one of the best tight ends in the country. He had caught thirty-four passes for 381 yards and five touchdowns in 2008 to help the Gators finish 13-1 and win their second national championship in three years. Florida beat the top-ranked Oklahoma Sooners 24-14 in the BCS National Championship Game in which Aaron was the Gators' leading receiver with five catches for 57 yards. Scouts were beginning to look at him as an NFL prospect.

Aaron was also pushing the boundaries of what Urban Meyer would allow, particularly when it came to housing. Aaron told me that after his sophomore season he wanted to move off campus away from the players' dorm with his best friends, twins Mike and Maurkice Pouncey, both now NFL Pro Bowl centers. Moving off campus was forbidden to underclassmen, but Aaron threatened to transfer to the University of Miami if he didn't get his way. Meyer relented and Aaron and the Pounceys were allowed to move into their own apartment where Aaron could be the bad boy he wanted to be.

Though Aaron was developing into one of the best tight ends in the country, Meyer was growing frustrated with his continuing marijuana use and his not attending classes. It was Tim Tebow, the Heisman Trophy–winning quarterback, who came to Aaron's defense when Meyer wanted to throw Aaron off the team after he failed a drug test prior to his junior season. The two athletes had been close since their first meeting during Aaron's recruiting visit. After that Tebow always looked out for his tight end from Connecticut. Aaron described Tebow as caring and compassionate, and said he always had a soft spot for Aaron, knowing the impact his father's death had on his teammate. According to Aaron, Tebow told Meyer: "If you throw him off the team you're going to have to throw me off. We want him on the team."

During the entire time I knew Aaron Hernandez, and based on everything we investigated and saw, everyone who knew Aaron absolutely loved him. Aaron may have broken a lot of rules but the fact is he was so genuine, sincere, and likable that people didn't hesitate to go to bat for him. They did so despite all his flaws. He never made excuses for them, he owned them, and his candor just made people like him even more. That was the Aaron most people didn't know.

After Tebow's ultimatum, Meyer relented and agreed to keep Aaron on the team but it came with a condition. Aaron said Meyer told him: "We'll let you stay on the team for your junior year. But that's it. You're going to have to turn pro after that." Aaron told me he literally didn't have a choice to come back for his senior season; he knew his junior season would be his last at Florida. Meyer had done all he could. He had counseled Aaron about losing his father, introduced him to the Bible, turned him into a star player, but he also knew chances were great Aaron would not be around for his senior year because of either poor grades or failing more drug tests. Seldom does a coach tell a talent like Aaron he can't come back for his senior year, but Meyer couldn't keep Aaron out of Bristol or the Bristol out of Aaron.

"Unfortunately, you can't lock them up and keep them away from their homeboys," Meyer once said.

When I asked Aaron about this, he had no idea what I was talking about. "Man, I barely ever went home, I didn't have the money. The trouble I got into really wasn't much trouble. It was slacking off on the rules. I was a kid in a candy store and there was no one other than the coaches around to tell us we couldn't do what we wanted to do."

This made perfect sense. Urban Meyer's program was rife with players getting arrested and getting into all kinds of trouble. One year during Aaron's tenure at the University of Florida, the team not only set records on the football field for wins, they also set the record for most arrests of players in the program. Ironically, for all the talk I have heard and read about Aaron being such a bad boy in college, he was one of the few players who never got arrested.

Aaron went on to have a monster season his junior year, catching sixty-eight passes for 850 yards and five touchdowns. The 2009 Gators finished the regular season unbeaten at 12-0, but lost to eventual national champion Alabama 32-13 in the Southeastern Conference Championship Game, ruining their chances to be back-to-back national champions. They would end up 13-1 and ranked number three in the national polls. Aaron was named first team All-American and won the John Mackey Award for being the best tight end in college football.

He achieved all that while smoking weed regularly. He justified his drug use to me by saying weed made his head clear; he would get into a zone where he felt he was faster and operating on another level.

"Every time I was on the field I was high on weed," he told me. "I could not play without weed."

The medical benefits of marijuana are becoming more acceptable now, and there are even calls from some within the NFL to legalize the drug as a form of therapy. In August of 2017, the NFL sent a letter to the NFL Players Association indicating it was willing to work with the association to study the potential use of marijuana for pain management. The letter indicated areas for potential research, including pain management for acute and chronic conditions.

Aaron was way ahead of his time when he claimed smoking weed helped him heal faster from his injuries and even prevented injuries. "Before when I played high school ball it would take a few days to recover from the bruises and everything," he said. "But when I started smoking weed, I never really had those issues."

What many people don't realize is just how prevalent marijuana is in football, and not just with the pros. I have represented multiple college football players over the years and gone to visit them several times at various dorms; each and every one of these dorms smelled like a marijuana dispensary, and the coaches and organizations knew it. You can't walk within twenty feet of a team dorm or hotel room and not smell the weed. It is a part of the game and the players all swear by its medical benefits. But in order for football to keep its squeaky clean image for sponsors and league officials, they act like it doesn't exist and have blocked marijuana from the list of approved substances players can take.

Teams continue to conduct ridiculous piss tests to detect drug use and act on the results at their own discretion. Good players are given multiple chances. If a player has no value to the team, a positive test can be used as an excuse to dump him and release his scholarship, all while maintaining the public position that the player was dismissed for violating team rules. Whenever you see a player getting dismissed from a major college program for violation of team rules, I will bet the house the player was no longer needed on the team and he got popped on a piss test.

There were a couple of times in college when Aaron said he tried not to smoke so he wouldn't get popped and disciplined by Meyer; but he just didn't heal as fast. The way he explained himself was "I did it because I wanted to do it. But the healing just kind of reinforced it for me."

He never trashed Urban Meyer to me. Aaron accepted responsibility for what went on at Florida. "I was fucking up," he said. "I could have been more mature and I wasn't."

Aaron left Florida after the Sugar Bowl in January 2010 to prepare for the draft. He spent two and a half months in California getting ready for the NFL Scouting Combine held that February in Indianapolis and then the pro day at Florida that followed a few weeks later. Aaron worked out at the training facility owned by his agent Brian Murphy. As he did with all of his clients, Murphy oversaw Aaron's preparation program, which included strength training and classroom instruction on how to handle the interview process.

Bradley became Aaron's primary weed dealer whenever he was back in Bristol for a visit. Sometimes Aaron paid him for the weed, sometimes he didn't. Once Aaron got drafted by the Patriots and he moved to an apartment in Plainview, Massachusetts, the two started to hang out with each other more. Bradley visited Aaron's home up to three to four times a week. They would play video games, smoke weed, drink, and frequent nightclubs in Boston,

Rhode Island, or Springfield, Massachusetts. Bradley said he and Aaron became "best friends" and would text each other every day.

"You want to step?" one or the other would ask, and off they would go.

Most of the time when they went out it was just the two of them. Aaron's other friends didn't like Bradley and didn't trust him. They thought Bradley was just using Aaron for his money and celebrity. They heard about the way he ran his drug business and saw him as bad news. However, Bradley served two purposes: in addition to supplying Aaron with weed, Bradley was also his muscle.

Before Aaron signed his $40 million contract in August 2012, he was making the league minimum. While he may have been the best college tight end in the country, his immaturity and discipline issues in college caused his draft stock to fall, and he wasn't selected until the fourth round. He was the 113th overall player selected, far lower than his real talents warranted. If he was going to make money in the NFL he was going to have to earn it. Until then his $320,000 base salary as a rookie, $200,000 signing bonus, and an additional $76,000 for making the roster would have to do.

While that amount is more than most Americans make in a year, take into consideration the cuts taken by his agent, financial planner, and trainers. The advances given to him to prepare for the NFL combine also had to be repaid, leaving a struggling college dropout with just enough to party away in a few months. Unfortunately for the players, they become instant celebrities in the cities they play in and if they act their age, they are going to go out and act like big spenders.

Aaron, like most players, could not afford security so he did what most players do. They hang out with their boys from the neighborhood, and many times these boys are thugs and gangsters. People do not usually mess with them, and no one was going to mess with Sharrod.

Many professional athletes also dabble in the drug trade. While Aaron did not sell drugs himself, he did invest in them. There is even a name for it: floating. The sad fact of life is there are very few ways to get out of the ghetto. Sports is one of them; rapping is another. A few people break out through education and other unique opportunities. Many turn to the illegal drug trade. It's a quick business and usually people already know the customers.

All aspiring dealers generally need to make it big in the drug trade is for someone to "float" them some money to buy the drugs. They then mark up the drugs so high that not only do they make a living, but there's enough left over for the floater to make serious money. The return is higher than anything they'd make on Wall Street.

The athletes who get involved with floating are usually players of color who come from predominantly minority-based neighborhoods and have $20,000 to $50,000 to spare. All they have to do is hand the money to someone they trust and wait for the return. There is little to no risk because many times no mention of drugs is made; the floater makes the loan knowing only that they will be getting a hefty return.

Aaron was no exception. When Aaron joined the Patriots in 2010 out of the University of Florida, he was given the number 85, but in 2011 a flamboyant wide receiver formally known as Chad Johnson joined the Patriots after ten seasons with the Cincinnati Bengals. By that time, Johnson had legally changed his name to Ocho Cinco, Spanish for the number 85.

Aaron figured Ocho Cinco might want to wear number 85 with the Patriots, so he approached Ocho Cinco and offered to sell him the number for $75,000. Mr. Cinco balked at the price and countered with $50,000. Aaron accepted, gave him the number, and went back to the number 81 he had used in college. Aaron took the money and floated it to his cousin's husband T. L. Singleton, who gave Aaron back $120,000.

I asked Aaron why he would risk everything for what would be comparatively little, and his response made more sense than I expected. He said, "I had no idea what he was going to do with it.

Of course I suspected, but we never spoke about it." All I had to do was give Aaron a look and he folded like a lawn chair and said, "Okay, I knew what he was going to do with it, but it is not something we ever spoke of. He just paid me back. I was broke as fuck. I can't tell you how many times I've gone out to eat or drink with teammates and didn't have the money to cover the bill." He was talking about the baller life and the peer pressure of keeping up in order to be considered a good teammate. I have asked Aaron and other players about floating, and was told by multiple sources that everybody has either done it or does it. Chances are if you come from the hood and you come into some money you have floated one time or another.

I often wonder how many times the NFL has turned a blind eye to floating, with all the resources they spend investigating players for the draft. Does it ever consider where players' money goes? The NFL has to know floating exists given the sheer number of players doing it. I'm reminded of the Humphrey Bogart movie *Casablanca* when police captain Louis Renault claims to have just found out there is illegal gambling going on at Rick's. He says, "I am shocked, shocked to find that there is gambling going on in here" just as an employee walks up to him and says, "Your winnings, Captain." He quickly says, "Oh, thank you very much" and tucks the money away as he shuts down the bar for gambling.

Many people thought of Bradley as a hanger-on and that Aaron led and Bradley followed. The dynamic was really more the other way around. Aaron was usually broke. Bradley, who was several years older, was not. In fact, Aaron would often borrow money from Bradley. While most people from the neighborhood were hitting Aaron up for money because he was a big-time NFL superstar, Bradley was not. He didn't need Aaron's money and he also protected Aaron from people who would try to bother him.

When football players go out at night they run into all different types of people. Yes, there are the adoring fans and girls, but there are also those who want to bother you, ask for pictures, talk your ear off, not allow you to have a good time. Then there are thugs who want to make a name for themselves, and kicking an NFL football player's ass or snatching his chain goes a long way in earning them street credit.

Being with Bradley protected Aaron from all of that. The second anyone stepped out of line, Sharrod the Shooter was there. Most people knew who he was and those who didn't learned the hard way.

Bradley's girlfriend Kelly Kay didn't like the relationship with Aaron. She lived with Bradley in a state supported-housing complex along Lake Avenue, and Kay didn't like how much time Bradley was spending with Aaron, nor their frequent visits to nightclubs. She might turn a blind eye to Bradley's drug business, but Kay knew Aaron was a celebrity athlete and figured wherever they went there would be women chasing the two of them. It wasn't long before she kicked Bradley out of the apartment and ended the relationship.

Bradley, a single man now, was able to spend more time with Aaron. Aaron even provided Bradley with tickets to Patriots games during the 2011 season and Super Bowl XLVI in Indianapolis, where New England lost to the New York Giants 21-17 at Lucas Oil Stadium. The loss was a bitter defeat for Aaron, who had always dreamed of being a Super Bowl champion, and going out in Boston meant being reminded by fans they had lost the biggest game of the season.

Bradley viewed himself as a bodyguard and confidant of Aaron. But the weed was always the bond. Bradley continued to supply Aaron with marijuana, while Aaron supplied Bradley with access to the life of a celebrity. When they went to nightclubs they didn't have to stand in line. They didn't have to pay a cover charge and often didn't pay for their drinks. Aaron was a Patriot, a member of one of the most famous franchises in professional sports. Bradley with his size looked like he could be a professional athlete too. Even though he was in his early thirties, if he was with Aaron, Bradley convinced most clubgoers that he must be a baller too. Bradley liked that.

The beautiful friendship ended in West Palm Beach when Bradley felt betrayed by Aaron for setting him up with those "Florida niggas." Back in Bristol with only one eye to show for it, Bradley was going to get his revenge in the best way possible: through blood and money. Bradley began texting Aaron incessantly, constantly accusing Aaron of shooting him, and demanding money as compensation.

Aaron immediately called Brian Murphy and told him about the situation. Murphy hired civil lawyers for Aaron and ordered Aaron not to reply to *any* of Bradley's texts. Even so Aaron would occasionally respond and deny he shot Bradley. In between demands for money there were threats to Aaron's life. Bradley knew where Aaron lived. He also knew where everyone related to Aaron lived in Bristol.

This was hands down the most frightening time of Aaron's life. To have someone like Sharrod the Shooter haunting you, calling you, threatening to kill you can unnerve even a man as street smart and physically imposing as Aaron Hernandez. Aaron tried to protect himself. Soon after moving into the mansion in the winter of 2012 with Shayanna and Avielle, who was born that November, Aaron immediately installed a complete surveillance system with cameras everywhere, inside and out. He wanted to make sure Shayanna and the baby were safe. He also began arming himself because many of Bradley's texts bragged about his "weaponry."

Aaron struggled with how to tell. And what to tell. Aside from his agent Murphy, who could he trust? At what point would he have to tell Coach Belichick? "I knew once I told Coach, it would be over; my whole life would be over, so I put it off as much as I could." Aaron told me.

Aside from arming himself Aaron needed new muscle, someone he could trust, so again he reached out to his boys from the hood: Ernest "Bo" Wallace, a close friend of the family, and Carlos Ortiz. Both had extensive criminal backgrounds, and neither was afraid of Bradley. Both would now watch Aaron's back for a not so small fee.

Bradley's life was also unraveling, if not just as fast then maybe faster. After returning to Bristol from West Palm Beach his patience grew thinner and began to manifest itself through violence. In April 2013, fresh off surgery, Bradley got arrested for domestic violence against his girlfriend Kelly Kay. He continued hounding Aaron, demanding money, but was getting nowhere. Aaron's civil lawyers were agreeable to settling the dispute but for nowhere near the $1.5 million Bradley was demanding. After unsuccessfully threatening to kill him, rat him out to the Patriots, contact the media, Bradley finally made good on at least one of his threats when he filed his civil lawsuit against Aaron on June 1, 2013. But before it could make any serious headlines, Aaron was arrested for the murder of Odin Lloyd on June 26, 2013.

The arrest was not good for Bradley's lawsuit, as all of Aaron's resources would now go toward his defense and any civil matters would take a back seat to his criminal trial. The shocking news of the Odin Lloyd murder accusations clearly overshadowed any news about Bradley losing an eye. Things were going downhill for Bradley fast.

The prosecutors in both Boston and Bristol County, Massachusetts, wanted to speak to Bradley, but how would this affect his lawsuit? He did not want Aaron to go down until he got his pound of flesh first, so initially he refused to cooperate. Then after he failed to appear at a grand jury proceeding in Boston prosecutors had had enough. They issued a warrant for Bradley's arrest and found him in the one place he was not supposed to be: Kelly Kay's house. There was a domestic violence order requiring him to have no contact with her.

Bradley quickly learned that Boston prosecutors and the Bristol police were not playing around. The police kicked down Kelly Kay's door to arrest him. After throwing him in jail for failure to appear on a grand jury subpoena and violating the protective order, the judge slapped him with an unprecedented $250,000 bond, which Bradley could not post. The walls were closing in on him. Aaron was already in jail for Odin Lloyd and Boston detectives were closing in on him and Aaron for the double murder of Abreu and Furtado. Bradley, ever the criminal genius, knew nobody cared about him. They all wanted the NFL superstar. With his chances of recovering money on a lawsuit dwindling, it was time to cut his losses, save himself, and offer up the only currency he had left—Aaron Hernandez.

11.

TRAPPING A RAT

Informants are common in our criminal justice system. They assist law enforcement in breaking open investigations by providing information police might not otherwise come to know. Usually informants are criminals who try to exchange information for leniency, a kind of "you scratch my back and I'll scratch yours" arrangement. But criminals are not always the sharpest tool in the shed. They make impulsive decisions that adversely affect their future (they are, after all, criminals). Sometimes the informants make good deals; sometimes they make terrible deals. I guess the success of the deal depends on whether the quid quo pro is even. Does the prosecutor have a stronger case against the rat or the target? What information is the informant offering? Does it make the prosecution's case? Can any of the information that would not have normally been obtained through an investigation be independently verified? These are all variables in the art of the deal for rats.

I have never been on either side of the table during this kind of negotiation, but I have had many cases involving jailhouse snitches and rats, and have had plenty of opportunities to cross-examine them.

Although after his acquittal Aaron gave me permission to tell his story, he did so with the clear understanding that I would not snitch or inform on anyone. This was not only for my protection, but also because I am fundamentally opposed to the way government uses confidential informants or snitches. My firm handles a limited number of drug cases, but when we do we have a strict policy of not representing anyone interested in snitching as part of a plea deal. There are multiple reasons for this. First, I cannot ask anyone to ever trust me if I assist a snitch in setting someone up, taking them away from their families, and destroying their freedom just because I have a client who did the crime but doesn't want to do the time. Second, I do not approve of the way law enforcement uses people they have arrested to entrap and many times set up other people who were not predisposed to commit a crime, just so they can make more arrests. Third, working with snitches is extremely bad for business, as many of those ultimately arrested or set up by the informant want to hire us to represent them, and that would create a conflict of interest for me.

A lawyer who represents a snitch never knows who their client is setting up. If the entrapped individual then hires the same lawyer, the lawyer would never know it was his or her former client that set up their new client. Making backroom deals is a dangerous game I refuse to play; it means living in a world of deception. I don't claim any moral high road here. Wheeling and dealing with people's lives just doesn't feel right to me. It goes against my nature.

The terms "rat" and "snitch" are used interchangeably but they are very different. Jailhouse snitches, or "bitches," as they are known, are inmates who call up police and tell them they have befriended a prisoner who couldn't help but pour their heart out to this stranger who for obvious reasons cannot be trusted. We did not have a jailhouse snitch in Aaron's case, but in high-profile cases you have to expect them at any minute.

Rats are individuals who commit crimes and do not want to do the time, so they "rat" out their friends. This may all seem obvious, but what isn't so obvious is the way they are treated and the reliability and accuracy of their information. I understand when prosecutors use rats to make their case, but I am a firm believer that they need to make sure they can independently verify the information they are being given. To do this they really need to do their homework on who they are dealing with to ensure they are not putting a violent criminal on the streets while letting the least culpable person in the crime go to prison.

The opportunity for criminals to get away with murder triggers a race to the prosecutor's office to see who flips first and gets their deal. This is a pathetic way of dispensing justice. I know for a fact that prosecutors all across America are betraying the public trust by allowing deals to be made without exercising proper discretion. Such was the case with Alexander Bradley.

Everybody seemed to be getting immunity in Aaron's case. The one who benefited the most was Bradley. Bradley was no fool. He had been dealing drugs for about ten years when he finally felt the walls closing in on him; he was looking at a potential double-murder charge in Boston for which he was exposed to a life sentence without the possibility of parole. Until now he had moved in many circles in the underworld and managed to become a major drug trafficker in Connecticut without spending any real time behind bars.

His priors all consisted of minor charges for possession, traffic offenses, and a domestic violence case involving Kelly Kay. This is important to note because someone in this position usually avoids prison in one of two ways: by being smart about his or her dealings and avoiding detection, or by becoming a confidential informant.

I never had any evidence that told me Bradley was a confidential informant. The fact that he never did any real time was certainly a red flag. So was the shooting in Bristol with Jamar, after which the cops just called him on the phone to ask if he was involved. That is the way informants are protected; while they can be useful to law enforcement, they aren't investigated or prosecuted to the full extent of the law. But again, I never had anything concrete that told me Alexander Bradley was a rat prior to the Aaron Hernandez case.

The deal he cut with Boston prosecutors was a good one. Since he was facing life in prison if tried and convicted of the double murder, his immunity agreement was literally the deal of a lifetime. Prosecutors had the option of charging Aaron Hernandez and Alexander Bradley with murder and proceeding on what Massachusetts law calls the *joint venture theory*. This is a law that allows the prosecution to prove someone guilty of murder even if they don't know who pulled the trigger, as long as there is evidence the person knew about the crime and participated in furthering the crime in some way. So even if Bradley was telling the absolute truth, his actions by running the red light to catch up to the BMW where Abreu and Furtado were shot constituted an overt act that furthered and enabled the crime to happen. Under this theory he could be convicted for first-degree murder and serve life in prison even if Aaron was the one pulling the trigger. This is the same concept of law prosecutors used in Bristol County to convict Aaron of Odin Lloyd's murder.

On October 8, 2013, Alexander Bradley sat down with law enforcement, prosecutors, and his own lawyer and *proffered*, the legal term for telling them what he knew. Under the grant of immunity, he told prosecutors his story in exchange for not being charged for the murders of Daniel de Abreu and Safiro Furtado. This agreement was committed to writing and became the centerpiece of my cross-examination of Bradley, because I felt it said so much not only about Mr. Bradley and his motives, but also those of the prosecutors for the Commonwealth of Massachusetts.

The agreement starts off with the lead prosecutor laying out his understanding of Bradley's participation or nonparticipation in the crime by stating:

It is my understanding that Alexander Bradley operated a motor vehicle of which Aaron Hernandez was a passenger. It is my further understanding that Mr. Bradley made certain observations of the fatal shooting at the intersection of Herald Street and Shawmut Avenue in Boston. It is also my understanding that Mr. Bradley did not discharge a firearm at any time on July 16, 2012. Based on these representations the following sets forth the agreement entered into.

As you see, the agreement sets out from the very beginning that in order for Bradley to get this deal he must say first, that he was the driver; second, that he saw the shooting, meaning of course Aaron; and third, that he never fired a gun on that night. On its face the statement may seem harmless, but what this document essentially does is cover the prosecutor's butt and ensure Bradley is going to say Aaron is the shooter; otherwise Bradley has no deal.

The agreement also repeats the following ad nauseam: in order for Bradley to get this deal he must provide "complete and accurate information." Every paragraph uses wording like "complete and truthful," "not withhold nor provide false information," and "testify truthfully." The grant of immunity basically uses every synonym for the word "truth" in the English language, and explicitly requires Bradley to tell it.

Then the document states: "If after Mr. Bradley testifies before the Grand Jury. . . ." Notice that they are already anticipating a grand jury to indict Aaron without even hearing his *full* story. ". . . the District Attorney learns that Mr. Bradley did not give complete and truthful information, the District Attorney may declare this agreement null and void. Should the District Attorney declare this agreement null and void because of the false information provided by Mr. Bradley, the District Attorney may institute a prosecution for perjury."

Keep in mind that the first words out of Bradley's mouth about that night were the fake motive of the spilled drink. Was that complete and truthful information? Did it sound complete and truthful to the prosecutor? Only he knows. Then Bradley says Abreu and Sanches left Cure, crossed the street, and followed him and Aaron to another bar despite video showing conclusively that the Cape Verdean group never left Cure until closing time. Was this complete and accurate information? No. Did it matter to the prosecutor? Apparently not.

Alexander Bradley, the drug dealer with blanket immunity, first tells police that he drove the 4Runner out of the Tufts parking garage. Police had to show him that it was Aaron who drove the car out of the garage. Was this complete and accurate? And did it matter to the prosecutors? No.

In his first statement to police Bradley tells them that Aaron's whole body was out the window when he was shooting into the BMW. Then in his second statement Bradley says it was just his arm. Later at trial Bradley tries to suggest that Aaron's arm equates to his whole body. The list of inaccuracies and false statements given by Bradley from the very beginning goes on and on. That's before we even get into the craziness of the 104-year-old murder weapon.

None of this should have surprised prosecutors who knew what they were dealing with from the moment Bristol detective Peter Dauphinais said, "That's Sharrod." Bradley could be heard during his calls from jail telling his associates to go around and make collections and not let "those niggas think they can get away without paying." Prosecutors knew all this but ignored the obvious because Bradley was giving them Aaron.

Here is the danger in giving criminals immunity. Shortly after making his deal Bradley was set free. He wasn't given any orders to stop dealing drugs. Police or prosecutors did not go to his home and confiscate any bulletproof vests, or guns that he was threatening Aaron with. He wasn't charged for his confession that he had purchased a gun for Aaron. He was set free to do what he pleased, and do it he did.

On February 3, 2014, less than four months after making the deal of a lifetime with Boston prosecutors, Alexander Bradley was in a bar called Vevo Lounge on Meadow Street in Hartford, Connecticut, and got into a dispute with a man named Leslie Randolph. The two had a disagreement over money and the conflict spilled into the streets. Bradley was shot three times during the scuffle, including once in the groin. Video footage shows Bradley threatening people after being shot, and going to his car where he retrieved a hidden gun. Sound familiar? Then in the most reckless disregard for human life, Bradley went back toward the nightclub. As bouncers tried to lock the door, Bradley emptied the magazine of a .40-caliber semiautomatic pistol into the crowd.

The video shows Bradley walking with the gun up to the door and trying to open it. When he is not successful, he starts shooting into the crowded nightclub through the window. The video inside of this nightclub, which police successfully recovered, shows men and women tripping and falling over each other as shots ring out throughout the club. I am from Orlando, Florida, where on June 12, 2016, twenty-nine-year-old security guard Omar Mateen murdered forty-nine people and wounded fifty-eight others in a terrorist attack/hate crime inside Pulse, a gay nightclub in Orlando. All I could think about was the Pulse shooting as I saw video of these young people at Vevo falling to the ground or running for their lives.

Fortunately for those inside the lounge, Bradley did not kill anyone with his random attack. He returned to his car, tossed his gun, and drove off, only to be stopped later by Hartford police and taken into custody.

The message should be clear: Bradley goes to Cure Lounge, two people get shot; he goes to Tootsie's, he gets shot; he goes to Vevo, he gets shot again and shoots up the whole bar. Bradley and bars do not mix.

If all of that wasn't enough, police tracked the gun Bradley used in the Vevo shooting to another shooting in Bridgeport, Connecticut, that occurred just a year earlier. Where did this occur? Yep, you guessed it: a bar. Several shots were fired into a bar called Expression Café in Bridgeport, striking one male and damaging nearby buildings and cars. I don't know how else to say this other than if you ever see Bradley in a bar, run for your life.

Despite Bradley's record and temper, Boston prosecutors kept his deal in place as long as he ratted on Aaron. There was never a threat it would come off the table. Bradley ended up making another deal of a lifetime in the Vevo case. In January 2017 he was sentenced to only five years in prison for shooting up the Hartford bar. That's less than six months per bullet. Bradley was allowed to plead no contest to criminal possession of a firearm, first-degree reckless endangerment, and third-degree criminal mischief.

Boston and Hartford prosecutors claim they never made any special deals in the Vevo shooting so Bradley would testify against Aaron. I believe Pat Haggan; he is an honest lawyer. But maybe someone else made a call and Pat didn't know about it. Maybe somebody gave a wink and a smile. I have no evidence to support the fact that Boston cops or prosecutors ever gave Bradley a pass on the Vevo shooting. Yet in all of my years of experience, I have never seen a case where a crime was actually caught on video and someone got only five years for emptying a gun into a crowded area. Is he that lucky? Does he have a guardian angel? This guy keeps getting shot and lives. I believe what I would later say in my opening statement: Boston prosecutors made a deal with the devil.

12.

PATRIOT GAMES

By the time Aaron returned from his photo shoot in Phoenix, he had endured an endless stream of threatening texts from Bradley.

"When I get home you know what time it is," was one of the texts Bradley admitted to a grand jury that he sent Aaron. "I told him I would kill him. I told him I can't wait to see him. I told him I was going to sue him, then kill him."

Bradley was losing it. How could things get this crazy? Aaron told me that at this point in his life he wondered how he could keep his family safe. Bradley's method of retribution was to shoot up the houses of people who owed him money or who he felt had wronged him. What if he tried to shoot up Aaron's house?

Aaron thought of someone who might be able to give him some advice: the man he respected most in this world. He was all knowing, feared, respected, and loved within the football family that was a major part of Aaron's life. The first thing he would do was make sure Shay and Avielle were safe. Then he would call the head coach of the New England Patriots, Bill Belichick.

I once asked Aaron why Belichick and the Patriots were so successful. "It's Belichick," he said. "It's his way or no way. You can be
the best player on the team, but if you don't do it his way, you're
gone. That's the one thing Belichick liked about me is I did things
exactly the way he wanted. I put in my work. I was always in the film
room. [Tom] Brady would know exactly where I was at all times and I
made sure I was where he needed me to be. We all bought into that."

About a week after Bradley was shot in West Palm Beach,
Aaron contacted Belichick, desperate to schedule a meeting. A
plan was made to meet in Belichick's office at Gillette Stadium in
Foxborough, Massachusetts, on Monday, February 18, 2013. Gillette Stadium, which replaced the old Foxboro Stadium, is located
twenty-eight miles southwest of Boston and is where the Patriots
have played since 2002. The team offices are in the stadium; the
practice fields are located outside.

Belichick carved out time to meet there with Aaron, but the
tight end didn't show up for the appointment. Belichick would
tell detectives that Aaron said he missed the meeting because of
"something that happened in California," though exactly what that
meant is unknown. Belichick said Aaron contacted him and asked
if the meeting could be rescheduled.

This was a busy month for Belichick, who had won three Super
Bowls since becoming the Patriots head coach in 2000. He had just
missed a chance to be in his sixth Super Bowl appearance, losing
the 2012 AFC Championship Game to Deonte Thompson's Ravens
28-13. He was already preparing for the 2013 season.

Belichick initially asked if they could discuss whatever it was
Aaron wanted to talk about over the phone. Aaron insisted on a
face-to-face meeting; he was anxious and persuasive. Belichick
sensed the urgency in Aaron's request and agreed to a meeting in
Indianapolis during the weekend of February 23–24, 2013.

Six months later, after Aaron had been arrested for the shooting of Odin Lloyd, North Attleboro police captain Joseph DiRenzo,

Massachusetts State Police lieutenant Michael King, and Eric J. Benson of the Bristol homicide squad visited Belichick's office at Gillette Stadium to find out the details of that February meeting with Aaron.

When I read the police report outlining the police interview I could immediately see that the coach received star treatment. A reporter from the *Boston Globe* once told me, after he heard we might be calling Belichick to testify, that to New Englanders calling Belichick was like calling the pope to testify. That is how much Belichick is revered.

The first thing I noticed was that the meeting took place in his office with his attorney Andrew Phelan, a former federal prosecutor, present. That in itself was not a big deal, but the fact that Belichick refused to be recorded made it clear the cops were there as fans, not investigators. Cops don't need anyone's permission to record their conversations in the middle of a murder investigation. They could have done it without his knowledge and consent. They were more concerned with being on good terms with the coach than they were about getting a complete and accurate account of the meeting. What a witness says is so important; a case can turn on a word or two. Like so many critical moments in life, it's not just what a person says, but how they say it that's important.

The great Bill Belichick told the homicide detectives sitting his office on August 15, 2013, that he and Aaron met privately that February in his room at the Westin Hotel in downtown Indianapolis. The police report from the interview with Belichick said Aaron was concerned about the safety of his "daughter and his girl." Aaron went on to explain to his coach that he was being threatened by people who might potentially harm his family. Aaron was not concerned about his own safety because he had money, Belichick told the officers, but he was concerned that his recently purchased home did not have a gate or any security.

The police report also states that Belichick told the detectives Aaron expressed an interest in relocating. I don't believe Belichick told the whole truth here, or if he did it wasn't documented. Aaron told me the purpose of the entire meeting was for him to ask Belichick to be traded. He wanted to get as far away from Bradley as possible, even if it meant playing for another team. Aaron told me he told Belichick he did not feel safe and wanted to be traded to a team on the West Coast.

Belichick wasn't about to entertain that request. Aaron told me the coach was incensed by the idea, and reminded Aaron that the team had made a significant investment in him and had secured long-term deals with him and Rob Gronkowski. The Patriots planned to build their whole offense behind their future Hall of Fame quarterback and two of the best tight ends in football, then rule the football landscape for years to come. Belichick wasn't about to change those plans because of some threatening text messages. Aaron would just have to work out his security concerns.

Since cops refused to record Belichick during the meeting we will never know whether the police report accurately reflects what Belichick said. Of course, Belichick could have just been coy when talking with the cops because of the Odin Lloyd murder; he knew civil law suits were pending.

Belichick told the detectives he directed Aaron to contact Kevin Anderson, who at the time was the Patriots director of player development and normally assisted players when they looked for a new residence. According to the report, Belichick also referred Aaron to Chief Operating Officer Mark Briggs to address his security-related concerns.

Belichick told detectives he didn't speak with Aaron again until just before the start of off-season workouts on May 1, 2013, when Aaron called to confirm when he needed to be back. By then Aaron had undergone shoulder surgery in California, where he spent two months rehabbing three thousand miles away from Alexander

Bradley and all his threats. Knowing he had to return to New England, Aaron wound up working with Anderson to get a run-down apartment with minimal security while upgrading the security and surveillance of his home in North Attleboro.

The Patriots ended their off-season minicamp on June 13, 2013, but five days later the coach learned Aaron was at the team's complex getting treatment for his injuries sustained during the previous season.

By this time Aaron's name had surfaced in connection with the Odin Lloyd shooting, and Belichick wanted to know the truth. The coach told the detectives he summoned Aaron to his office and asked the player "point blank" if he had any involvement in the homicide. Aaron, according to Belichick, said he was "absolutely not" involved in the homicide but explained that he and Lloyd knew each other because the sister of Aaron's girlfriend was dating the victim and Aaron had rented a vehicle and given the keys to Odin Lloyd.

That five-minute conversation would be the last Belichick had with Hernandez, who was arrested while the Patriots head coach was on vacation in Europe. When he returned, the father figure wasted no time in distancing himself from Aaron, who by then had been formally charged with Odin Lloyd's murder.

"It's a sad day. It's really a sad day on so many levels," Belichick said while reading a statement just before the start of the Patriots training camp in 2013:

> Our thoughts and prayers are with the family of the victim. I extend my sympathy to everyone who has been impacted. A young man lost his life and his family has suffered a tragic loss and there's no way to understate that. When I was out of the country I learned about the ongoing criminal investigation that involved one of our players. I and other members of the organization were shocked and disappointed in what we had learned. Having someone in your organization that's involved in a murder investigation is a terrible thing. After consultation with ownership we acted swiftly

and decisively. Robert and his family and I since I got here in 2000 have always emphasized the need for players and our team and our organization to represent the community the right way both on and off the field. We've worked very hard together over the past fourteen years to put together a winning team that's a pillar in the community and I agree 100 percent with that. The comments that Robert's already made on the situation, I stand behind those as well. This case involves an individual who happened to be a New England Patriot. We certainly do not condone unacceptable behavior and this does not in any way represent the way the New England Patriots want to do things. As the coach of the team, I'm primarily responsible for the people that we bring into the football operation. Our players are generally highly motivated and gifted athletes. They come from very different backgrounds. They've met many challenges along the way and have done things to get here. Sometimes they've made bad or immature decisions. But we try to look at every single situation on a case by case basis and try to do what's best for the football team and what's best for the franchise. Most of those decisions have worked out, but some don't. Overall, I'm proud of the hundreds of players that have come through this program. But I'm personally disappointed and hurt in a situation like this.

Robert Kraft, CEO of the New England Patriots, also wasted no time rushing to judgment and telling reporters during a press conference that the decision to release Aaron was made *before* his arrest. "We decided the week prior to Aaron's arrest that if Aaron was arrested in connection with the Lloyd murder case that we would cut him immediately after," Kraft said. "The rationale behind that decision was that if any member of the New England Patriots organization is close enough to a murder investigation to actually get arrested, whether it be for obstruction of justice or the crime itself, it is too close to an unthinkable act for that person to be part of this organization going forward."

During that forty-minute press conference, Kraft produced the letter Aaron sent to the Patriots a week before the 2010 NFL Draft discussing his alleged use of marijuana. In the letter addressed to Nick Caserio, the Patriots director of player personnel, Aaron agreed to be drug tested and have his salary based on the results of those tests.

Dear Mr. Caserio,

I am writing in regards to some of the feedback I am receiving from my agents, Florida coaches and other personnel. These sources have indicated that NFL teams have questions about my alleged use of marijuana. I personally answered these questions during the pre-draft process, but understand that NFL teams want to conduct thorough due diligence before making the significant financial investment inherent in a high draft pick. I have no issue with these questions being asked, but thought that it made the most sense to communicate with you directly regarding this issue so you would not have to rely upon second-hand information.

Any information I volunteer to you about my past will be looked at with great skepticism as I am trying to get drafted as high as possible by an NFL team. As such, I thought that the best way to answer your questions and your concerns was to make a very simple proposition. If you draft me as a member of the New England Patriots, I will willfully submit to a bi-weekly drug test throughout my rookie season (8 drug tests during the 2010 regular season). In addition, I will tie any guaranteed portion of my 2010 compensation to these drug tests and reimburse the team a pro-rata amount for any failed drug test. My agents have explained that a direct forfeiture provision in my contract along these lines would violate the CBA rules. However, I have instructed them to be creative in finding a contract structure that would work. In the worst case scenario, I would donate the pro-rata portion of any guaranteed money to the team's choice of charities. My point is simple—if I fail a drug test, I do not deserve that portion of the money.

I realize that this offer is somewhat unorthodox, but it is also the only way I could think of to let you know how serious I am about reaching my potential in the NFL. My coaches have told you that nobody on our Florida team worked harder than me in terms of workouts, practices or games. You have your own evaluation as to the type of impact I can have on your offense. The only X-factor, according to the reports I have heard, is concerns about my use of recreational drugs. To address that concern, I am literally putting my money where my mouth is and taking the financial risk away from the team and putting it directly on my back where it belongs.

In closing, I ask you to trust me when I say you have absolutely nothing to worry about when it comes to me and the use of recreational drugs. I have set very high goals for myself in the NFL and am focused 100 percent on achieving those goals. So test me all you want during my rookie year . . . all of the results will be negative while I am having an overwhelming positive impact on the field.

Good luck with your preparations for the NFL Draft and feel free to contact me or my agency (Athletes First/David Dunn) with any questions.

Sincerely,

Aaron Hernandez

University of Florida

Kraft admitted he was initially impressed by the letter, but now the Patriots were trying to erase Aaron from their memory. They even organized a jersey exchange so fans could trade Aaron's jersey for that of another player at the team's pro shop at Gillette Stadium. "We made a mistake," Kraft said. "We're facing it head on. Obviously, it wasn't the correct decision. It's sad. Very sad."

It was a disingenuous ending to what had once seemed like the ultimate sports story: hometown kid makes good with hometown team. Though he had won the John Mackey Award as the best tight end in college football during his junior year at the University of Florida, Aaron's draft stock fell amid rumors of drug use and a propensity to run with the wrong crowd. There was also lingering concern about a bar fight in Gainesville in 2007 when Aaron allegedly punched a bar manager, but was never officially charged in the matter.

The 2010 NFL Scouting Combine didn't help Aaron raise his draft stock. Some teams had concerns about the results of his psychological profile that suggested under his weaknesses: "He enjoys living on the edge of acceptable behavior and may be prone to partying too much and doing questionable things that could be seen as a problem for him and his team." The 2010 profile was written by Human Resource Tactics, a testing service that profiles elite military units along with six hundred college football prospects each year for twenty National Football League teams. Aaron's results were supposed to be confidential, but were published in the *Wall Street Journal* after his death.

What often goes unmentioned, and what the Patriots might have been attracted to most, was the number of strengths listed in Aaron's profile.

Hernandez is a dedicated player who will challenge himself to get better. He knows that hard work has been an essential element of his success to date, and he will continue to give his best in practices; when studying film, and when participating in off-season strength and conditioning programs. His willingness to give his best from start to finish suggests that his performance will improve from year to year. Hernandez sees himself as being a football player above all else. He will place a high priority on football and what it takes to be successful. Compared to other players, Hernandez is very confident of his skills and ability to reach some of his football goals. His confidence will be consistent throughout a game; he will quickly recover from mistakes and bad breaks. Even when things aren't going his way he will continue to believe in himself. Hernandez's high expectancy for success can be a significant building block in helping him become as good as he can be in the future. All of the mental ability dimensions that we address show good potential for his position. Hernandez's Matrices and Wonderlick scores are above the typical minimum for his position, and SIGMA scores indicate that he will be able to focus during meetings and practices, and that he can concentrate on executing during games. His excellent mental processing speed will also be a plus for him in that he will be able to quickly make his reads and properly execute. Hernandez appreciates the contribution coaches have made to his career and will be willing to listen to their technical critiques and try to follow through on what they want him to do on the field. Hernandez will not be confrontational and divisive in his statements about his teammates and coaches. He will try to not say things that could cause problems in team chemistry.

Five tight ends—Jermaine Gresham (1st round/21st overall/ Bengals); Rob Gronkowski (2nd/42nd/Patriots); Ed Dickerson (3rd/70th /Ravens); Tony Moeaki (3rd/93rd/Chiefs); and Jimmy Graham (3rd/95th/Saints)—were selected before the Patriots took Hernandez as 113th pick overall in the fourth round.

At the time it looked like the Patriots had gotten a steal. More to the point, they got a bargain. Not only did they get first-round talent at fourth-round prices, but Aaron had already agreed to certain stipulations that limited the team's financial risk in signing him.

Aaron held up his end of the bargain, using his rookie season to become a dedicated team player who stayed out of trouble. It wasn't long into his first training camp that Aaron was noticed by quarterback Tom Brady, who began giving the rookie advice on how to execute certain plays. By the first preseason game, Aaron was catching warm-up passes with veteran receivers like Randy Moss and Wes Welker.

It also didn't take long for Aaron to gain attention around the league. In just his second game as pro, Aaron starred against the AFC East rival Jets, catching six passes for 101 yards in a 28-14 loss in the Meadowlands. Aaron played in fourteen games and started seven his rookie season, catching forty-five passes for 563 yards and six touchdowns. By the end of the 2011 season he and Rob Gronkowski were being credited for changing the game of football.

With Aaron paired with Gronkowski, the Patriots featured the best tight end combination in football, overwhelming defenses with their versatility and talent. Gronk was the most celebrated of the pair. In 2011, he set the single-season record for touchdowns (TDs) by a tight end with seventeen receiving TDs as well as the single-season record for receiving yards by a tight end at 1,327. He was also the first tight end to lead the league in receiving touchdowns.

Aaron wasn't bad either. Having changed his number from 85 to 81, he also emerged as a future star, catching seventy-nine passes for 910 yards and seven TDs. He also ran the ball five times for forty-five yards as the Patriots began using him as a hybrid running back. The media was captivated by Gronk and his antics, but hard-core followers of football saw something just as special in Aaron. Together fans were calling them the "Boston TE Party."

Former Patriots safety Rodney Harrison was interviewed by the *Boston Globe* after the 2011 season. "Obviously, they're both great players, but I think when you look at Aaron Hernandez, he's a kid that they used in a lot of different roles last year—he played wide receiver, he played in the slot, he played tight end, he played some running back, and really showed his versatility," he said. "[There are] just so many different things he can do."

The 2011 Patriots would lose the Super Bowl to the Giants in Indianapolis, but Aaron's value to the future of the team became evident when New England signed him to a $41 million contract extension just before the 2012 season. The signing bonus of $12.5 million was the largest ever given to a tight end and the team's second-largest extension after signing Gronkowski to a $53 million deal.

Aaron publicly thanked the Patriots for the new contract and immediately donated $50,000 to the Myra Kraft Giving Back Fund, a charity named after the deceased wife of Patriots owner Robert Kraft. "He didn't need to give me the amount he gave me and knowing he thinks I deserve that and he trusts me to make the right decisions, it means a lot," Aaron said following the signing. "It means he trusts in my character and the person I am, which means a lot."

During that time, Aaron told Comcast Sportsnet: "You can't come [to the Patriots] and act reckless and do your own stuff. That was one of the reasons that I came here. I might've acted the way I wanted to act. But you get changed by Bill Belichick's way. And you get changed by the Patriots way. And now that I'm a Patriot, I have to start living like it and making the right decisions for them."

After signing the contract everything seemed perfect in Aaron's life. He was happy with his team, including his relationship with Brady, who "I love to death and always will." When Aaron talked to me in prison about Brady, he told me: "You wouldn't know it, but Brady and I were really close because Brady always wanted to know where I was at all times. He would always tell me, 'Stop hanging with those guys. Get your shit together.' One of the things I regret is not listening to him more."

He loved Gronk too, calling him "the best TE ever to walk on a football field." This was when Gronk was coming under intense scrutiny for his late-night shenanigans.

I OFTEN WONDER how different things might have been if the Patriots had listened to Aaron's concerns for his safety and the insanity going on in his life. Instead of showing him any kind of real support, the Patriots used a violation of the morals clause in his contract to cut him once he was arrested, and kept the remaining $3.25 million of his original $12.5 million signing bonus. It was money he could have used for his defense in the Lloyd trial.

Things might have been different if they had considered trading him. He certainly would not have been with Odin Lloyd on the evening Lloyd was killed. Without that case, the Boston case would have remained cold. Would Bradley have traveled across the country to execute his revenge? That's probably unlikely. We won't know because the Patriots didn't want to break up the greatest tight end tandem in football.

The Patriots are known as the most thorough organization in the NFL. Why not take a second look when a player travels halfway across the country to meet in the off-season with the head coach and tells him he is concerned about his life and that of his family? I have to imagine that doesn't happen every day. NFL teams spend an obscene amount of money investigating college football players to decide whether they should draft them and spend millions of dollars on them. But this organization did nothing when one of their own came to them with concerns for the safety of his life and that of his family. In a game in which these players risk their lives and personal health with every play, it's nice to know who has your back and who doesn't.

13.

WHO SHOT ODIN LLOYD?

When Aaron first learned he was a suspect in the June 2013 murder of Odin Lloyd, he called his agent Brian Murphy. An athlete's agent is the person who takes them from rags to riches. The athlete trusts his agent with everything. Brian Murphy is one of the better agents I have met; my dealings with him before and after the trial showed me all I needed to know about "Murph." He puts his athletes first, so naturally he named his agency Athletes First. He was one of the few people who never turned his back on Aaron. To this day, he remains concerned about Shayanna and Avielle because he knows that is what Aaron would have wanted.

I believe Murphy genuinely cared for Aaron, so the first call he made was to his former law firm Ropes & Grey and connected Aaron with the best criminal defense lawyer they had, which was Michael Fee. The problem was that most of Fee's experience was in white-collar matters and health care compliance cases. He was also a former federal prosecutor, but prosecuting cases and defending them are about as different as murder cases and health care compliance cases. I believe that for this reason he brought in two veteran criminal defense lawyers, Charles W. Rankin and James L. Sultan of Rankin & Sultan. They offered much-needed experience, but the lead lawyer is the one who normally calls the shots.

I cannot comment on the team dynamic as I never spoke to Michael Fee, but I did have extensive conversations with Charles and Jaime (as James is known); both were true gentlemen and from what I could see good lawyers as well. They faced challenges and dealt with them the best way they could. As good as they were, I still think I would have tried the case differently.

Aaron knew Odin Lloyd through his fiancée Shayanna, because her sister Shaneah had been dating Odin for approximately a year. Aaron and Odin were not close but were getting to know each other through a mutual interest in marijuana. Odin supplied Aaron with weed on a number of occasions, though they had only gone out to party together a couple of times.

After establishing a relationship, the prosecution did a good job of presenting its timeline during the night of the murder, with a combination of cell tower records, call records, and video surveillance. It was airtight, and it basically excluded any defense other than mere presence. The timeline was as follows:

JUNE 16, 2013, ABOUT 9:05 P.M.: Hernandez texts Lloyd: "I'm coming to grab that tonight u gon b around I need dat and we could step for a little again."

9:34 P.M.: Hernandez texts again: "Waddup."

LLOYD RESPONDS: "Aite [meaning "all right"] where?" Hernandez: "idk [I don't know] it don't matter but imam hit you when I'm dat way like las time if my phone dies imam hit u when I charge it which will be in a lil."

9:35 P.M.: Hernandez texts Wallace: "Get ur ass up here."

10 P.M.: Lloyd texts Hernandez: "Aite idk anything goin on." Hernandez replies: "I'll figure it out ill hit u on the way."

10:21 P.M.: Hernandez receives a text from Ortiz "the other male associate" saying, "On r way a . . . God bless." Hernandez responds: "Bet hurry up tell fish [meaning Wallace] to drive nigga."

10:23 P.M.: Hernandez texts Wallace again: "Hurry ur ass up nigga."

JUNE 17, 12:22 A.M.: Lloyd texts Hernandez: "We still on."

ABOUT 12:40 A.M.: Surveillance video, shows Shayanna with Hernandez as Wallace and Ortiz enter Hernandez's home. Hernandez is also seen holding a gun, which the prosecution later put on evidence, was possibly a Glock. [No murder weapon was ever recovered.]

ABOUT 1:09 A.M.: Surveillance video shows Hernandez, Wallace and Ortiz leave Hernandez's home in a silver Nissan Altima. Police think Wallace was driving.

1:22 TO 2:32 A.M.: Lloyd receives five phone calls from a number later traced to a cell phone used by Wallace.

ABOUT 2 A.M.: On their way to pick up Lloyd, Hernandez, Wallace and Ortiz stop at the Blue Hill Express Service Station on Route 138 in Canton, Massachusetts. Hernandez purchases Bubblicious blue cotton candy bubble gum. This kind of gum with Hernandez's DNA is later found in the Altima along with a .45-caliber shell casing, the same caliber used to kill Lloyd. But the gum was found by police attached to the shell casing, thereby rendering Hernandez's DNA on the shell casing useless. [This provided the defense with good arguments attacking the sloppy police work, but it should have never seen the light of day in the courtroom. I believe the judge should have excluded this evidence because the DNA results were meaningless and this only served to confuse the jury. I do not believe the defense challenged this in pretrial hearings. I would have tried to exclude it.]

2:33 A.M.: Surveillance video from a camera at a home across the street from Lloyd's house on Fayston Street in Boston shows Lloyd getting into the car with Hernandez, Wallace and Ortiz.

3:07 A.M.: Lloyd texts his sister [Shaquilla] Thibou: "U saw who I'm with."

3:11 A.M.: Lloyd texts Thibou again: "hello."

3:19 A.M.: Thibou texts back: "my phone was dead who was that?" Lloyd responds: "Nfl." Thibou later tells police she understood "Nfl" meant Hernandez.

3:22 A.M.: Thibou texts Lloyd again: "lol your aggy" (meaning Lloyd was aggravating her).

3:23 A.M.: Lloyd sent his last text to Thibou: "just so you know." [All of the text messages to Lloyd's sister were excluded by the judge in pretrial.]

ABOUT 3:25 A.M.: Lloyd is shot and killed in an industrial park roughly a half-mile from Hernandez's home.

3:26 A.M.: The Altima returns to Hernandez's home. Hernandez was driving.

3:27 A.M.: Home surveillance video shows Hernandez, Wallace, and Ortiz entering through the garage.

MANY PEOPLE ASK ME: "Do you believe Aaron Hernandez shot Odin Lloyd?" Well, I can tell you Aaron told me he did not. My honest answer, despite the fact that I knew Aaron, represented him in the Boston case, and even liked him, is I don't know for certain. However, after examining the case and how it was tried, I have a reasonable doubt that he did it. Now let me show you why.

First and foremost, many people do not know that Aaron Hernandez was tried on what is known as the *joint venture theory*, a legal loophole that allows prosecutors to hold someone liable for murder even if they don't know they are the person who did the actual killing. Huh? Yes, that's right. A person can be convicted of murder even if the prosecutor cannot prove they did it.

Bristol County prosecutors went on a dual theory in his case. They believed Aaron was the shooter but weren't sure enough to charge him on that theory alone. Dual theories to me scream reasonable doubt. I tell juries all the time: under the law, you are not to guess what happened or figure out a mystery. The government must prove beyond and to the exclusion of every reasonable doubt. It is the highest legal standard in American jurisprudence.

To understand the reasonable doubt standard you have to compare it with other legal standards. A lower standard of a *preponderance of the evidence* is the criterion for a verdict in civil cases. This is the only standard quantified at 51 percent; meaning if the case is proven 51 percent in one direction, jurors must render their verdict for that side.

In some evidentiary proceedings there is *clear and convincing evidence*, which is still lower than *beyond a reasonable doubt*. Now think about that for a second. If you don't know who the shooter is, how in the hell is the evidence proven beyond a reasonable doubt? Think of the injustice of being convicted of murder when the prosecutor in your case doesn't even have to prove you pulled the trigger.

Most defenses counter the joint venture theory by arguing what is called *mere presence*, which means that a person, under the law, cannot be convicted of a crime just because they are merely present when a crime occurs, even if they knew it was about to occur. People who are present aren't forced to act and put their own life in danger. Otherwise we might have more casualties. To be convicted, the accused must have participated in the crime and had the intent to commit it.

Now that you understand the framework of the law the jury had to follow, let me walk you through the evidence as it was presented in court.

The prosecution was extremely weak on motive, so what do they do when they don't have motive? They throw everything against the wall to see what sticks. In this case the prosecution provided the following motives. First, that Aaron was angry at Odin because when they went out a few days before the murder, Aaron saw Odin talking to some of his friends at the Rumor nightclub and that made Aaron so mad he killed him. (Yes, I'm serious. That was their best motive.) They spent days playing video from inside and outside Rumor, showing various interactions, trying to show an angry Aaron as he contemplated killing Odin for talking to a friend of his. Complicating this theory was the fact that after that night Aaron had loaned Odin a Chevy Suburban to drive around Boston, despite being enraged enough to kill him. By the way, Rumor is part of the same ownership as Cure, but in this case all videos were properly obtained without incident.

The second motive prosecutors put forth was that after partying that night, Odin and Aaron took Aaron's babysitter and her sister to the apartment the Patriots helped him rent for his safety. They spent the night there after the babysitter refused Aaron's advances, the theory being that Odin might have told Shayanna about Aaron hitting on another woman. This was absurd, considering Shayanna is no fool. She is not only an intelligent woman, but she also totally knew that Aaron the celebrity athlete was not the poster boy of fidelity. Plus, under that theory Aaron would have had to kill off the babysitter too, right?

Finally, they even had Alexander Bradley testify that on one occasion, while at Aaron's house, Odin and Shayanna's sister Shaneah came into the house and walked upstairs without saying hello, and Aaron remarked that it was rude. This encounter would somehow enrage Aaron several months later and motivate him to hang out with Odin a few times and then kill him.

The lack of real motive was a gaping hole in the prosecution's case. Aaron's lawyers did a decent job of attacking this weakness at closing arguments, but I'm not sure if the point was hammered enough throughout the trial.

What does all of this evidence show? It basically shows that four guys went into a gravel pit and three came out, but only one gun was used. That means you have only one shooter. The prosecution could never prove who it was, so they tried to paint Aaron as the ringleader, thereby arguing that if he didn't shoot Lloyd, he participated by organizing the outing and driving him to the gravel pit. He was also the only one shown on video with a gun at his house. Sounds pretty damning, but let me poke a few holes in this thing so you can see the reasonable doubt.

You first have the so-called organizing of it all. There was zero evidence showing when and how the criminal intent was formulated. Without a motive, as I mentioned earlier, it's anyone's guess what these four guys were going to do that night and at what point things turned to murder. That's huge. The prosecutor argued that they were going to Aaron's house. Well, that indicates innocence. Why do all this elaborate organizing only to bring the police to your front door? The more logical explanation is these guys got in the car, realized it was too late to go to a club, so they decided to go to Aaron's house and chill in the man cave. Hanging out in a mansion was quite a treat for these guys, so the idea is not far-fetched.

Why stop at the gravel pit? Maybe they wanted to go somewhere private and get high? Ortiz and Wallace were known to use PCP, which Aaron would not have done considering the NFL penalties for using PCP would have astronomical consequences. He could have been suspended for up to four games without pay. Aaron would also not want anyone using it in the house in case Shayanna walked in on it.

There's also the possibility that something happened on the way to Aaron's house; perhaps a dispute between Lloyd and another member of the group. Who? That would be for the prosecutor to prove. But if some conflict had indeed erupted, how do we know they didn't pull over to fight it out and someone took out a gun and shot Lloyd? You see, without motive or any evidence of intent, these are two very plausible scenarios; had they been considered, jurors would have had a hard time convicting not only Aaron, but also Wallace and Ortiz. You can't just say Aaron had the opportunity to kill Lloyd and that's why he's guilty. No, you have to show either incriminating statements made by Aaron or some type of forensic evidence that ties Aaron to the murder weapon, and the critical gum on the shell casing doesn't cut it.

What helped the prosecution the most was their video evidence, much of which Aaron provided through the cameras in his home. But the pink elephant in the room was Alexander Bradley. No one knew what was going on between Aaron and Bradley. The defense had to make a strategic call here to exclude any mention of what happened in West Palm Beach and of course Boston. So the jury would never hear the reason Aaron had this elaborate surveillance system in his house was because he feared Bradley killing him, Shayanna, and the baby. They would never hear the reason Aaron was going everywhere with Ernest "Bo" Wallace and Carlos Ortiz was because he needed backup. The reason Aaron had armed himself with a gun wherever he went was because he feared being lit up by bullets at any moment by Bradley and his henchmen. Instead, the prosecution seized this as an opportunity to paint Aaron as a gun-toting thug who hung around unsavory characters when he had the world at his fingertips. That's the image most of America had of Aaron Hernandez.

There was also footage of Aaron holding a gun before he left that night and after he returned. On the face of it the video was a blow to the defense. They tried arguing that Aaron was actually holding an iPad or a phone or a remote control. This I think was a mistake. You instantly lose credibility with a jury when you try to mislead them in this way. The defense was in a bind here because they wanted to protect Aaron by excluding all the Bradley business. But it was the Bradley saga that explained much of the behavior that made him look guilty. Therefore much of the evidence presented by the prosecution went unrebutted and out of context. The jury did not know that after the Bradley war began, Aaron always armed himself before he left his home.

A jury trial is about the prosecution and defense painting two different pictures of the accused, and how his personality, circumstances, and actions played out during the event in question. Without understanding why Aaron had extra protection, guns, and cameras, and with no background about why he might have acted the way he did, jurors could assume this was just who he was. Now add the media's focus on lurid details and their tabloid spin to the story, and you have the perfect storm for a conviction, evidence be damned.

The jury was not sequestered in this case, and Bristol County is a small area. Aaron didn't stand a chance. I don't criticize the defense for excluding this information. I am not sure they had much choice: it was pick your poison. Let Bradley tell his story or exclude him altogether. They chose the latter, and it didn't work out.

The prosecution also submitted a couple of uncharged crimes into evidence when they put on evidence, and these too struck me as missed opportunities for the defense. Right after getting back from West Palm Beach, Aaron sent money to some of the guys he met down in Florida to transport some guns up to Massachusetts so he could arm himself against Bradley's "weaponry." This load of illegal guns came in as evidence, but no one knew why Aaron was buying guns. None of this was relevant to whether or not he shot Odin Lloyd. But prosecutors needed to paint Aaron as a thug, and the war with Bradley gave them all the ammo they needed, literally.

When I saw the illegal gun buy, I thought the opposite. If Aaron was such a gangster thug why would he need to get guns from Florida from guys he just met? Shouldn't he be able to get plenty of guns from the guys he knew in Bristol? This showed me that Aaron was an amateur bad guy, and I was reminded of one of my favorite lines from HBO's *Boardwalk Empire* when Jimmy Darmody tells Nucky Thompson: "You can't be half a gangster." Aaron's sloppiness could only come from someone who had no idea what he was doing in the violent world of guns and murder.

You might be thinking, I'm sorry, but being in and around two shootings is too much of a coincidence. However, most people who live outside the turbulent world of guns and drugs have no idea just how frequently shootings happen. It is not uncommon at all for someone with Aaron's background to be in a few shootouts. Odds are that eventually one of those bullets hits you and you're not around to see any more shootings unless you have nine lives, or your name is Alexander Bradley.

14.

PRISON LIFE

At 8:45 A.M. on June 26, 2013, about a dozen officers and detectives from the Massachusetts State Police and North Attleboro police arrived at Aaron Hernandez's home in North Attleboro, Massachusetts. Seven of them walked up to the door. One of them knocked.

Aaron and Shayanna were in their bedroom playing with Avielle. Shayanna was still in her nightgown; Aaron was wearing gym shorts with no shirt or shoes. They were enjoying a leisurely morning at home until they heard the knock at the door. Aaron answered, not expecting these would be his final moments as a free man.

The police, with looks of self-satisfaction, announced they were there to arrest him for the murder of Odin Lloyd. They let him put on a pair of black sneakers, but didn't wait for him to put on a shirt before handcuffing his wrists behind his back while reading him his Miranda rights. The plainclothes cops then stretched a V-neck T-shirt over his head before escorting him out of his home.

Television crews that had been camped outside his home for several days finally captured the moment they had been waiting for. One detective held his right arm while another detective held his left arm as Aaron was walked to a police cruiser. He had no emotion on his face. Yet in a last act of defiance, he spat on the side of the road before getting in the police cruiser.

The arrest that was national news came nine days after Lloyd's body was found by a nighttime jogger in an industrial park less than a mile from Aaron's home. The police had spent those nine days building their case against Aaron, the star tight end for the Patriots. They had searched his home multiple times, police dogs had sniffed around his property, and scuba divers had checked a nearby pond. The search warrants needed to do all this became public knowledge as the media was fed every update that pointed to Aaron as a suspect.

As helicopters tracked his arrival, he was taken to the North Attleboro Police Department for booking as media began feasting on the story line of a rich athlete blowing it all by committing a heinous offense.

The video of his arrest was played worldwide, much to the satisfaction of homicide detectives working the case. They could have arranged for Aaron to turn himself in. Very commonly, as a professional courtesy, arrangements are made well in advance to allow high-profile suspects to turn themselves in privately.

I do not know Michael Fee, who became Aaron's attorney when police first began questioning him as a primary suspect. Everything I know about him and how smart he is tells me this was done behind his back. The very public, publicized arrest was just the kind of bush-league move that would be made by amateur cops looking for their fifteen minutes of fame.

Everything I have seen come out of Bristol County since then has shown me that this small town held the limelight and let media interest dictate the way they conducted business. The way Aaron was arrested is a perfect example.

As ministers of justice, prosecutors are also charged with protecting the integrity of the system, including the presumption of innocence. Knowing full well that cameras were rolling and a media blitz would sway public opinion, they should have allowed Aaron to turn himself in. The fact that they didn't reveals a win-at-all-costs mentality that should give everyone pause. If they allowed a man who should have been presumed innocent until proven guilty to be arrested with such fanfare in front of the whole world, imagine the things done in lesser-known cases where no one is watching.

The following day in a courthouse in Fall River, Massachusetts, Aaron's attorneys James Sultan and Michael Fee argued that Aaron should be released on $250,000 bail. They pointed out that he had no prior criminal record of any kind, that he grew up in Bristol, Connecticut, and that he was a professional who had devoted much of his time and energy to playing football. They also pointed out that he was a homeowner with a fiancée and the father of a young child.

Judge Renee Dupuis didn't want to hear it. Her demeanor implied she had already passed judgment on Aaron based on the circumstantial evidence. "The facts as they've been presented to me, if believed by a jury, is that this gentleman either by himself or with two other people that he requested come to the Commonwealth basically in a cold-blooded fashion killed a person because that person disrespected him—and if that's true and based on the presentation it seems to be—I'm confident that type of individual obviously doesn't comply with societal rules and the idea that I release him on a bracelet and he would comply with court rules is not something that I'm willing to accept." She added: "He also has a means to flee and a bracelet just wouldn't keep him here."

As I reviewed the case and watched video of Judge Dupuis denying the defense's motion for bail, I was especially stunned by her comment "if that's true and based on the presentation it seems to be." What happened to the right to the presumption of innocence or innocent until proven guilty? Judge Dupuis was telling everyone, including a potential jury pool, that based on the evidence she had seen, "it seems to be" true that Aaron Hernandez committed the crime for which he had been charged. She totally disregarded the fact that Aaron was from Bristol, had not left Bristol when he was named a suspect, had cooperated with every search warrant, had recently purchased a home, and had an eight-month-old daughter he adored. Instead, she not only said he was basically guilty, but that he would likely flee, and put him in jail until the trial.

The obvious fact is that home confinement would have been absolutely effective in his case, as the media was parked outside his home and he was clearly a recognizable figure. He couldn't step outside without twenty cameras trained on him. The purpose of bail is to ensure someone's appearance for court, not to punish the accused. Establishing bail is really the system's first opportunity to show the presumption of innocence is a living and breathing constitutional right, not just some obscure theory. But not a word was said about the judge's inflammatory ruling, and Aaron spent every night for the rest of his life behind bars.

The denial of bail puts a great hardship on the defense team as well, especially in a high-profile murder case where such things as text messages and cell phone usage would play such crucial roles. Instead of having full access to a client, who can help in clarifying things and preparing for trial, preparation is limited to select hours during jailhouse visits under the eyes and ears of the corrections department.

If that wasn't bad enough, the boss of the Bristol County jail near Dartmouth was a publicity-seeking sheriff named Thomas Hodgson. With his white slicked-back hair and bushy white mustache, Hodgson took full advantage of the media interest that came with Aaron's arrest. He agreed to multiple interviews and gave a half-dozen personal tours of the jail where Aaron was sent after his 2013 arrest, and even after he was transferred to the Souza-Baranowski Correctional Center in 2015. He even speculated on Aaron's mental health.

A die-hard Republican-appointed sheriff in 1997, Hodgson was in charge of about a thousand inmates when Aaron arrived, most of them either awaiting trial or serving two-year sentences or less. He fancied himself to be the toughest jailer in Massachusetts, an old-school lawman whose way of administrating jailhouse justice bordered on archaic.

This is a guy who over the years intentionally made sure meals were bland and unsatisfying, and who in 1999 instituted a chain-gang work crew, shackling inmates when they worked in the community picking up trash. He cut coffee and orange juice from the budget and eliminated televisions, weight-lifting equipment, and smoking from the jails. In 2002, he started charging inmates rent of $5 per day until a judge overruled him in 2004.

Hodgson, an elected official, was as much a salesman as a sheriff. He never met a camera he didn't like and didn't hesitate to toot his own horn. He took every opportunity to bolster his tough-guy image by telling reporters how unpleasant Aaron's life was behind bars with all of its restrictions.

While other sheriffs tried to rehabilitate inmates through education and improving self-esteem, Hodgson preferred the tough-love approach, saying it was an appropriate way to discourage children from a life of crime. Perhaps most galling were Hodgson's attempts to provide a fatherly influence for Aaron, saying he encouraged him to read the Bible and open up about his past. I know for a fact that this was a total fabrication on his part. Aaron was no fan of the police, especially after being arrested with the threat of life in prison. The last person he wanted to talk to was a cop. He had three lawyers visiting him on a constant basis. I know from examining their work closely that they were not asleep at the wheel, and would not have forgotten to mention something as basic as *do not speak to law enforcement.*

I asked Aaron about this guy and he said, "There's no way I would talk to him. He would always come around my cell trying to talk to me. He would say, 'I think if you open yourself up to me you would feel better and life would be better for you.' I would just flip him the bird." In fact that became almost a daily ritual. Hodgson would pass by his cell trying his best to get Aaron to talk. He would walk by his cell and say, "Hey, Aaron, how are you today?" "Fuck you, that's how I'm doing," Aaron would answer.

"Okay, see you tomorrow," Hodgson would press.

"Okay, fuck you very much," Aaron would respond.

This guy wouldn't shut up. He was still talking to the media years later when I came on the case, and he continued giving radio interviews after television cameras were long gone from his tiny jail. At one point I came close to filing a motion against him and making a public statement, but I really didn't want to validate him by giving him the time of day. I'm sure he's still out there granting interviews to anyone who will listen.

Aaron wasn't looking for a father figure while in jail. He was looking to survive, and that meant putting up a tough facade. Despite being isolated from most of the general population, he had plenty of fights and conflicts. At one point during his stay in the Bristol County jail, he was charged with assaulting an inmate and threatening a guard. That's when Sheriff Hodgson decided he would be Dr. Phil and tried to diagnose Aaron. "I'm not a psychologist," he told Boston radio station WEEI on the day of Aaron's death. "I don't have any background in it, but I do think [Aaron] had some sociopathic tendencies."

Aaron couldn't get away from Hodgson fast enough. A little more than a year after he was first arrested, his request to transfer away from Bristol County jail was approved by a Massachusetts judge in July 2014.

NOT LONG AFTER the Odin Lloyd trial began, Aaron guessed the outcome wasn't going to be favorable. He started to get dejected. After an eleven-week trial the jury deliberated for seven days before returning a guilty verdict on April 15, 2015. The first-degree murder conviction in Bristol County Superior Court in Fall River, Massachusetts, carried a mandatory sentence of life in prison without parole and automatically triggered an appeal to Massachusetts's highest court. Aaron had hoped to be going home that day. Instead he mouthed to Shayanna, "Be strong. Be strong" as he was led away. A week later, he was transferred to Souza-Baranowski Correctional Center, a maximum-security prison in Shirley, Massachusetts. He had gone from a $40 million contract to less than zero. He was twenty-five years old.

Being behind bars is difficult enough for the average person, but it's compounded when you're a celebrity and you're big. Aaron was an ex-Patriot in a maximum-security prison where everyone knew it. Souza-Baranowski opened in 1998 as one of the most technologically advanced prisons in the United States. It was named after two corrections officers, James Souza and Alfred Baranowski, who were shot in July 1972 by an inmate whose wife had smuggled a gun into what was then Norfolk Prison Colony. Souza-Baranowski, located forty-two miles west of Boston, housed just over a thousand criminally convicted adult males.

Since its opening the prison has seen suicides, attacks on the staff, fighting between inmates, and a riot on January 9, 2017, when a fight between two gang members erupted into forty-six prisoners rioting in a housing unit for nearly three hours. It took a special operations unit using pepper spray to end the melee.

When Aaron arrived at Souza-Baranowski following his conviction in the Lloyd case, he thought he had to project a tough-guy image to survive. "I'm fucked. My life is over," he told me of his attitude at that time. "I'm going to spend the rest of my life here."

In order to fit in and get some protection, he decided to join a prison gang. I should note here that when Aaron first got arrested he was evaluated to see if he had any gang affiliations, and it was determined that he was not part of a gang. I have seen multiple reports and stories, including one written in Rolling Stone magazine, saying he was a member of the Bloods. This was directly contradicted by law enforcement investigation. The only gang he was a member of when he got arrested was the New England Patriots.

However, prison survival was a different story. He thought maybe being part of a gang would give him some sense of belonging. When fights broke out, he'd know which side he was on. Within a month of being at Souza-Baranowski, he was disciplined for his involvement in a fight. According to an incident report released by the prison, he served as a lookout for another prisoner who had gone into another inmate's cell where they fought a bloody battle until guards broke it up.

Within his first twelve months in prison, Aaron was found with a six-inch shank-like weapon. After that incident he was removed from the general population and placed in a segregated unit; there inmates were kept separate from all other inmates.

He didn't care. After I took over the case, I can't count the times I would get word from him that he was placed in the hole because of people challenging him in prison and trying to break him; or they perceived him as weak, a sure way to get killed or abused in prison.

Aaron tried to maintain his tough front even though he had gone from a seventy-one-hundred-square-foot home to a seven-by-ten jail cell. According to another incident report, he told officers: "This place ain't shit to me. I'll run this place and keep running shit. Prison ain't shit to me."

At Bristol County jail, Aaron was charged with twenty-one disciplinary offenses arising from twelve separate incidents, according to records. At the Souza-Baranowski prison, from his arrival in April 2015 to his death two years later, there were seventy-eight more disciplinary offenses and twelve major incidents. There were at least four physical altercations. One time mace was used to break up a fight he was involved in.

Prison life was awful. Keeping up a tough-guy image was taking its toll. At one point he was so despondent he got a large tattoo on his neck that read LIFETIME. He got other tattoos as well, though they were against prison rules.

He was known to experience periods of extreme frustration when he would kick and pound the door to his cell. He could also sit quietly by himself for long periods. Sometimes he had headaches; sometimes he just wanted attention. "He is constantly kicking his cell door and screaming at the top of his lungs, utilizing profanity at times when he wants something regardless of how miniscule it is," one Bristol County guard wrote in a report. "It is not uncommon for Hernandez to kick his cell door constantly until an officer approaches his cell, merely to ask the officer for the current time."

I wish I had reviewed these records when I started to represent him. I now believe these were clear signs that something was wrong with his brain.

Angry, frustrated, and defiant, the only things Aaron looked forward to were his visits with Shayanna. After one such visit he thought about how much he loved Shayanna and Avielle and how much he wanted to be with them again. He decided that he didn't have to die in jail. He started to read the Bible, the way his coach Urban Meyer and his quarterback Tim Tebow had shown him in college.

Aaron found faith. He found hope. He told me that's when he decided that "I want to fight this." He wasn't ready to give up; he told his fellow gang members he was out. "I'm not rolling with you anymore," he said. "If a fight breaks out, don't count on me."

He would be tested again and he would have to fight again. But Aaron had a new outlook.

He had another trial coming up in Boston. By May of 2014, a grand jury had indicted him on two counts of first-degree murder, three counts of armed assault with intent to murder, and an additional count of assault and battery with a dangerous weapon in the deaths of Daniel de Abreu and Safiro Furtado in July 2012.

When Aaron contacted me he told me: "I hear you're the lawyer that wins cases that can't be won. I need your help, Jose. If I don't get it I'm going to die in here."

Yes, it was a long shot. But hope was the only thing keeping Aaron alive on the inside and he wasn't ready to give up.

15.

FAMILY MATTERS

One aspect of the double-homicide trial that bothered me and my team was the lack of support Aaron received from his family members. Shayanna was there, driving from Rhode Island to Boston every day to attend the trial. Aaron was always so happy to see her. He would often turn to her and mouth "I love you" or blow kisses to her.

But she was the only one there consistently supporting Aaron; the families of the Cape Verdean victims were there daily. This concerned me because it sent a message to the jury that Aaron was the kind of person even his own family didn't love.

The absence of family support upset Shayanna greatly. "I feel like they gave up on him," she would tell me. "The money stopped. They didn't have their hometown hero like they wanted. I don't believe in that. There's no way I would have left him. There's no way I could have left him."

Maybe his family thought it was a foregone conclusion that he was going to be found guilty in the Boston shootings after being convicted for the murder of Odin Lloyd. But to me it was more evidence of the dysfunction that engulfed a family once close knit and prominent in their community.

Aaron's father, Dennis, was the rock of the family. He was Aaron's hero. Dennis Hernandez was the son of Puerto Rican immigrants Bienvenido and Josephine Garcia Hernandez. He was born athletic and smart and had big dreams.

Dennis was a football star long before his son tried to follow in his footsteps. He and his twin brother, David, excelled for Bristol Central High School in the 1970s. They were three-sport stars who were also good at fighting, being two of the few Puerto Ricans in an Irish-Italian community. Dennis was nicknamed "the King," a sign of respect for the confident way he carried himself and the way he was revered. No one messed with the King. Dennis and his brother received scholarships to play football at nearby UConn. But Dennis liked to party and dabble in petty theft, and wound up leaving the university before fulfilling his true potential.

He would meet and marry Terri Valentine, a school secretary in Bristol, and they produced two boys, first DJ and then Aaron, born three years later on November 6, 1989.

Employed as a custodian at Bristol Eastern High School, Dennis took great pleasure in watching his sons play sports and attending their games. He set up a gym where the boys could lift weights. Outside, there was a makeshift basketball court where they worked on their hoop skills into the night.

Dennis was also fond of motivational sayings. He had not fulfilled his own destiny, but he would ensure his boys pursued theirs. One of his father's favorite quotes was tattooed on Aaron's arm: IF IT IS TO BE IT IS UP TO ME. Everyone in Bristol knew the Hernandez boys. "Watching his sons play sports was Dennis's greatest joy," Terri once said.

It was Dennis's vision that his boys would excel in sports, and each did. DJ, named for his father and grandfather, played three years as quarterback for UConn before being moved to wide receiver in 2007. Aaron looked to be following him.

Wearing number 15 for the Bristol Central Rams, Aaron was a "can't miss" Division 1 prospect. At six foot one, he had good size and great hands. He also had speed, allowing him to break tackles and run through defenders. He was coachable and a good kid. All he wanted was to make his father happy and his older brother proud.

Aaron and DJ were always mentioned in the same breath, even though DJ was older. They were joined at the hip while growing up, sharing the same bedroom and learning the lessons of being an athlete from their father. Their competition with each other made them better. They played football and basketball in the backyard, challenging each other the way brothers do. They worked out together and they raced against each other, running through the hills of Bristol chasing their father's dream.

Terri was the disciplinarian of their single-story ranch-style home at 189 Greystone Avenue. She made sure the boys did their homework and were where they said they would be. With Dennis coaching the boys and her taking care of the home, they were a model American family. But in 2001, when Aaron was twelve, Terri was arrested in a statewide sting for booking bets on sports. The *New York Daily News* reported she was a bookie for Marty Hovanesian, a restaurant manager in Bristol. She reportedly was paid $300 per week to accept wagers on professional football and baseball games as well as the NBA and college basketball. According to the *Daily News*, the feds estimated more than $70,000 was wagered during one four-day span. She would then calculate the winnings and losings.

A wiretap of her phone led to a search warrant, which led to her arrest. Hovanesian eventually pleaded guilty and was fined $10,000 for racketeering. Terri did no time, but in a small community like Bristol everyone knew what had happened, and her actions brought shame on a family that had been highly regarded for the football prowess of her two sons.

DJ tried to defend his mom, telling *Sports Illustrated* that she needed the money to buy her kids clothes and bicycles. "I'm not

Since I didn't have an office yet in Boston, sometimes we had to sign and file motions on the fly. *Courtesy of Linda Kenney Baden*

Sitting in the SUV, realizing there's no way Aaron could be the shooter because of his size. *Courtesy of Linda Kenney Baden*

Why the fuck didnt you fly up and demand me to hire you on my 1st trial — Fuck, im mad at you, even tho I needed this time in jail to straighten myself out (not literally lol)! You would have had multiple millions to work with and I would have gave you my last of it all. It all worked out perfectly and will but I wish you came up and demanded it! But I got you regardless in time!

Aaron's note to me, written in the middle of the trial. As each day went by he was happier and happier, as his dream of freedom became more viable. *Courtesy of the author*

Shows the trajectory of bullets hitting Aquilino Freire, supporting our argument that he was hit by two bullets, not one.

Shows how the shot would've been fired given the range of motion and Aaron's bulk.

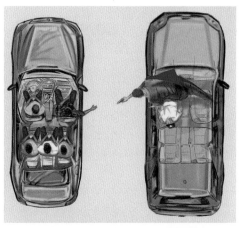

We took precise measurements of Aaron's body, the available space in front of a driver, and the trajectory of the bullets to illustrate the impossibility that Aaron could have been the shooter. *All illustrations by Sheldon Borenstein*

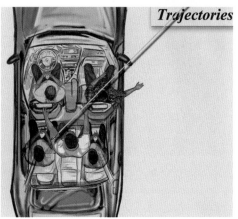

Trajectories

As deliberations began, everyone was feeling optimistic. Michelle Medina, Linda Kenney Baden, Ronald "Sully" S. Sullivan Jr., Jerry Lyons, me, George Leontire. *Courtesy of Linda Kenney Baden*

Heading out to closing arguments with interns Jeon Favors and Jake Meiseles with exhibits they'd been working on all night. *Courtesy of Linda Kenney Baden*

Early morning, before closing arguments, putting final touches on my video. *Courtesy of Linda Kenney Baden*

Shay and Aaron at her Sweet 16 party.
Courtesy of Shayanna Jenkins-Hernandez

Shay and Aaron, engaged and expecting.
Courtesy of Shayanna Jenkins-Hernandez

Aaron as a new father. *Courtesy of Shayanna Jenkins-Hernandez*

4/18/17

Jose,

What's up, brotha? Well, I wrote this letter following my aquittal and wanted to voice how I felt and let some people whos music helped me get through hard time know that it did. Wrong or right — who knows — I just follow my natural instincts and how it guides me. Pros or cons, didnt weigh them, but im sure youd let me know your view. Besides that, I want you to know you have me forever like you never understood and time will reveal that I'm not perfect but my love and loyalty is like you've never seen! I appreciate all your work, time, effort, and never let that slip your mind! In time you will see how appreciated you are, as well as all the others equally! But never forget I will whoop your ass if you get to crazy haha! But we could grab a drink after! All jokes aside, I hope your son is well and all your loved ones!

I need a favor — if you have any contacts for any artists like Gates, meek mill, Russ, Jay, Game ... etc, I would like to send you letters so you can send to their information or whichever way you think best. I dont want any media really getting into me trying to just send my love to all the artist who got me through my tough times and sending my respect to a few of the real ones out there, so I think thats the best idea through you. Its something I have to do and id appreciate if you could do that for me, if possible! If not, ill figure something out. Well, get at me, love ya brother!

Aaron

Aaron's last message to me, written the night he died. *Courtesy of the author*

Avi,

You are the most beautiful girl ever born and you're an angel. Love everyone as yourself and know im always with you. I love you so much but im smiling because i know im now with you every second of everyday.

All my loved ones I love you all!

DJ, MA, PARKER, ALL HERNANDEZ'S, ALL MY FAMILY!

NOT MUCH TIME

IM BEING CALLED!

JOHN 3:16

(*This page and next*) Part of Aaron's last messages to those he loved. *Courtesy of the author*

I love you all equally I we are all eachother I Dont shed
one tear, for I am with all of you and never went I
DO NOT GO BACK TO LIVING WHILE worshipping False
Idols in which I warned you about!

SHOUT OUT TO Those In which spoke to my soul and I heard
myself!!!

YO GOTTI   "LAST SONG"
                    [BIG SEAN: SUNDAY MORNING JETPACK]
MEEK
JAY
ROSS
YFN LUCCI   STAND FOR WHAT YOU BELIEVE
THE WEEKND   IN AND FOLD FOR NOTHING!
FRENCHIE
GAME   ITS TIME!!!
Pusha T
NIPSEY   THE REAL LIVE FOREVER
NAS
LYFE JENNINGS
KENDRICK LAMAR
K. GATES
JADA
STYLES
GUCCI
WAKA (ELM LOVE)   GODBODY
FUTURE
DRAKE
KHALED
DJ NS i e

The memorial card
from Aaron's funeral.
Courtesy of Shayanna Jenkins-Hernandez

saying it was right what she did at all," he said. "I don't think it is. But this woman did this because I was crying every single night. She didn't do it for the thrill. She didn't do it to pocket money. She did it to provide for me and Aaron."

Not long afterward Terri shook the family again, when it came to light that she was having an affair with a landscaper named Jeffrey Cummings. Cummings moonlighted as a drug dealer and happened to be married to Dennis's niece Tanya Cummings, Aaron's cousin and his most loyal friend besides Shay. Being caught in a bookmaking scheme was bad enough. Now Terri was cheating on his father and betraying his cousin.

Tanya was more like a sister to Aaron and shared his innermost secrets. He never quite felt that his mom was trustworthy. "Why do you think me and Tanya are so close?" Aaron once asked her during a telephone conversation from prison. "That's one of the reasons."

Those feelings hardened when his father died in January of 2006. Dennis underwent a routine hernia operation and died unexpectedly from complications that began with an infection. He was forty-nine. Aaron was just sixteen and devastated.

"It was more like a shock," Aaron said at the time. "Everyone was close to my father, but I was the closest. I was with him more than my friends. When that happened, who do I talk to? Who do I hang with? It was tough."

More than a thousand people attended the funeral services held at Saint Matthew Roman Catholic Church in Bristol. Any donations were asked to be sent to the UConn Alumni Association. Everyone expresses their grief in different ways. DJ bawled his eyes out; Aaron hardly shed a tear during the funeral.

"I saw a kid who was devastated," DJ would tell *Sports Illustrated*. "I think he was confused. He was lost. Crying is not always the answer, but being an emotional family, for him to put up a wall during the services . . . it was shocking to me. He was holding everything in."

Shayanna didn't really know the impact of his father's death until one day years later when she and Aaron were in California enjoying a quiet moment on the water. "We were talking and I remember him getting emotional and crying," she said. "I saw Aaron cry maybe three times the entire time I knew him. We were talking about his father and he was saying how much he missed him and how much he meant to him. With everything going on with him and his mother and who she married [Cummings], everything was coming to light. At that moment, I realized how much he was holding in and how much the impact of his father reflected on his life. I had no idea."

Aaron felt alone and abandoned when his father died. His mother was already seeing another man, and his brother was in college. The situation at home grew worse when Cummings moved into the house where Terri lived with Aaron on Greystone Avenue. The couple got married as soon as he divorced Tanya, who at one point confronted Terri in the stands during a high school football game. Terri's connection to Cummings put a strain on Aaron's relationship with his mother and strengthened his bond with Tanya. Aaron remained very close to Tanya throughout her divorce ordeal and long afterward—her children became his godsons, and later when she was diagnosed with terminal cancer, he promised to look after them.

With Cummings around, Aaron took to the streets, hanging out in the rougher areas of Bristol. That's when he began to smoke marijuana more frequently to mask his pain.

Still, he continued to excel in sports. He was a star player on the basketball team and a terror on the football field. At the end of a record-breaking career at Bristol Central High School that included 3,437 receiving yards and forty-five receiving touchdowns, Aaron earned first-team All-State honors and led the Rams to the 2007 Central Connecticut Conference Southern Division Championship.

He had verbally committed to UConn. But then Urban Meyer and the Gators called and Aaron thought it might be good to get away from the cold and all the family drama and attend college at the University of Florida in Gainesville. He was recruited by Steve

Addazio, an assistant coach at Florida who grew up just outside of Bristol. Aaron visited the campus for the 2006 spring game where he met Tim Tebow, a freshman quarterback from Jacksonville. Overwhelmed by the atmosphere of big-time football and the chance to play for a national championship, Aaron committed to Florida.

Aaron left Bristol in January 2007, and like most freshmen he was homesick and not sure he could handle the demands of school and playing sports. The death of his father still lay heavy on his heart; his father was his best friend. Aaron was depressed, and he carried that depression with him to Gainesville.

Aaron spent the early part of his first year locked in his room sleeping. But later, after he got a taste of the nightlife and the perks of being a Gator, he started going to bars. He smoked weed and stopped going to class. He was the starting tight end for the Gators. He was still going to play because the team needed him, but the rest of his college career was in shambles.

Meyer knew Aaron was still despondent over the death of his father and encouraged him to attend Bible study, which he did from time to time. The coach also asked Mike and Maurkice Pouncey, twin offensive linemen, to make sure he stayed out of trouble, and also asked Tebow to keep an eye on him. That was often easier said than done.

There was a well-publicized incident in 2007 at a bar near campus. Aaron, in a group according to records that included Tebow, reportedly had an argument with a waiter, Michael Taphorn, who suffered a ruptured eardrum in an ensuing scuffle. No charges were filed, and in the larger context of college football misbehavior, the conflict was a nonevent. But word made its way back to the coach.

Aaron came under scrutiny again when he was suspended for Florida's 2008 season opener against Hawaii. Meyer would later say Aaron was benched because he failed a drug test. This was the only drug test on record that Aaron officially failed, though he was known to be heavy into weed and would later have to address it at the NFL Scouting Combine.

Meyer has taken criticism for covering up Aaron's transgressions while at Florida. But in my opinion, he shouldn't be blamed. Coaching should be about helping kids grow into emotionally strong men and women, not just physically strong athletes. But every member of the university administration, not just coaches, should encourage their student athletes to seek counseling for their personal crises. The fact is being a college football coach means not only preparing students for game days, but also steeling yourself for their arrest warrants. During an interview with HBO's *Real Sports*, Meyer acknowledged there had been thirty-one arrests of twenty-five players under his watch at Florida. Charges aren't often pursued if the team is winning national championships; but regardless, college programs have law enforcement on speed dial for when athletes get in trouble.

Truth is, Aaron had a good relationship with Meyer and his wife, Shelley. She told *Real Sports* when she saw Aaron arrested in the Odin Lloyd case that her immediate thought was "That's not the Aaron Hernandez I know." She said, "Aaron Hernandez was in my home many, many times, sitting with my kids, playing with my kids. Yes ma'am, Miss Shelley. It's just excruciatingly sad to see a kid that we know that was part of our family make decisions that are just horrible."

When Aaron was arrested in the Odin shooting, every questionable deed he committed in Florida was brought to the surface. He was also mentioned in the double shooting that took place in Gainesville in 2007, where five gunshots were fired into a car containing three passengers stopped at a traffic light. The occupants of the car described the shooter as a "Hawaiian" or "Hispanic" male with a large build and many tattoos.

Aaron was contacted by police, but he invoked his right to counsel and refused to talk to them. No charges were filed, largely because police reports indicate every witness to the shooting, other than those directly involved, identified the shooter as a black man under six feet tall with cornrows and wearing a green polo shirt. Aaron said he was innocent, but the idea he was the shooter persisted.

I was among those who assumed he was involved, but Aaron insisted he wasn't. He told me he had interacted with the group that day; that somebody had snatched a chain off one of the Pounceys and there had been a lot of tough talk back and forth. But there was another group of guys who had a beef with the victims, and they must have done the shooting. He had not.

"I'm serious," he said.

Aaron had told me so much at this point—good, bad, and ugly—that he seemed shocked that I didn't initially believe him.

"Why do you think I would lie to you like that?" he asked.

"C'mon," I told him, "you were at least in the car. You were at least part of it."

"No," he said. "I literally had nothing to do with that. I wasn't anywhere near the shooting."

I guess I was just as guilty as everyone else passing judgment on him, assuming he was involved. He said he had participated in the initial talking shit part. But after that he and the twins took off. I believe him now. There were times he told me things he didn't have to tell me: behavior of his that was questionable. There were many times when I expected an innocent answer and he would respond with a shockingly candid admission. That's why I felt he was always ultimately truthful with me.

While there may have been doubt about his behavior off campus, there was little question about his performance on the football field. He was playing well and getting along with teammates. His Gator teammates nicknamed him "Chico" because he was the only Puerto Rican on the team. Aaron liked the nickname and even got a little jealous when players started calling a new equipment manager Chico too. "I thought I was the only Chico," Aaron complained.

After catching nine passes for 111 yards in Florida's 51-24 win over Cincinnati in the Sugar Bowl, Aaron announced in January 2010 that he was declaring himself for the NFL Draft. Meyer had already told him he wouldn't be welcomed back for his senior year, but he had played well enough during his junior season to be considered one of the best prospects at tight end.

"It is really special for me to take this first step toward my lifelong dream of playing in the NFL on the fourth anniversary of my father's passing," Aaron said at the time. "I know he would be proud of not only me, but of my whole family, whose love and support are the only reasons I am where I am today. My three years in Florida provided me with the foundation I need to succeed as a player and a person."

Aaron signed with the sports agency Athletes First and began to prepare for the NFL Scouting Combine in Indianapolis. This is the annual showcase where all potential college candidates for the upcoming NFL draft assemble and are put through physical and mental exercises for careful evaluation. Coaches, scouts, and general managers from every franchise in the National Football League are on hand to dissect every player's statistics and test scores and use the information to decide which players they will draft in April. The prospects are there by invitation only and have often spent several weeks training daily in preparation for the showcase, hoping a good showing will increase their draft stock. Since rookie contracts are tied to draft position, the higher a player is drafted, the more money he'll make. Some players are just hoping to be drafted during the seven rounds of selections. Those who go undrafted are free to sign with the team of their choice if they're wanted.

When it came time to perform in Indy, Aaron couldn't. A back injury prevented him from competing in the drills, but he did go through interviews with several different teams interested in him. He would work out during a pro day at the University of Florida, but concerns about his drug use and off-the-field incidents lingered, and Aaron dropped to the fourth round, where he was selected by the Patriots. His first professional contract would earn him $596,000 as a rookie and $650,000 the following year.

A few days after being drafted, he showed up on Shayanna's doorstep. They had attended South Side Elementary School

together, but didn't really interact until they were classmates at
Memorial Boulevard, a middle school in Bristol that no longer exists. They became sweethearts in high school. Aaron was already
a jock and a class clown, while Shayanna was captain of the high
school dance team and a sprinter on the track team. Their relationship was off and on while he was in Florida, but Aaron, who had
moved to Plainview, Massachusetts, after leaving college, was a pro
now and looking for stability.

"Ultimately, we ended up with each other," said Shayanna, who
was working as a phlebotomist. "I moved to Plainview with him
and I was driving back and forth from Massachusetts to Connecticut for my job."

Meanwhile, in 2010 police were summoned to the home Terri
and Cummings were sharing. Cummings had grabbed an eight-inch
knife and made a three-and-a-half-inch cut on Terri's right cheek
after pushing her to the floor during an argument in the family
kitchen. Cummings was arrested and ultimately sent to prison for
two years. The couple divorced, but renewed their volatile relationship once Cummings was released.

Aaron kept his focus on football, and in his second season the
Patriots reached the Super Bowl and the Hernandez family was the
toast of Bristol again.

There was a celebration in the gym at South Side Elementary
where Terri worked as secretary to the principal. There were bal-
loons, banners, and posters. Teachers wore T-shirts that read: GO
PATRIOTS! FROM THE HOMETOWN OF AARON HERNANDEZ. Terri
was given a bouquet of flowers and a sash that read: SUPER BOWL
MOM.

A video featuring Aaron was played as tears fell onto the cheeks
of his proud mother. "Make sure you listen to your teachers," Aaron
said in the video.

Somewhere in the heavens, Dennis had to be smiling. His son
had reached the ultimate stage in football just like he had envisioned. What began in the backyard of their home in Bristol had

reached the Super Bowl. Aaron caught a touchdown pass in the Big Game, but the Giants won, sending the Patriots home as losers and denying Aaron a Super Bowl ring. But he had played well enough over his first two seasons to earn a $40 million extension, which he signed during the offseason. He was living his father's dream.

Unlike most ballers who have just struck it rich, Aaron didn't immediately go out and buy his mother a house. Instead, Terri remained in her home with Cummings. Aaron bought himself a house, the large mansion in North Attleboro into which he eventually moved with Shayanna.

They got engaged in October 2012 during her baby shower. Everyone knew what was about to happen except Shayanna. "He sat next to me and was helping me open the last of the gifts," Shayanna recalled. "I thought he was getting up to thank everybody for coming and he started with a speech and I figured out what was going on. It was a special moment for us."

On November 6, Avielle arrived on Aaron's birth date. The grinning football star was there "from the beginning of my contractions to the birth of Avielle," Shayanna would say. "He seemed more interested in the process than anything."

A few days after Avielle's birth, the family gathered everything they owned and moved into "the big house," as Shay called it. "Everything happened really fast," she said. "Him signing the contract, us getting pregnant, and us moving into our home happened within a few months."

Their dreams of a wonderful life as a family were turned upside down that morning in June of 2013 when Aaron was arrested and charged with the murder of Odin Lloyd.

WHEN AARON WAS CHARGED with shooting Odin Lloyd, Terri was still working at South Side Elementary and wondering how things had gone so wrong. Despite the strained relationship with her son, she was a daily presence during the Lloyd trial and constantly maintained her son's innocence. "All I can say is that he will be cleared of all these charges in the end," she said at the time. "Let it play out until the end."

She was there weeping alongside Shay when the guilty verdict was read. When a husband, son, or brother is torn from their home and jailed, it's not just the prisoner who suffers; the entire family is affected. But after that it seemed Aaron's family wanted to distance themselves from him. Aaron's mother was never seen at the Boston trial, an absentee figure I'm sure was noticed by the jury. DJ wasn't really there either.

After the conviction, DJ started going by "Jonathan," his middle name. Jonathan presents a story of an older brother who never abandoned his younger brother. He told *Sports Illustrated* that he often talked to his brother by telephone at the Souza-Baranowski Correctional Center. But when Aaron needed him at the Boston trial, he was reluctant to attend.

DJ, or Jonathan, showed up for one day of the Boston trial. But that was only because the prosecution had subpoenaed him as a potential witness to testify. Aaron was happy to see his brother, but knew the real reason he was there. It wasn't really to support him.

Aaron told us that when he and DJ were kids they were competitive, and Aaron always felt he had to do something to earn his big brother's attention and love. He felt that with other members of his family there was always something he had to do or give to gain their love. He once told my associate Michelle Medina that he never felt he was loved without a string attached. Now that Aaron was in prison, he could see who really supported him because he had nothing to give back.

Aaron smiled at his brother the one day he showed up. Little did either know it would be the last time they would see each other.

We could never get his mother, Terri, to the trial. My office called her several times asking her to come down to see Aaron. She would call our office and leave messages with concerns about security at the courthouse and what the media would say about her attendance and how the media would portray her. Here was a man fighting for his freedom, who needed his mother's love, but she was more concerned about what the press would say.

Aaron was frustrated by his mother's absence and assumed she didn't show because she didn't want her arrest for being a bookie to be rehashed again. Aaron always thought his mother was an informant who cooperated with the cops, because she got a slap on the wrist while others were convicted and fined. He knew she must have cooperated with authorities, and deep down he wasn't proud of that.

I can tell you that Aaron did love his mother. But he was so frustrated by the way she showed her love. A transcript of a phone conversation the two shared while Aaron was in prison shows the dynamic:

AARON: "There's so many things I'd like—I would love to talk to you [about] so you can know me as a person, but I never could tell you and you're gonna die without even knowing your son. That's the craziest thing about it. You know what I mean? It's crazy."

TERRI: "Well if you feel you can't talk to me . . ."

AARON: "How could I? How could I? You are not trustworthy at all."

TERRI: "Well . . ."

AARON: "It's so sad. You know?"

Later in the conversation Aaron says, "I just wish I could be closer with you, but I can't and it kills me, but I can't . . . it's just—it is what it is. I just have to deal with it."

TERRI: "But, babe, after nine years we're both hurt."

AARON: "It's not even about being hurt, ma. It's just like, I don't know. There's just so much stuff I would love to just talk to my mom about, but I can't . . . 'cause I know you'll tell."

Near the end of the conversation, Aaron says again: "You'll die not knowing your son and I think that's really sad."

Terri never made it to the trial. Aaron's uncle David came to court once, and brought his wife and kids. David was going through cancer treatment and was very sick. His cousin Jennifer was there for a day and brought along Tanya Singleton's kids, Jano and Eddie, the two names Aaron referred to in one of his notes the night he committed suicide. He had promised Tanya he would take care of them when she died of cancer. Besides Avielle, they were his world.

Aaron was the kind of man who would ask everyone he met about their families. He would ask how my kids were doing, and he wasn't just paying lip service. Family was important to him. In the end Shay and Avielle were his family. He would often pull out the picture of Shay and Avielle he carried with him in his coat pocket during trial as a good-luck charm. He would brag about Avielle and say, "She's so beautiful. She looks just like me, right?"

Every time he saw Shay in court supporting him, he would say, "I love this girl." He was always trying to turn around and say to her "I love you." That's what drove him: love and hope. That's what drove Shayanna too.

"Every single time he came out of the holding cell into the courtroom and saw me, Aaron lit up," she said. "Stuff like that gives you butterflies. You're thinking how could I ever not support this man? I didn't understand how a family that was once so supportive and so loving and so tight could leave him like that. I wish I had a better relationship with them so I could ask them. You're supposed to fight for what's right. They just quit. There was a lot of selfish behavior . . . you can't be there all the time. But not once? It's just sad."

16.

WOULD YOU PLEASE CONVICT
IF THERE'S NO EVIDENCE?

As we began speaking to potential jurors individually, I could immediately see how different picking a jury was going to be in Boston. Boston is a mecca of American higher education, home to universities like Harvard, MIT, Boston College—the list goes on and on. This natural abundance of higher education was reflected in its jury pool.

We started taking hardship requests from jurors, and I couldn't believe the number of doctors and surgeons who had commitments that precluded them from serving. We were reviewing requests in a small anteroom outside of the main jury-pool room. While many potential jurors had legitimate reasons to be excused, an almost comical number seemed to feel they didn't have to perform their civic duty simply because they were doctors. The absurdity reached its zenith when a pharmacist walked in and said he couldn't serve because he was a pharmacist.

"If you were required to serve, how would you be affected?" Judge Locke asked.

"Well, my patients would not receive their proper medication and there could be many sick people who desperately need their medicine," answered the good pharmacist.

"And are there no other pharmacists that work in the pharmacy where you work?" Locke pressed.

"Well, yes, but I know how to fill the prescriptions better because I know how my patients like their prescriptions," answered the man.

That one left us all scratching our heads. Locke made him wait until the end of the day before excusing him.

All students got a free pass, as many would miss class and finals, and with all the universities and specialty schools in Boston, that eliminated about half our pool right there. The process was painfully slow and careful. We had done months of preparation for jury selection. We had a detailed questionnaire prepared that all jurors were asked to fill out, and we had a team of interns in a hotel room nearby working around the clock to search public and not so public records to get further background information on potential jurors. We had another group of kids scouring the internet and social media sites to get all the available information we could. George Leontire was in charge of compiling all the data and identifying the group of jurors we were looking for.

Once we were done with the hardships, we moved straight to the individual questioning of each potential juror. The mood was fairly light throughout the week until a Hispanic-looking man walked in looking quite somber. He spoke with a thick accent, and I quickly realized he wasn't Hispanic; he was Cape Verdean. That was an immediate disqualification for the defense, but we could not excuse someone because of race, or in this case, ethnicity. Soon we realized he not only knew the Cape Verdeans in the BMW, but he was Daniel de Abreu's uncle. I felt terrible for the man as we questioned him and he broke down and began to cry. The man clearly wanted to do his civic duty. He felt it was an honor to serve on a jury. Yet he was honest enough to know there was no way for him to be fair to Aaron. Then he shocked the entire room when he turned to Aaron, looked him in the eye and said, "I want you to receive a fair trial."

The next issue we covered was how much press coverage the potential jurors had seen. We were sure not to mention the Odin Lloyd case until the potential juror indicated he or she had seen media coverage of both cases, and an overwhelming majority of them had.

I was shocked by how much of the Odin Lloyd case some of these potential jurors recalled. Some could even recite some of the witnesses' names and what their relationship was to the people involved. But some didn't know much at all, and a few knew even less than they thought. A well-dressed, middle-aged white woman walked in and was questioned about her exposure to the media. When asked by Judge Locke if she had been exposed to some of the media coverage about this case, she responded proudly, "Yes I have."

"What exactly have you seen?" Locke asked.

"Well, isn't this the case about Deflate Gate?"

This drew laughs from everyone, including the press, who were familiar with New England Patriot quarterback Tom Brady's suspension from the NFL for allegedly deflating some footballs during games in order to gain tactical advantage. The poor woman's face was flushed with embarrassment when Locke broke it to her that she was not there to pass judgment about deflated footballs.

Jury selection should really be called jury deselection, because it's more a process of elimination than anything else. The way the process works is that each side can strike a juror for *cause*. Cause is usually a constitutional challenge questioning whether the person should serve; for instance, they admit they can't be fair or they have some form of bias.

Either side can move to strike a juror selection, or the judge can do it. Then each side is given a certain number of cause challenges, allowing them to question why the other side has struck a juror. Most states give each side twelve strikes, called *peremptory challenges;* these allow a party to strike a juror for any reason they choose other than for race, religion, or gender, which would violate the juror's constitutional rights.

Peremptory challenges are one of the few tools given to a defense lawyer because prosecutors always, and I mean always, strike African Americans from juries. That's mainly because African Americans face so much discrimination in our criminal justice system that most are predisposed to distrust the police, the main witnesses for the state. What I find amusing is that prosecutors will never admit to excusing jurors because of their race, but the practice is plain as day, and they get so upset and indignant when you call them out on it. Again, like Captain Renault from *Casablanca*, they are "shocked, shocked" if you insinuate their actions are racist, but they do it anyway. I never let a prosecutor strike a person of color without forcing them to state their reasons; this is called a *Batson challenge*. Never. Because I want the prosecutor to know that I will guard against racism like a pit bull.

Prosecutor Mark Lee, who was leading the jury selection process for the prosecution, was a bit thrown off when I made my first Batson challenge.

Once we raise the Batson challenge we then request that the prosecutor give a race-neutral explanation for why they are excusing the juror. If the judge finds the reason to be race neutral, he will allow the strike. If not, then the prosecution cannot strike the juror, and the juror is guaranteed to sit on the jury.

As we kept going I kept raising objections, and I could tell that Mark, of Asian descent, was getting more upset by the minute. He finally burst out with a statement about how offended he was. "As a person of color, I am offended by Mr. Baez's insinuations," he barked.

"You're a person of color?" I responded, just to piss him off.

"Yes! I am," he said as his face turned red.

"Do people cross the street to avoid you when you walk down the street at night?" I couldn't resist.

"All right, that's enough," Locke interrupted.

This was the first of many skirmishes I'd have with the prosecution, and it gave me a good sense of how to upset Mark Lee. Let's save that for later, I thought to myself. Overall, the effect of all the Batson challenges paid off, because after Mark's "I'm a person of color" speech the prosecution did not strike any more Hispanics or African Americans, even those clearly biased for the defense. We ended up with an overwhelmingly minority jury of four Hispanics and four African Americans.

Prosecutors also tipped their hand in a big way during jury selection. I always look for clues as to how prosecutors are going to try their case by listening to some of the questions they ask potential jurors. It wasn't too hard to figure out their plan, since Mark Lee asked every single juror the same three questions:

1. *"Could you convict if there wasn't any forensic evidence tying the defendant to the crime?"*
2. *"Could you convict if you didn't believe the motive for the crime?"*
3. *"Could you convict if the state's chief witness cut a deal for himself?"*

Basically, they kept asking the jurors, could you convict Aaron Hernandez, even though there is no evidence against him and our main witness is a snitch who cut a deal to save himself?

I had to keep fighting not to smile every time I heard these questions. Did they think these people were stupid? And wouldn't they see right away that something was up? I knew right then and there I would have to scratch my opening statement and center it around these questions. The opportunity to preempt their argument was just too good to pass up.

Patrick Haggan would deliver the opening statements for the prosecution. As expected he was good, really good. He began by describing the early morning hours of July 16, 2012. His theme was that of "two worlds colliding": the world of hard-working immigrants, the Cape Verdeans; and the world of a privileged celebrity athlete. He described how Daniel de Abreu was a former police officer in Cape Verde, a fact detailed nowhere in the evidence turned over to the defense; and Safiro Furtado was a former tour guide who had been in this country only months before that fateful night. He described how these two worlds by mere chance interacted with one another in Cure; how these hard-working immigrants had to pay a cover charge yet the celebrity football player did not.

He began painting Aaron as a hothead, a self-entitled prick, while these poor immigrants were just out for a rare night on the town; one of them would bump into this celebrity who frequented nightclubs and lived the good life.

What Haggan was doing was trying to get the jury to hate Aaron. Deep down inside many people hate professional athletes because they appear to have it all: youth, money, fame, all for playing a game. What we don't see is the hard work that goes into being one of the very few who actually make it in professional sports; the sacrifices they make as children, as their parents push them to fulfill the dreams they never could. While other children are playing video games and riding their bikes, these future stars are running more laps, catching more passes. I knew after hearing Haggan describe Aaron this way that I would have to remind the jury of the sacrifices Aaron made.

"Nobody gave Aaron anything. Whatever he gained in life he had to work for, and it should not be held against a person because they decided to work hard enough to fulfill the American dream," I would later tell the jury. I tried to emphasize how "athletes do this at a great risk of their current and future health, just so we can enjoy a game." Little did I know how true that was in this particular case.

Haggan then moved on to Bradley, describing him as Aaron's best friend and future godfather of Avielle. What a crock, I thought to myself as the words came out of Haggan's mouth. I made sure I did not show any expression on my face as he said this. Years earlier in the Casey Anthony trial, I noticed out of the corner of my eye that the prosecutor Jeff Ashton was laughing as I was delivering my arguments. He had been doing it throughout the trial and I had asked the judge to instruct him to stop on multiple occasions. But the judge kept saying he didn't see him laughing, so when I saw him doing it at closing I pointed to Ashton and said, "It doesn't matter who is asking the questions, whether it's me, or this laughing guy right here."

It was a powerful moment in the trial because mocking an opponent's arguments is an incredibly stupid thing for a lawyer to do. Jurors hate that, as *they* are the triers of facts, not the lawyers. There would be none of that in this trial—Haggan was the consummate professional and I knew better—but my mind could not help but wander as I imagined Bradley, the gun-toting drug dealer, in church. Ridiculous, I thought as I jotted down a reminder to point out the inaccuracy to the jury.

Most lawyers have a set script of what they want to tell a jury during opening statements. I use only an outline because my mentor Rick DeMaria, from the Miami-Dade Public Defender's Office, would always tell me that nothing is more persuasive to a jury than when you take what the prosecutor says during opening and use it against them. Responding to the prosecution in the opening has been a habit of mine ever since, and I truly believe the strategy has served me well. I think that psychologically for the jury it sets the stage for the dynamic to come: the prosecutor will tell you one thing, but I will be the one to show you the true meaning of that evidence, or show you something else entirely.

Haggan next tried to cushion the blows we would aim at Bradley by explaining that Bradley was "honest to a fault," or perhaps "too honest." Can you believe that? A prosecutor was warning the jury that their star witness was going to be "too honest." As if that was a bad thing.

Haggan knew Bradley had baggage, and lots of it. This was his way of diffusing the power of Bradley's criminal record, which no doubt would give any jury pause. He then concluded that the proof or corroboration of Bradley's testimony would come in the hundreds of text messages between Bradley and Aaron after the West Palm Beach shooting, when Bradley was attempting to extort money from Aaron. He forecast that the process of reviewing texts would be long and tedious, but in among all the messages they would find not only the truth about what happened in West Palm Beach, but "at least one reference to the double homicide in Boston."

My ears perked up; I had read those messages multiple times and knew every word that was said. I looked over at Michelle Medina, my right-hand "woo-man," as I jokingly call her. Michelle goes through all the evidence in my cases with me as a second set of eyes. She is my secret weapon, and has been with me for years. I would not have close to the amount of success I've achieved in the practice of law if it were not for her. As I turned to her, she looked at me at the same time, and she knew exactly what I was saying inside to myself, as she had heard it a million times before:

Michelle, what the fuck is he talking about?

Our eyes met and she shook her head slightly so only I could see, telling me it was *not* true. I could then relax and focus on my opening, which was coming up next.

I cannot even begin to tell you how many of my courtroom rants poor Michelle has withstood. A trial is by far the most stressful event I can possibly describe. A person's life hangs in the balance, on every word said in the courtroom, and we as humans are bound to make mistakes. I really have to take this opportunity to publicly apologize for all those times in the middle of all those battles when I completely freaked out and made her the focus of my wrath. Sorry, Mishy. She is directly responsible for *all* of my courtroom victories, and there will never be a better example than the Aaron

Hernandez trial and those "goddam text messages," as a prosecutor would later call them.

Finally it was my turn, and as I rose I immediately tackled the three questions prosecutors asked all of the jury members during selection.

1. *"Could you convict if you didn't believe the motive as described by Alexander Bradley?"*
2. *"Could you convict if there was no forensic evidence tying Aaron Hernandez to the crime?"*
3. *"Could you convict if you didn't believe Alexander Bradley?"*

My third question was a little different than the one prosecutors had actually asked: "Could you convict if the state's chief witness cut a deal for himself?" But the issue remained the same: you couldn't convict Aaron Hernandez unless you truly believed Alexander Bradley. These were all major weaknesses in the prosecution's case, and I was not about to let the jury forget it. The words of my mentor Rick DeMaria echoed in my mind. *Take what they say and use it against them.*

I outlined the defense case as best I could, constantly reiterating my theme: "Could you convict if there wasn't any evidence?" Putting my hands together in a prayerlike motion, I talked about the missing video from Cure, and I could see the surprise in a couple of jurors' faces. I talked about the missing photo taken by the fan inside Cure and how the cops never looked for it. Now I was seeing anger in their eyes. I talked about the crime scene and how the bodies of Abreu and Furtado were disrespected, and I could see the eyebrows of a couple of jurors coming together in disbelief. I pointed out all the inconsistencies and lies in Bradley's testimony in both Boston and West Palm Beach. Apparently, as I was giving my remarks a fire alarm was going off in the background as loud as could be. I didn't hear it and neither did the jury. The room was as quiet as the alarm was loud. I left nothing unaddressed, from the mysterious behavior of the guys in the BMW to Bradley's mountain of lies.

I thought I hit all the points I needed to, but the press thought my opening argument was a big flop. The next day, March 2, 2017, Bob McGovern's article on the front page of the *Boston Herald* read: "Strong Offense Not the Best Defense for Aaron Hernandez." He went on to write: "Jose Baez has multiple ways to try and get former New England Patriot Aaron Hernandez out of double murder charges—but showing a brutal lack of respect to prosecutors, police and Bay State investigators isn't a smart tactic." I don't know a single person in this world, if they were accused of murder, who would want their lawyer to hold back good evidence-based arguments against the prosecutors or police. The fact is I was not there to make friends with the prosecutors or police. I was there to defend a man facing life in prison, and he didn't say, "While you're doing it, please be nice." To the contrary. When I was done I began walking back to the defense table, and while my colleagues were patting me on the back and offering words of encouragement, my eyes were fixed on Aaron's. I saw a brightness there I had never seen before.

He was pleased. I didn't know it at the time, but in the middle of my opening statement Aaron handed Michelle a note that read: "OMG, Jose is so fucking good." "Duh!, Who the hell did you think you hired," Michelle wrote back.

When Michelle showed me the note, it warmed my heart. Nothing pleases me more than when my clients are happy with my work. I never take the trust they put in me lightly. It's an awesome responsibility; actually a mind-wracking, stressful one. For the first time I saw hope in Aaron's eyes, followed by those famous words he uttered when we first decided to go on this journey together: "Fuck yeah!"

17.

INDEPENDENT AND
NOT SO INDEPENDENT WITNESSES

The prosecution began its case by putting on families of the victims to do what Massachusetts law calls "humanizing the proceedings." I have never been a fan of this. What they do is start the trial by calling a tearful family member to testify and entering into evidence a photograph of the victim. The trial begins with an obvious effort to pull the heartstrings and emotions of the jury. Before you go thinking that I'm cold, look at it from this perspective: the law has a theory, which is that the jury should base its decision on the evidence, not on emotion. I cannot agree more with this concept. We do not want jurors making decisions based on emotion.

I believe this concept took root in the 1960s, when criminal justice reform was enacted after a series of miscarriages of justice during the civil rights era. Dispensing justice based on emotion was another form of lynching. You aren't taking someone out of their cell and hanging them in front of the courthouse. But what you are doing is putting them on trial, making the jury angry about this horrible crime, and then pointing the finger at the accused. Someone must pay for this horrible crime.

Recent case law has trended away from this line of thinking, and for good reason. Think about it this way: you have a prosecutor putting family members on the stand to evoke sympathy from the jury, yet at the end of the trial you have the judge instructing the jury that they are to base their decision on facts, not feelings.

After the victims' families took the stand and offered little information about who could have committed this crime, the prosecution shifted focus to the crime scene. We all spent the next two weeks listening to each and every officer on the stand confirm three main things: that they knew little about how to properly process a crime scene; that they had no idea who had placed the sheets on the bodies or where the sheets came from; and that all of them had heard from another officer that a street sweeper had passed by, but no one had seen it, and no one could identify the officer who had.

Next up were the eyewitnesses, including numerous people involved throughout the investigation. There are two very important things to remember when relying on eyewitness testimony. One is the difference between *independent* witnesses and *interested* witnesses. The descriptions are pretty straightforward: independent witnesses do not have a dog in the fight. They have no interest in the outcome of the litigation. The interested witnesses, simply stated, have a motive or a reason to slant their testimony one way or the other. The problem with high-profile cases is that independent witnesses can evolve into interested ones due to peer pressure or a sense of moral duty, or the prospect of financial gain if they feel they can make money off their story.

We are all human beings motivated by wants and desires, and while making a statement under oath is meaningful to all of us, I have often seen a person's commitment to the truth start to wane in the glare of the spotlight. This is something we had to look out for throughout this case.

The best example of the interested witnesses would be the three surviving Cape Verdeans inside the BMW. I will begin with Raychides Sanches. You may recall that Sanches was seated in the rear passenger side of the BMW. Aside from Safiro Furtado, who was killed, Sanches should have gotten the best view of the killer. But while in the BMW Sanches wanted one of his rap songs to be played, so I don't know how much attention he was paying to the SUV next to him. By his own account, he testified he was not paying much attention.

He didn't go to the police station until the day after the incident because he fled the scene the night of the shooting. He took a cab home covered in blood and then burnt his clothes. He discussed the case with fellow victim Gerson Lopes before going to the police station to give a statement. On July 16, 2012, Sanches described the driver as a white boy, American looking, wearing a white hat with a logo of a different color. He did not see the driver's face. He believed the passenger was female and the gun was black but could not give any further description.

Now this description should be analyzed in the following way. First, Rachides Sanches did not have a strong command of the English language and did not use an interpreter when speaking to the police. This was a colossal blunder on the police's part. A perfect example is the term "white boy." Sanches is dark-skinned black. Later on in the same statement he used the term "white boy" to describe Daniel de Abreu, who Americans would describe as either light-skinned African American or dark-skinned Hispanic.

Both guns described in this case were chrome, not black, and nobody wore a white hat, although Aaron had on a gray hat at various points in the evening.

Brian Quon, an independent witness, was a security guard who saw the SUV before it ran the red light, and did not have to endure a stressful event like Sanches. He testified the driver was African American, did not wear a hat, and was not young, maybe thirties or forties. Aaron was twenty-two at the time and Bradley was thirty and a light-skinned African American. Quon also said the passenger "might have been a female," and had "long shoulder-length hair with beads and cornrows." Quon's description of the passenger was more detailed than Sanches's description but not inconsistent with it.

Donald Gobin, the driver in the car with Quon, gave a similar description. Bear in mind that when witnesses have an opportunity to talk about what they saw they almost always give the same description. That takes us to Gerson Lopes, who did not testify at trial but spoke to police. He had been seated behind the driver in the BMW and had the opportunity to talk to Sanches as they went to the police station together. He also said the driver was white. Again keep in mind that the prosecution was arguing that Bradley, a light-skinned African American male, was the driver. Yet Lopes described the driver as wearing a green hat and in his twenties.

Lopes's statement would never see the light of day, as a few days later Gerson Lopes returned to the police station and told a tale that did not match what everyone else was saying. He said he got a partial license plate, which he put in his phone as the shooting was occurring, and that after Abreu and Furtado were shot the SUV then sped off, turned around, and shots were fired at the BMW from the front. It was a bizarre tale the police questioned immediately. Lopes did believe the shooting was drug related, saying he recognized somebody at the club who thought Lopes was involved in a shooting at a weed house in Dorchester, Massachusetts. This grabbed my interest, as Bradley was a marijuana trafficker and this would have explained everything. But Lopes's tales just spun bigger and wilder.

After Aaron was named in the media as a suspect, Lopes described Aaron to a tee and said he actually got into a fight with Aaron in Cure because Lopes was hitting on Shayanna—at the time of the shooting Shayanna was in Florida—and he and Aaron had been fighting, rolling around on the club floor. He said he feared for his safety because every time he walked down the streets of

Roxbury, a town on the outskirts of Boston, the Puerto Ricans began throwing furniture at him. My star witness was disappearing before my eyes. I certainly didn't want the jury to start throwing furniture at me if I called him to the stand, so off he went, not to be called by the defense or the prosecution.

Aquilino Freire was seated in the middle rear seat of the BMW and could not give any description at all, except that he heard the SUV pull up and somebody say, "How are you guys doing?" He said he believed someone in the SUV might have been a female but could not tell the race or give any descriptions of those in the SUV; that is, of course, until Aaron Hernandez was named as a suspect. Then his story changed and he claimed the driver of the SUV was white Hispanic with lots of tattoos on his arms and wore a black hat. Freire went on to state that the driver said, "What's up, Negros?" not "How are you guys doing?"

As he testified before the grand jury in the Boston shootings, Freire admitted to researching Aaron on the internet and TV news and stated that Aaron's voice was exactly the same as the guy who said, "What's up, Negros?" And that the shooter was in fact Aaron Hernandez. The one constant in Freire's testimony was that he saw someone in the car who looked like a female.

Sanches would also change his testimony after Aaron was named as the suspect, saying the driver was Hispanic and had tattoos. He further stated that the driver's gun was an automatic. And the shooter was shooting with his left hand. It should be noted that after Aaron was named as a suspect, the website TMZ had posted a photograph of Aaron taking a selfie with his phone in his right hand and a semiautomatic pistol in his left hand. Sanches would later admit to seeing the photograph. I think it was clear he thought Aaron was left handed because in the photo he had the gun in his left hand. The only two constants in *all* of the witnesses' statements, constants that remained unchanged even after Aaron was named as a suspect, were that the shooter was the driver and the passenger looked like a female.

As you can see, the witness statements were all over the place, and Massachusetts has really strong case law that allowed us to move to exclude the descriptions that both Sanches and Freire were about to give after being influenced by media accounts and stories. We filed the motion and to my surprise Judge Locke granted it. I say to my surprise because most judges in *all* cases, high profile or not, rarely grant defense motions. They're granted occasionally when the cameras are not present, but next to never when the news is watching. No judge wants to be seen as soft on crime, or as letting someone off on a technicality. I knew right then and there that Judge Locke was going to give us a fair trial, and I liked our chances even better.

The ruling didn't really tip the scale in our favor all that much, actually, because I would have been able to point out the discrepancies in their stories to the jury during cross-examination, and Sanches and Freire would have looked like liars. Maybe Locke was doing the prosecution a favor by excluding them, but I don't think so. Locke seemed to try his best with all his rulings and I respected him immensely for it. He called them like he saw them and didn't give consideration to how a ruling made him look.

One night, after a long day of court about midway through the trial, I went to get a haircut. As I was sitting in the barber's chair my phone went off. I didn't answer because the man had a pair of scissors right next to my ears. The ringer went off again, and again. I realized something was up, so as soon as he was done I checked my messages. My office had forwarded a voicemail from a guy in California. He was a realtor who was watching the trial on the internet and heard my opening statement. He heard my arguments about the police not wanting to look for the picture of Aaron and the fan taken inside Cure that night. He took it as a personal challenge to find the picture, and find it he did.

The guy scoured the internet and found it on the Facebook page of a guy named Antoine Salvador, or "Junior." I was shocked. I had Jerry Lyons, my investigator, pull every driver's license taken from the Cure video scanner and talk to everyone he could find. Some of the IDs were not clear on the video and for some he couldn't find phone numbers. I also had several interns look all over the internet, and nothing. This guy in California combed the internet and checked friends of friends and so on and eventually found what no one from our team could.

While I was excited to get the information and the photograph, I have to admit I was kind of bummed that we didn't find it ourselves. Not being the one to find this critical piece of evidence was a total blow to my ego, but better this guy in California than nobody at all. The client comes first.

I immediately sent Jerry and Jeon Favors, our head intern and recent Harvard Law School graduate, to talk to Junior Salvador. I gave them strict instructions to not leave his house without a recorded statement because I knew once we turned this evidence over to the prosecution, Mr. Salvador was going to get a little visit from Boston detectives. "The Fan," as we originally called him, turned out to be a psychology doctoral student. He had no idea the trial was going on or even that he held one of the most important pieces of evidence in it.

Junior was at Cure with a few of his friends that night celebrating his birthday. He was standing at the main bar when he immediately recognized Aaron Hernandez as he walked in with what looked like a group of guys. He said as soon as Aaron walked in, he walked away from the large group of guys and went to the bar to get a drink. Junior said he could see Aaron was still with one guy, but the guy was standing a few feet away. After a couple of minutes of building up the nerve, he finally walked up to Aaron and asked him for a picture. Aaron politely declined. Junior then told Aaron it was his birthday and Aaron quickly relented. But Aaron insisted they walk somewhere private so others could not see him taking a picture. Junior walked up to Jaime Furtado and asked for access to the back room, which Furtado denied. Seeing the look on Junior's face, Aaron asked Furtado himself. Furtado finally agreed and was the one who took the picture.

After getting his photo, Junior thanked Aaron profusely then went back to show his friends. He told us he was amazed to see Aaron return to the bar instead of some VIP area. He watched him for about a minute as Aaron waited at the bar for his drink. Junior said he then walked up to Aaron again to thank him once more and offered to buy Aaron a drink. Junior told us Aaron politely declined. Junior said that Aaron's drinks arrived and he left the bar right after with his drinks in his hands. This is confirmed by the video near the entrance/exit of Cure, which shows Aaron walking out alone with two drinks in his hands. He chugs them before exiting through the door. Bradley is seen several steps behind him walking out on his own, contrary to his testimony, which was that he had to usher an angry Aaron outside of the bar.

Just like that we had a star independent witness, one who had no interest in the outcome of the case, who could testify about almost every second of the nine minutes Aaron spent in Cure. No spilled drink. No interaction with Abreu. No fight. Nothing but a rather uneventful nine minutes.

Junior would tell the jury that his entire interaction and observation of Aaron lasted approximately seven to ten minutes. But the prosecution was not about to take this blow to their case lying down. On cross-examination, prosecutor Mark Lee tried to break down every second as if he held an imaginary stopwatch, asking, "So you saw him walk down the stairs and that took about thirty seconds?" A puzzled Junior answered, "I suppose so."

"And then another thirty seconds to walk to the main bar?" Lee asked.

"Sure," replied Junior.

Lee was timing every detail in Junior's story and coming up with a total that was more like four or five minutes, the implication being that Junior could not in fact account for all of Aaron's actions in the bar, and there could've been an altercation he missed. Lee's Perry Mason moment culminated with: "So it was actually four or five minutes that you observed Aaron Hernandez and not seven to ten as you testified to under direct examination?" A perplexed Junior shrugged his shoulders and said, "Okay."

My co-counsel Sully responded brilliantly by showing Junior a photograph of himself that evening. "Mr. Salvador, what is that thing around your neck that is depicted in this photograph?"

"A tie?" Junior answered with a "where the fuck is this going" look on his face.

"It's not a stopwatch is it, sir?" asked Sully.

"No," Junior responded.

"So you weren't in the nightclub walking around with a stop-watch checking every action and timing it, were you, sir?" Sully asked sarcastically.

"No, sir, I wasn't," Junior shot back.

This exchange was followed up with probably one of the most impactful moments of the trial when Sully asked: "Sir, all of this back and forth about four to five minutes or seven to ten minutes, do you have any idea what it's all about?"

"No," Junior said while shrugging.

The point was made loud and clear: this guy was just there to tell the truth. All he did was ask for a picture with a football player and three years later he's sitting in a courtroom with no reason to lie and not a care as to who wins or loses. After all the back and forth of what happened inside the club, Junior had one more bombshell to offer. After he exited the club the outside club video showed him walking across the street toward the W Hotel. At the same time, about a hundred yards away, there were two shadowy figures near the Tufts garage that prosecutors said were Aaron and Bradley.

But Junior would tell the jury that minutes later he saw Aaron Hernandez walking with another guy toward the W, not the garage. Junior was the second witness, after Cure bouncer Ugo Ojimba, to testify to this fact. The third would be another bouncer at Cure, now a firefighter, named Andrew Wallace. This made a grand total of three independent witnesses who all saw Aaron over by the W at and around the time of the murders. The message was clear: Aaron couldn't be in two places at once, and testimony that proved Alexander Bradley was lying was beginning to sound like a broken record.

18.

THE STREET SWEEPER

You can go into a trial thinking you have every *i* dotted and every *t* crossed only to face an unexpected setback, or an unexpected stroke of luck, in the form of a surprise witness. Junior Salvador and his photograph was an example of the latter, and so was Warren McMaster the street sweeper.

McMaster was a twenty-six-year-old street-smart kid from South Boston, or a "Southie." He had driven a sweeper for American Sweeper for about five years, working the 11:00 P.M. to 7:00 A.M. shift during which he cleaned a different route each day of his five-day workweek.

He was driving on the right curb of Marginal Road the morning of July 16, 2012, when he turned left on Shawmut Avenue and hugged the right curb heading toward Herald Street. He could immediately see a BMW ahead that had just been shot at, and right next to it was a white or light-colored SUV. As two men stumbled out of the car, McMaster saw what he said appeared to be a woman with her head sticking out of the sunroof of the SUV, apparently recording the scene with an iPhone. The SUV then bolted about a

180

minute before Warren's sweeper passed within fifteen feet of the BMW.

As police started to arrive, McMaster continued on his route before receiving a call from his supervisor telling him to go back and speak to the police, which he did. We might never have known about the street sweeper had Officer Thomas O'Donnell not included it in his report from the night of the shootings. Officer O'Donnell was one of the first officers on the scene and apparently the only one who bothered to mention the street sweeper among the thousands of reports filed.

I may have never in my life heard of a street sweeper driving through a crime scene before, but what was the overall significance of this? I figured we would use the fact to show that if people in the BMW had fired shots at the SUV, the street sweeper would have swept away any evidence. Additionally, the fact that a street sweeper went through and nobody investigated it thoroughly was just plain sloppy, and whenever you have sloppy work cops always try to cover it up. What's the saying? The wrong deed is never the problem; it's always the cover-up. That was it.

I never believed the street sweeper was going to be more significant than that. But little did I know the prosecution was worried about his potential testimony and was going to try and sweep him under the rug (pun intended). When you push your opponent about careless police work and question their evidence enough sometimes they do something really stupid, and in this case the prosecution did just that.

Unbeknownst to me, in the middle of the trial, probably around the time we were attacking everyone for allowing the street sweeper to drive through the crime scene, the prosecution subpoenaed the street sweeper to come to court under the guise of having him testify. I say the "guise" because there's no way they were going to call him. His testimony was not going to help their case, plus they were already past reviewing the crime scene personnel and into another area of their case, so I believe it was complete and total nonsense.

What they really called McMaster in for was to force him to sit down with detectives to make a recorded statement about what had happened nearly five years earlier on the night of the Boston shootings. The prosecution was obligated to turn over the transcripts of this interview and did so one day after court.

Initially, I didn't think much of it. I just put the papers in my briefcase and headed back to the defense team apartments on Devonshire Place, where we always had our meetings to review what went on that day in court and prepare for the next day's events. After our meeting, I sat down to review the transcripts and could not believe my eyes. The interview was conducted by the co-lead detectives on the case, Detectives Paul MacIsaac and Detective Joshua Cummings, another officer assigned to the case. McMaster began telling them the story of how he drove through the crime scene and saw a woman with her head sticking out of the sunroof of the SUV, holding a cell phone.

"Oh my God," I blurted out. "He was the first to come up on the scene and actually saw the immediate aftermath." It's no wonder all the officers testifying about the crime scene did not see the street sweeper. He drove by *before* the police arrived.

McMaster was now the third independent witness who would describe someone that looked like a female in the passenger seat of the SUV where the prosecution was saying Aaron sat. I don't care how you slice it or how bad your eyesight is, there is no way you could mistake Aaron for a female or a guy with shoulder-length cornrows. We also had the three witnesses, the fan Junior Salvador and the two bouncers from club Cure, saying he was over by the W at the time of the murder.

What McMaster saw was not the only bombshell he had to offer. When Detective MacIsaac asked him why he didn't say anything about a woman hanging out of the sunroof of the SUV on the night of the shootings, McMaster responded: "I'm . . . a hundred percent positive of this. I stated that there was a girl. Honestly,

Boston PD was kind of treating me kind of like dreadful. . . . They said, keep your mouth shut or you're gonna be arrested."

MacIsaac then asked during the interview: "Who said that to you?"

"An officer that said, 'Shut your fucking mouth. This is a homicide investigation. You'll be under arrest blah, blah, blah.' Honestly, at the time I was like kind of frozen."

The detectives then inquired whether he had given a uniformed officer this information or a plainclothes detective. McMaster said he told them both. Detective MacIsaac immediately went into self-preservation mode by informing McMaster he was in fact one of the officers he spoke with that night and McMaster never told him anything of the kind.

The problem with Detective MacIsaac was that he now had a conflict of interest, as it was turning into what looked like a serious case of obstruction of justice or destruction of evidence issue. Detective Cummings should have excused Detective MacIsaac and continued the interview on his own. Instead, Cummings allowed MacIsaac to continue questioning and arguably coaching a primary witness in a murder investigation. MacIsaac continued with leading questions:

Q: All right. Do you remember it being me or do you remember speaking to a detective?
A: Yes.
Q: All right. 'Cause that night you didn't mention anything about this SUV and the girl hanging out?
A: I'm pretty, I'm pretty a hundred percent sure I stated that there was— [He's interrupted with another question.]

Notice MacIsaac is now telling him what happened, not asking him. This flies in the face of what a proper interview should be. It is to get information, not to give it. MacIsaac continues relentlessly:

Q: Yeah, but you never mentioned anything about a woman hanging out of an SUV.

A: I'm pretty a hundred percent positive of this. I stated that there was a girl— Honestly, the Boston PD was kind of treating me kind like dreadful . . . they told me not to say none of this to no one. They said, "Keep your mouth shut or you're gonna be arrested."

Q: Is that why you didn't tell me anything? [MacIsaac leads him to get himself off the hook.]

A: Yeah, and I just, I just kept my mouth shut.

Q: So you weren't treated properly, you thought.

A: No, no.

Q: And then when you spoke to me you just didn't tell me?

A: I just didn't say anything.

MacIsaac, a seasoned detective questioning this kid, knew exactly how to lead him down the right path. I say this confidently because throughout the interview the street sweeper made it clear he did not recognize MacIsaac or recall speaking to him that evening. McMaster followed up these questions:

A: I might not have told you but I know I told other, I told other officers there.

Detective MacIsaac continued to lead him and tell the street sweeper facts in an intimidating fashion. They were outright statements, not questions. Judge for yourself:

Q: What I'm saying, you and I had the conversation. You told me that you were coming off; you were on the far side; you went by; you saw the BMW; and you kept going on your route until you were called back. I mean, you never told me anything about this white BMW or anything like that—white SUV.

A: Honestly, I couldn't remember anyone because it was dark too and like there was a lot of people down at the time and there were lights, a lot of situations going on and like I really honestly, I can't remember talking to you, honestly.

Q: Well no, I mean I'm the one actually that actually spoke to you that night.

My blood was boiling as I read this. Here they were in a recorded interview trying to get a witness to back off a statement he made and telling him what he did and did not say that evening. One key fact you should note is that Detective MacIsaac filled out many reports in this case and noted every interview he did in the entire three-year investigation. He even had to turn over a notepad in which he jotted down things he did in the investigation. There is not one single mention anywhere, on any document in the thirty-four thousand pages in this case, that Detective Paul MacIsaac *ever* spoke with the street sweeper on the evening of the shootings.

HOW CAN THEY DO THIS, you might ask? Because they can. The very next day we filed a motion to dismiss, and four days later we stopped the trial and had a full-blown hearing in front of Judge Locke, without the jury present.

I got my first look at Warren McMaster out in the hallway before he entered, while I was speaking to prosecutor Mark Lee. The animosity between them was quickly apparent. I wasn't sure if McMaster's animosity was against Lee or all of us, so I thought I really needed to take a soft approach with McMaster.

As he took the stand McMaster's frustration was apparent: you could see him rolling his eyes, fidgeting in his seat, and answering all of Lee's questions with an attitude. I wasn't sure what Lee was attempting to accomplish with his direct examination other than to get a brief overview of the events and what McMaster told law enforcement on that evening and during his interview with Mac-Isaac and Cummings. Lee's questioning wasn't clear but one thing was certain, and that was that McMaster wasn't happy with how police treated him the night of the shooting. "The police were being rowdy to me," he declared with a thick Boston accent.

"And how were they being rowdy to you?" asked Lee.

"By telling me to shut the fuck up; sit the fuck down; tie four fucking shoes."

Lee pressed on: "But what exactly did they say to you?"

"It was fuck this, fuck that, fuck, fuck, fuck, fuck!"

An undiscouraged Lee continued as if it was going to help his cause: "So you said hi and they said fuck?"

"Pretty much, they said hi back, then it was fuck, fuck, fuck, fuck! . . . They kept getting in my face violating my rights, telling me if I told anybody anything they were going to have me arrested," said McMaster, who wasn't backing down.

As I rose I knew I was not going to make the same mistake, so I let McMaster take me where he wanted to take me. After making it clear that he in fact did tell multiple police officers on the night of the shootings that there was a white or light-colored SUV on the scene and what could have been a woman outside the sunroof with a phone or recording device, we moved over to the interview with the detectives at the courthouse.

Lee had tried unsuccessfully to get McMaster to admit he remembered speaking to MacIsaac the night of the shootings, so I began there. "Did you feel that they were trying to get you to say what they wanted you to say?" I asked.

"Yeah, this one guy kept trying to get me to say that I remembered him from that night, but I honestly don't remember speaking to him at all," McMaster responded calmly.

"And did he try to tell you that multiple times?" I asked, already knowing the answer.

"Yes," he answered unequivocally.

Then I got a piece of information we didn't have. Warren mentioned that the prosecution and cops spoke with him the previous day to try and coach him some more. "What was the purpose of this meeting?" I asked.

"They were trying to prep me; you know, prep me towards their side of the case," McMaster said in what could have been the best James Cagney impersonation I had ever heard.

"And what were they doing in this meeting?" I continued.

"They started getting rowdy to me and I kind of got rowdy back, because I wasn't going to say things the way they wanted," McMaster said of his meeting with prosecutors a day earlier.

"Did they record this meeting?" I asked.

"No, they talk to you different when they're recording you," he responded, offering another gem.

"How are they different?" I asked.

"They're much nicer when they record you," McMaster mumbled quietly.

I then asked a question I didn't know the answer to: "Were any prosecutors there?"

"I don't know what prosecutors may have been there," he answered unclearly, so I pressed.

"Were any of the three prosecutors sitting here in this courtroom there yesterday?"

McMaster took a second, leaned back, twitched his mouth to the side, and nodded his head with a grin. "Yeah, Mr. Wang or Mr. Chang over there," he said, pointing at Mark Lee.

It was at this moment I had to remind myself I was a grown-up and wasn't allowed to laugh, but that didn't stop the entire courtroom, including the press corps, from laughing.

"And was he getting rowdy with you too?" I couldn't help but ask.

"Yeah, and he kept talking down to me like I was stupid or something," he concluded.

Warren McMaster in all of his colorfulness could not have been a more important witness for the defense. He was a living and breathing representation of the culture of police work shaping this investigation. I specifically limit my comments to this case because I have not worked on enough cases in Boston to say this is an agency-wide problem, but clearly in this case we were in the Wild West.

McMaster's statements thus far had come during his interviews with police, prosecutors, and the hearing with the judge. While it would be difficult, I knew we were going to have to get McMaster in front of the jury, but it would be a gamble. The jury could be turned off by his colorfulness and just think this was a "rowdy" kid with a beef with the police, and discount the important information he had to give. So rather than have him blow up on me in front of the jury, I entrusted him to Michelle Medina, my right hand and trusted associate. "Do not coach him, but get him to calm down and be more presentable," I told her. She did just that.

After taking the stand with the jury present, the street sweeper was the talk of the town and on the internet. People thought he was the funniest thing since Eddie Murphy, but they also accused him of being on drugs. He didn't like it. He was, by all accounts we could find, a very street-smart young man, a good kid who had the same job for several years and always helped provide for his extended family.

McMaster repeatedly said he felt pressured and disrespected by the police. So Michelle explained to him that when we called him it would be his opportunity to make it right and come across like a sincere and honest young man. However, I felt we needed more than Warren McMaster. I felt we needed some type of corroboration of his testimony. I gave our interns an assignment to track down the police officer who actually saw the street sweeper. In a stroke of luck we found him, Officer O'Donnell, the only officer to mention the street sweeper in his report from the night of the shootings.

When we called him to the stand during the trial, Officer O'Donnell told the jury that upon his arrival near the scene he saw the street sweeper pass the BMW and turn onto Herald Street. Officer O'Donnell was a straight-up, by-the-book veteran of the Boston Police Department, bald headed, portly, with silver-rimmed glasses and all business. He said that once Sergeant Clifton McHale arrived and took charge of the crime scene, O'Donnell told him about seeing a street sweeper drive past the BMW. That led to McMasters's supervisor calling and telling him to get back to the scene.

In my closing arguments you can be sure that I pointed out what I knew the jury was thinking: Why did the prosecutors call approximately fifteen police officers to the stand, some testifying to very little other than they were there that night, but they didn't call the guy who saw the street sweeper? They called the first officer, the fourth officer, the tenth officer, and so on, but never considered calling Officer O'Donnell, who arrived second and immediately following the incident.

The inescapable fact is they knew the street sweeper was going to hurt them, and they were going to try and keep him as far away from the jury as they could. After Officer O'Donnell stepped down from the stand we called the street sweeper.

Warren McMaster took the stand in front of the jury; he was nicely dressed, clean shaven, and as clear and concise as could be. He told the jury what he saw and what he told the police and what they told him. He did slip at one point and refer to Mark Lee as Mr. Wang again, but it was under his breath and I'm not sure anyone even heard it. The following day during a courtroom break I joked with Mark Lee about it, and he rolled his eyes. Always good humored, he said, "You know, I can't fucking shake that nickname. My own wife is now calling me Mr. Wang."

19.

MARINATING THE JURY

Technically the prosecution doesn't have to prove motive, but I believe they were extremely concerned about the weakness of their argument from the start. Patrick Haggan made a point of telling the jury during his opening statements that "none of this would make sense." This was his way of saying he really had no motive: "The reason Aaron committed murder is not going to make sense to you, but you should believe that he did it anyway."

Meanwhile, I was trying to keep the jury focused on these questions: Why are we all here? Why are we spending weeks of our time trying to connect Aaron Hernandez to a crime he had no reason to commit? Why are we trying to invent a motive? I was pounding the weakness of the prosecution's case.

A high-profile trial is a big deal. I knew it would be hard for jurors, who make great sacrifices and endure tremendous inconveniences to perform their duty, to believe they were there over a spilled drink. Proof that a drink was spilled on Aaron, and that it made him angry, was critical to the prosecution's argument.

One thing that never became public, and we kept pretty close to the vest throughout, was that before the trial began a gentleman serving in the army in Kuwait had emailed our office and told us of an encounter he had with Aaron in the summer of 2012, around the same time as the Cure incident. He told us he was home in Boston on leave and was in a club (he believed it was Rumor or Cure) and a hot girl walked by with a really "nice ass." He said both he and Aaron were so distracted that he accidentally spilled his drink on Aaron. Rather than blow up, Aaron laughed it off and told the guy, who was apologizing profusely, not to worry about it. Aaron even went so far as to buy the guy a drink to replace the one spilled on him.

The army combat veteran seemed more than willing to testify but at some point got cold feet. He started to avoid us, and we went to great lengths to try and get him served with a subpoena in Kuwait. But after contacting the State Department and calling in favors from some very influential people, he was successful in hiding on his base in Kuwait and never getting served.

His commanding officer did not want to accept service for him, so we were ultimately unsuccessful in calling him. My theory is this guy really wanted to help Aaron out during his trial, but his superior officers wanted no part of it and pressured him to stay away. Having served in the military, I know there is nothing more persuasive than a commanding officer putting pressure on an enlisted man, especially while serving abroad.

Based on the timing and the descriptions given by this witness, I believe this incident was actually the inspiration for Bradley's spilled drink story. I believe it really happened, and that Bradley was with him when it did. Many lies start out as truths and grow from there. When I questioned Aaron about the encounter he remembered the guy but never put two and two together that this is where Bradley might have gotten the story.

We also planned on calling Patriots coach Bill Belichick to talk about the request to be traded that Aaron made during their meeting in Indianapolis. When we finally served him, he was in Miami attending a pro day at the University of Miami, preparing for the NFL Draft.

Lots of things happen behind the scenes of high-profile trials that would make headlines across the country if the public knew about them. In my opinion, prosecution's late-game decision to throw a Hail Mary pass to establish motive was one of the most explosive. Just before the trial started we got some police reports indicating that Boston PD flew to Arizona to interview a woman who had created a pen pal relationship with Aaron. This woman was in her forties and I believe even married. But she was completely infatuated with Aaron.

She would deposit money in Aaron's commissary account, they exchanged letters often, and the relationship got a little deeper than they expected. But it was still just a correspondence. I really don't believe Aaron had any genuine feelings for her, but clearly it felt good to be cared about and this woman expressed her love for him in many ways. Maybe she was fulfilling some kind of fantasy for him as well.

Police went to pay her a visit. For what purpose I still don't know, other than to try to find as much dirt as possible on Aaron, or at the very least get another little trip on the tax payer's dollar. The woman told them Aaron had ended their relationship. Aaron told me as well that he had ended it because he knew the trial was coming up and if the media went snooping into his phone calls or correspondence, news of the relationship would hurt Shayanna. Shayanna may have been a bit more forgiving while Aaron was free but their relationship was strained by his incarceration, and Aaron was afraid he would lose her once and for all.

So he sent this woman, who I won't identify, a Dear Jane letter that she claimed to no longer have in her possession. Why wouldn't she have kept the letter? I wondered. Anyway, the woman told police that in the letter Aaron told her he could no longer be with her because he was having feelings for men, and that it would not be fair to her to continue a relationship or love affair because he did not look at women in that way.

He also supposedly told her he was angry because of this built-up frustration and inability to be who he really was. He, according to her, was angry all the time but did not know why.

At some point in the trial Pat Haggan approached me and told me the commonwealth was considering calling this woman to the stand to tell her story, thus creating a motive for the shootings. Haggan told us she would testify that Aaron was a closeted homosexual; the frustration and anger of being a closeted homosexual made him overcompensate as a man, so whenever anyone challenged his manhood, like Daniel de Abreu supposedly did when he spilled his drink on Aaron, he would overreact and get angry enough to kill.

In essence, being a closeted homosexual made Aaron a killer.

This was by far the biggest reach I had ever seen a prosecutor make in an effort to establish motive, which the judge instructs the jury the prosecution does not have to prove. Usually salacious details about someone's sexual preferences or relationships are kept out of a court of law because they can be more prejudicial against the accused than probative. But Haggan and company did not care. They were all in, and with things turning out the way they were, the prosecution was flat-out desperate. When we went into chambers Judge Locke agreed to discuss this off the record.

Haggan laid out his theory and I watched the look on Locke's face, one of growing confusion. "So what you're saying is that men who are in the closet are more prone to kill than men who are openly gay or straight men?" asked Locke.

"That's exactly what he's saying, judge," I chimed in, even though I was not invited to do so.

"No," Haggan said. "What we are saying is that Aaron Hernandez was angry all of the time. He didn't even enjoy playing football anymore either."

Now, I knew this was bullshit. Aaron and I would talk for hours about football, and he talked about it like a kid getting ready to go to the park to play. Where was Haggan coming from? Apparently the police had gotten that from Bradley, and this woman had confirmed it. I could see "Coach" MacIsaac was at it again.

"And how do you plan on proving this? Are you thinking of calling some kind of expert to talk about this?" Locke asked. The judge was trying his best to be noncommittal but his questions were clear; he wasn't buying it and Haggan's new motive was falling by the wayside just as fast as the first one. At the end of the meeting Haggan said he was going to discuss it with his team and we all realized we would have to have a "gay hearing" on this issue, so both sides should be prepared to argue their points with supporting case law.

George Leontire, or "Mr. Devonshire" as I liked to call him—based on the way he pronounced the name of the building we were staying in, with his thick Boston accent—was openly gay. He was the most aggressive and noneffeminate member of the team. He was livid. I'm not sure if Haggan and company knew George was gay. I don't really think anyone knew. I have never paid attention to these sorts of things, nor have I ever had to deal with such nonsense from the prosecution in a court of law.

When my team met on this issue George was ready to storm the prosecutor's office and show them that a guy out of the closet could kill just as easily as one in the closet. Fortunately cooler heads prevailed and I told George: "Let's not kill anybody just yet."

Instead, George began making a list of every significant member of the LGBT community he was going to start making calls to. The next day when we went sidebar to discuss the matter briefly, I was about to make a point when George, always at every sidebar but off to the side, decided this was the time to literally bump lead counsel out of the way and put his two cents in. When I tell you he bumped me out of the way, I mean it. George outweighs me by about seventy-five pounds. He literally got in Haggan's face and said, "If you guys even think about pulling a stunt like this, I promise you that I will have every single member of the LGBT community ready to protest outside and in this courtroom; you will start a firestorm that you, sir, would not be able to contain."

While I remember these words as if they were spoken yesterday, I still don't think I'm doing the incident justice. This was literally the last we heard of the prosecution's "gay motive."

The trial continued and so did the shenanigans. Aaron had tattoos all over his body; some were interesting motivational quotes, some were football related, but most were religious in nature. But eight months after the Boston shootings and a couple months after the West Palm Beach incident, Aaron got several tattoos, two of which were of guns. One was a cylinder of a revolver with five bullets in it; one hole was left empty. The other one was a muzzle of what appeared to be a semiautomatic weapon; a bullet was out of it and smoke was coming from the muzzle. Prosecutors would argue that these two tattoos were confessions written on Aaron's body.

I believe cops were tipped off about these tattoos because Aaron had received some text messages from the tattoo artist asking when he was going to come in for more tattoos. Three detectives then flew across the country to speak with the tattoo artist and all his colleagues, hoping Aaron said or did something that amounted to a confession. This was amazing dedication on law enforcement's part. You have to wonder. Would they have gone through this much trouble and expense to track these leads down to find the killer of Daniel de Abreu and Safiro Furtado had Aaron Hernandez not been the suspect?

That's the thing about high-profile cases. Cops will spare no expense and stop at nothing to get you. The prosecution's theory was that they recovered five bullets from the crime scene, and the gun used was the antique six-shooter. Only the killer would know there were five bullets in the gun. Their theory was that the tattoo depicted the gun used to shoot Bradley. The tattoo was literally their smoking gun. I have to admit that as crazy as their idea sounded,

I thought a jury just might buy it. After all, everyone has heard of gangsters who get tattoos of teardrops to signify how many people they have killed.

In fact, I tried a case just like that several years ago in Miami in which my client was an accused gangbanger called "YLO Negro." The YLO stood for Young Latin Organization, a local gang in a neighborhood just outside of Miami's Little Havana. YLO was accused of first-degree murder. He had these stupid teardrops tattooed below his eye, meant to signify the tears of his victims. We could not put him in front of the jury with those tattoos, so we came up with the clever idea of using makeup to cover them up. YLO was only twenty-two but he, like Bradley, had nine lives; he had been shot twice, stabbed multiple times, run over and left for dead on the side of the road. He managed to survive but was permanently disabled and walked with a severe limp similar to that of Kevin Spacey's character Verbal in *The Usual Suspects*. Apparently, the Young Latin Organization does not discriminate against the handicapped.

In walks the jury, and the prosecutor begins her questioning of the jury. Everything is going fine until the prosecutor starts to question the jury about the potential of feeling sorry for the "defendant for being handicapped." She then goes into this long story about how he was stabbed multiple times and left for dead in a fight. It was a very sad story. I began to think this might actually help us make YLO a little more sympathetic to the jury. Unfortunately, it made him look so sympathetic that several people began to tear up a bit, including YLO himself. As I turned to tell him to stop crying he wiped one of his tears, removing the makeup and exposing the tattoos. While he wasn't a convicted of murder, the jury was not about to let that guy back on the streets; they convicted him of a lesser charge.

I learned a lesson the hard way: jurors pay close attention to tattoos, and while some people get tattoos that actually mean something, many people get them just because they think they look good. I think Aaron did a combination of both. Aaron said he got the gun tattoos because he liked guns. That was that.

"Trust me, Jose. I know you think I'm stupid, but damn, I wouldn't be stupid enough to tattoo a confession on me and then go show it to millions of people every Sunday," Aaron quipped.

When I first learned the prosecution was going to pursue this angle, I knew we were going to fight its admissibility, because nowhere in any case across the country has tattoo evidence ever been admitted for the purpose of a confession or substantive evidence. Tattoos are commonly used to identify somebody, but no one has successfully proven the meaning of a tattoo. It's too subjective. We filed multiple motions and Judge Locke went back and forth trying to decide if he would admit the tattoos as evidence. In the end he admitted them and the fight was on to try and discredit the "tattooed confession."

The prosecution called the tattoo artist to the stand to testify about the tattoos and admitted photographs of them. Then they did something really clever. They took a picture of the gun with the cylinder open, put five bullets in it leaving one chamber empty, and put it side by side with the picture of the tattoo. The similarity was eerie and did not bode well for the defense; but still something was off. I just couldn't place it. I held a little contest among our interns and promised I would buy dinner for the one who could go online and find a tattoo exactly the same, but nobody could find one. So the night before I was to cross-examine the tattoo artist I went online myself, and as I was googling images I realized what was off about the tattoo. The artist had drawn the cylinder backward! The tattoo was just a picture of the cylinder, no gun, so I kept arguing that distinction.

I wanted to downplay the significance of the tattoo in front of the jury. I didn't want them to think we were afraid of it. I rose to cross-examine the tattoo artist. "Sir, did they really fly you out here to talk about tattoos?" I asked derisively. "Ahhh, I guess so," he answered. My point was made. Then I pointed out how the cylinder was drawn backward, and the bullets couldn't be loaded from the angle shown; they'd have to go in through the other side. "What does this mean to someone?" I asked the tattoo artist.

"I have no idea," he said. "Does it mean something has back-fired in his life?" I pressed. "I have no idea," he repeated. The next point we made I can't take credit for; it was all Aaron. When Aaron saw me struggling over the pictures of the tattoos he said, "Jose, you should point out the gun used to shoot Bradley was a .40 cali-ber; the muzzle of that tattoo is the muzzle of a Colt .45."

"What?" I asked.

"Yeah, look at it and you can tell. The muzzle of a Colt .45 is very distinctive." He said this word for word and for a moment I thought to myself, Damn this kid could have been anything he wanted to be in this world and look at him now.

"How the hell do you know that?" I asked.

"Duh, I'm the one who picked it out," he responded with a smile.

That was when I think we neutralized the tattoo evidence. Throw in the fact that he got several other tattoos, including one that read: CBS WBS, meaning "can't be stopped, won't be stopped"; and IWBTG, standing for "I will be the greatest." He also got song lyrics on his chest, and Shayanna got the corresponding lyrics tat-tooed on herself. We also pointed out that Aaron went into the store looking for what is called a "gun tree" that showed a tree with different guns hanging from it. Due to the lack of space on his body Aaron ended up choosing the other tattoos.

It turns out gun tattoos are very popular in the United States. They are symbols of strength and the refusal to be a victim. Their meanings are so subjective they should never have seen the light of day in a courtroom. I think Judge Locke really dropped the ball on that one.

FINALLY, the long-anticipated date arrived when the common-wealth called Alexander Bradley to the stand. Like Aaron he was taller than I expected. He stood about six foot two, around 230 pounds, in a muscular frame, much slimmer than he looked in the videos taken on the night of the Boston murders. He showed up wearing khakis and a black Burberry dress shirt that cost more than half of what our jurors made in a week. These were obviously clothes delivered to the jail by one of his baby mommas, Brooke Wilcox. That was a big mistake on Haggan's part. They did put reading glasses on him, which I thought was a nice touch.

Bradley's direct went extremely well for the prosecution. Bradley is an intelligent drug dealer. He is well spoken when he wants to be and he really came across as believable when not pressured in any way. Before the trial began I studied his testimony in the Odin Lloyd trial, and thought he was an excellent witness for the prosecution. He held up strongly during cross-examination. Of course, his testimony in that trial was not as significant as it would be in this one. But I could see his habits and gestures and knew what to look for as he testified. When on the stand his language was formal; for example, he always referred to males as "gentlemen." He would refer to the "gentleman wearing a red tie" as he identified someone. If he couldn't remember something he would say, "I can't quite recall that." I also saw that if he was confronted with prior inconsistent statements, he would not fight to explain. He would say something along the lines of "If that's what it says I said then, yes, that is correct." He clearly made an effort to clean up his act. I don't believe he was coached to do these things by a prosecutor; I think he was clever enough to know how he came across and never wanted to look "ghetto" on the stand.

After going through Bradley's story of what happened in Boston, Haggan took him through the events in West Palm Beach, then began the tedious task of reading and going through each and every text message between him and Aaron after he got shot in West Palm Beach. That day I wore a black suit and white shirt with a black tie. I guess it was my best "men in black" impersonation. I usually dressed with more color, and Mark Lee noticed. As soon as

I walked in he commented: "Jose, you look like you're dressed for a funeral." I responded: "Yes, I'm here for the Bradley funeral. We plan on burying him today."

Unfortunately, the opportunity would not come that day, as Haggan lasted all day with Bradley and we could tell at around two in the afternoon that the prosecution was going to use the old trick of "marinating a jury." Basically, it's when prosecutors draw their case out so they can end court on a high note for the day. That is exactly what they did with Bradley. Haggan was not going to let me anywhere near him until the following day, so the jury could go home and think all night about Bradley's testimony.

Unfortunately for them, they called Bradley more than halfway through their case. While he wasn't their last witness, he certainly appeared late in the second half of their case. I guess their thinking was that the jury would be hearing about Bradley day in and day out, and once he took the stand he would bring together all the pieces for them.

The problem with that approach was that we had been so strong in rebutting everything the prosecution was presenting that the jury had started getting used to hearing interesting theories from the commonwealth, only to watch them get slammed by the defense on cross-examination. We had the feeling, watching their facial expressions, that the jury were literally waiting for the defense to get up so they could finally hear what was really going on with the evidence and hear the "rest of the story," as famous radio personality Paul Harvey would say.

I really do believe that if the prosecution had put Bradley on first, the defense would have had a much tougher job. But they chose another route.

When they finally let me at him, I had seen enough of this prim and proper Bradley, so the first words out of my mouth were "Who are you really?" "I'm sorry, Mr. Baez?" he responded in his gentleman's voice.

"Well, are you, as you describe," reading from his text messages, "the OG nigga wit weaponry dat will make you cry fo yo mommy." I said that in the best "street" voice I could muster. "Or are you 'like the gentleman seated next to the gentleman with the red tie,'" I said in a mocking nerdy voice. This changed him instantly. He did not expect me to start mocking him from the beginning. I think he expected me to attack his statements and his actions and talk about his past. But I knew this was a man not used to being made fun of. He was dying to jump out of his seat and kick my ass right there.

I then went into his aliases including Sharrod the Shooter, which he denied going by. That didn't surprise me, but then he denied being called Rock, which I didn't expect because his jail calls were riddled with people calling him Rock because he liked to "rock people to sleep," meaning kill them.

When I confronted him with the jail calls he claimed that his family called him "Rocky," insinuating it was a term of endearment, like Joey is for Joseph. This was too good to be true. He now gave me the ultimate tool for mockery. Every time I wanted to piss him off I would call him Rocky, as if it was the funniest thing I had ever heard. He took the bait and started saying my name as if it was the silliest word he had ever heard; for example, he might respond to my questions with something like "That's correct, Mr. Bii-eeeeeezzz," mocking my name as best he could.

I had gotten him out of his comfort zone, but I knew I couldn't overdo it because he was smart enough to pick up on what I was doing. Plus I also knew that during breaks the prosecution would make him aware that I was trying to provoke him. So I saved my "Rockys" for when it mattered. Because of his intelligence I knew his cross-examination was not going to be a series of knockouts. Instead his was going to have to be a death by a thousand cuts. So I tried my best to go through the facts in a methodical manner.

I did want to set up the whole cross-examination by putting the deal that he cut with prosecutors front and center. We read through his proffer letter line by line, and I put the agreement on the projector multiple times. I focused on the fifty different places it said he had to give "complete and truthful information." Then I went through all the different ways his statements were not complete or truthful. After each statement he gave that was either not complete or truthful, I asked whether the commonwealth had revoked his deal like the agreement said it would.

I was a broken record until it became abundantly clear that he had way too many statements that were not complete or truthful, and the prosecution didn't care and were still sticking with him despite his lies. Two villains, Bradley and the prosecution, or the "twins of deception" as Johnnie Cochran used to say.

I then went through the text messages, pointing out that 90 percent of them were from him to Aaron. Aaron would chime in only on occasion to deny shooting him. Basically all of Bradley's texts were simply self-serving statements. Bradley also referenced having contacted a lawyer early on; showing these texts were in anticipation of litigation was important. This would help the jury understand the mindset of both men as these texts were being exchanged, because Aaron was being advised by his agent Brian Murphy not to respond.

The second day was more of the same. This time I went through Bradley's text messages pointing out some of the slang Aaron had translated for us, messages the prosecutor skimmed through as if they had no meaning. They were texts about Bradley having "wolves on deck," meaning Bradley had guys who were his "shooters," ready to kill Aaron. We also pulled out the text messages in which Bradley discussed his "weaponry," an array of assault weapons. Not only did we discuss them, but I also went online and printed out pictures of them and had them admitted into evidence, then placed them on the overhead projector so the jury could see the tools of the drug trade.

"Mr. Bradley, this gun that you reference in your text to Aaron is what kind of gun?" I asked.

"Mac 10," he answered dryly.

"And after you made your deal of a lifetime, when did the police or prosecutors go to your house and confiscate this Mac 10?" I
continued.

"They didn't. I still have it," he answered to a stunned courtroom.

"And what kind of gun is this?" I asked moving on to his next
weapon of choice.

"An AK-47," he responded.

"When did the police or prosecutors come and confiscate this
gun?" I asked.

"They never did," he answered.

Then I went over the bullet-proof vest he had, as if he was
working part time as a police officer somewhere. The picture was
clear. Here was the prosecution's star witness and all his weaponry
coming to a neighborhood near you in the not too distant future.
Bradley was a convicted felon, and possessing these assault weapons was a serious crime. Not to mention he was sitting there after
emptying a gun into a crowded nightclub. But prosecutors, intent
on winning at all costs, were going to allow him to keep these weapons and put him on the streets again.

His second day on the stand was the day the fireworks began. I
wanted to leave the jury with a lasting impression of Bradley, and
I didn't want it to be a pretty one. After cutting his deal with prosecutors, the police asked Bradley to help track down the text messages in which he claimed Aaron made incriminating statements.
While there were no such things, Bradley did turn over one of his
two phones, and when he did the police had him and his attorney
sign a release form. In the form it stated that he was waiving all
rights of confidentiality as they related to this cell phone. I could
see the puzzled look on the prosecutors' faces as I began reviewing
this form and showed it to the jury.

Now it was time to bring down the hammer on Rocky, once
and for all. I directed him to a text message Michelle had discovered among the deleted files on the phone: a message he sent to his

lawyer Robert Pickering when he filed his lawsuit against Aaron after the shooting in West Palm Beach. Bradley thought the text had long been deleted; he was about to get a huge surprise. I read out the text as loudly as I could: "Now u sure once I withdraw this lawsuit I wont be held on perjury after I tell the court *the truth* about me not recalling anything about who shot me."

The courtroom fell into complete silence. I could see Haggan's face turn red like a tomato. He was pissed at somebody and it wasn't me. I then went through and explained that not only was this a confidential message, which at the time he wrote it Bradley believed was protected by attorney-client privilege, but he also believed the text message would never see the light of day, much less the inside of a courtroom.

At that moment I too decided to play the marinating a jury game and suggested to Judge Locke that this was a good time to break for lunch. At some point later on in the trial Haggan and I had a moment of privacy. I said to him: "You acted like you didn't know about that text?"

"No, I didn't," he answered. "I told Teresa to check and double-check all of those text messages to make sure there was nothing in there that hurt us and she assured me that we were good." The person he was referring to was the third-chair prosecutor Teresa Anderson. She was their "law person." Usually a member of the team focuses on all the legal research and memorandums of law. They don't usually question any of the witnesses or take a big role in the trial, but their importance to the team can never be overstated. I don't mention her much because she was not as outgoing as Haggan and Lee. I think she said ten words to me during the two months we tried this case and I'm pretty sure nine of them were "good morning." She was of average build with red hair, pale skin, and glasses that seemed to eat up her face and any signs of a smile. But she was a head shaker. Whenever she heard something in the courtroom she didn't agree with she would shake her head like a bobblehead. She wasn't as bad as Jeff Ashton, the laughing guy in the Casey Anthony trial, but definitely cut from the same cloth.

Haggan then said to me: "Yeah, what's the old saying, you want something done right you have to do it yourself?"

"Nah, man, don't be so hard on her," I said. I was lying. He should have. That was a colossal blunder.

"It just proves my Michelle is better than yours!" I quipped.

"Apparently so," he said as he walked away.

As I mentioned earlier, nothing gets past Michelle.

During lunch the courtroom was buzzing. We actually thought there was a possibility they would arrest Bradley for perjury. Maybe there was even an outside chance they would drop the charges against Aaron. After all, here was Bradley admitting to his lawyer in a confidential conversation that he in fact did not know who shot him in West Palm Beach; a fact he had just spent the last two days testifying about unequivocally and under oath. Instead, to my disappointment the prosecutors doubled down. They wanted to try and exclude the text, claiming it was protected by attorney-client privilege. But Locke wasn't buying it; the waiver form was clear. Bradley had waived all privileges when he signed it and turned the phone over.

It was a good day. I know it was as close as I will ever come to a Perry Mason moment in a courtroom. We savored it for the night, not knowing the prosecutors would declare World War III in court the next day.

20.

DESPERATE MEASURES

After Bradley's "the truth" text surfaced, the next trick up the prosecution's sleeve was Aaron's sexuality. They knew they would suffer a backlash if it came out they were outing a man just to try and make some sense in their case.

Massachusetts is a very liberal state. It was the first state to legalize gay marriage. How far did they think their information about Aaron's latent homosexuality would take them? But this bit of juicy information couldn't be left unused. They decided after what appeared to be much contemplation to leverage it by trying to get Shayanna on their side. They believed that if they told Shayanna about this other woman, and the fact that Aaron was either gay or bisexual, somehow Shayanna would turn on him and reveal something they didn't know, or at least sway her testimony in their direction.

Meanwhile, police had also gone to visit another individual they believed had a relationship with Aaron. I am intentionally being vague here; all I will say is that the person I am referring to had connections to Aaron and was credible, and I confirmed the facts with both Aaron and the individual myself. This was someone known to both Aaron and Shayanna, and he had in fact confirmed to the police that he had a romantic relationship with Aaron.

They knew Shayanna would feel betrayed, and considering the fact that she was the only person standing by Aaron, adding pressure to their relationship might shake things up enough for something useful to come loose and help their cause in some way, shape, or form.

I got word that day from Shayanna's lawyer that the prosecution wanted her to come to court so they could talk to her. They had something "very important" to tell her, something that "she had to know, perhaps something life changing." I immediately confronted Haggan on the issue and asked him if he intended to tell Shay about the "gay issue."

He told me: "Yes, I think she has the right to know, and I don't want her hearing about it for the first time when we put her on the stand."

"Why and how would this ever come up on the stand? And how is it relevant to this case?" I asked in disgust.

"I can't tell you that," he said as if hiding a secret.

I had to act and act fast. The first thing I did was to tell Aaron. He was beside himself. I had never seen him like that before. He was so afraid of hurting Shay that he begged me to help him in some way. I told him: "Look we just have to deal with this. I know it seems like the most important thing in the world right now but, Aaron, it isn't. This trial is. We don't know what the future holds for you two. But we do know that your future depends on the outcome of this trial. So let's stay focused."

Aaron began to cry. "But, Jose, she'll be devastated," he wept. "I never meant to hurt her. I know I keep disappointing her. But she is my soul. She is all I have and all I ever will have."

His tears kept flowing.

"No, Aaron, Avielle is," I explained.

He then said, "They both are, and I can't have that taken away from me."

As he said this I cursed Haggan. "I will talk to her. I will break it down, and I know she will be big enough to get through this," I said.

"How do you know?" he said, looking hopeful.

"Because look at all this other shit you put her through. If she stood by you through that, she is not going to abandon you now, especially knowing you two have a child to raise together. Everything else pales in comparison to this." For some reason that gave Aaron solace.

As the day went on I didn't have any witnesses to cross-examine; Sully and Linda had most of the witnesses. I don't know what was being said in court that day, as I was in a complete daze. I had never been in a position like this before. This is the shit they don't cover in law school. In all the years I had practiced, I never thought I would have to have a conversation like this.

I immediately called Shay and told her I needed to speak to her in private *before* she came to court that day. She already knew the prosecutors wanted to speak with her, so she wasn't surprised that I wanted to talk to her first to give her the heads-up on what they were going to tell her. She was going to be late for court, so I told her to text me when she got in so I could pull her aside.

When Shay's text came in, I told her to go to the sixth floor and wait for me near the elevators; our courtroom was on the ninth floor, and I didn't want anyone seeing us talking or interrupting us. I literally walked out of the courtroom while a witness was testifying. As I slipped out I don't think too many people noticed, although a reporter did tweet about me leaving at such an odd time.

The sixth floor was practically deserted. It was as good a place as any to have the conversation. I paced back and forth as I waited for her to arrive. When she finally stepped out of the elevator my heart warmed. Here was this beautiful, sophisticated woman who had so much love and compassion for Aaron. I couldn't hold back my nervousness. As we sat down on a wooden bench, no different than any wooden bench in courthouses across America, I had to tell her the most salacious secret in the highest profile case in America at the time.

I explained to her about the woman the police had interviewed and what she told them. Then I told her about the man the police had used to confirm everything. While the news about the woman did not shake her, I could see the betrayal in her face when I mentioned the man. She knew him and had spent time with him and Aaron. She felt like a fool.

I want to be abundantly clear about something: I am not mentioning names for a reason. It is not my place to out anyone. What a person does in their personal life is their business and I would never have even written about Aaron's relationship had Shayanna not addressed the matter publicly herself. I don't feel it is anyone's place to do this except Shayanna. Even with Aaron, their relationship was hers just as much as it was his. Only now with her permission can I share what we talked about that day.

After Aaron passed she did a sit-down interview with Dr. Phil in which he asked her point blank: "It was reported that he was gay. You were his fiancée. Was he secretly gay?"

Shayanna didn't hesitate with her response. "The Aaron that I knew, no," she said. "I had no indication or any feeling he was such. He was very much a man to me."

I was a bit shocked by her answer, as I expected her to talk about our conversation on the sixth floor of the courthouse.

She later explained to me that "if he had asked me the question the right way, I would have answered it. But the way he asked me, I felt I had to answer with what I felt in my heart at that moment to me was true, which was, yes, he was very much a man to me."

In her second sit-down interview for a documentary series with the Oxygen channel she was finally asked about our conversation that day and this is a direct quote of what she said:

Q: Can you talk me through the moment of Jose talking you through bringing up Aaron's sexuality?

SHAY: Aaron's sexuality from what I've known?

Q: Just talk me through Jose coming out to talk to you.

SHAY: Okay, Jose speaking to me about Aaron's sexuality was an intimate moment between Jose and I. We met on a bench and he kind of broke it down slowly. It was emotional. I cried because I was confused; still kind of am. But I wouldn't fault Aaron for what he may, or may not have wanted. I think I was more upset because I don't think I've chosen the path. I feel like it's been chosen for me in a sense. It's maybe selfish. But I try to be very understanding. It may not be something that I want but it's something that he may have been.

Q: And you decided after Jose told you this that you're sticking with your guy?

SHAY: After Jose had broken everything down to me there was some unsure parts because no one had answers. Everyone was speculating. I was speculating and I think Jose was trying to protect me. But he let me know that I could go home and he would understand. Being the person that I am, I would not want him to go through anything by himself. I wouldn't want anyone that I care about going through anything by themselves. I was the only thing that he had at the second trial. Even at the first trial; but more importantly at the second one. There's no way that he sees me and that I don't come back in. Hurt or not and I was hurt. I had to fight through it. I had to fight through it and we—I can't even say that we discussed it thoroughly because we never had time to. But I was willing to. I was willing to accept whatever was coming to me. I want to say that he understood that but at the same time I think he was just too scared and I don't think that he knew how to confront me.

Q: It says a lot about you that you went back in [to court].

210

SHAY: Oh it took a lot, it took me a, a few minutes. But yes I, I couldn't leave him by himself.

Q: Can you talk about a reporter spilling out Aaron's sexuality to the public?

SHAY: Aaron's sexuality? I actually don't necessarily know about a specific reporter who leaked it. I was not familiar with that at all.

Q: Did you know that someone had leaked the story and it had gone public?

SHAY: I did know that, you know, a reporter had leaked the story about Aaron's sexuality. Yes.

Q: How did you feel about that?

SHAY: It's frustrating that it wasn't in the way that we wanted if we wanted to release that information. I feel like people form opinions immediately instead of hearing Aaron's side because you know that's the only person that can necessarily say how he was feeling. It's something of course that we were all trying to get through and figure out what exactly was going on.

Q: Did you feel like it was nobody's business in the first place?

SHAY: I think that Aaron's sexuality is absolutely no one's business. I think we're in a world now that things should be accepted regardless of how people want to live. I think there's things that should remain private.

Shayanna went home, but after much pain and soul searching she was back in court the next day showing her loyalty to Aaron. That is why this woman will always walk on water as far as I'm concerned. She's not perfect. No one is. Her compassion is an inspiration. Her love for him is something I will never forget.

After our discussion, she refused to talk to the prosecutors, and by the way Haggan never went near the gay issue when he called her to the stand toward the end of the trial. The big secret he couldn't tell me was just a bluff. Instead he attacked her as if she was the accused, eliciting testimony that made little to no sense to the jury.

THE REPORTER being referenced in the interview with the Oxygen channel is Michelle McPhee. McPhee is an ABC News producer and formerly a *New York Daily News* bureau chief. She is also an author of true-crime books. A couple of days after Aaron was acquitted she was invited on WEEI's *The Kirk & Callahan Show* to talk about her new book about an investigation of the 2013 Boston Marathon bombing. But she was also working on a forthcoming article for *Newsweek* that would break news about Aaron's sexuality, and she decided to share details with the so-called shock jocks before they went on air.

The shock jocks began her interview by bringing it up. "This rumor," Gerry Callahan said on air, "this Aaron Hernandez rumor, which is so juicy. . . . It is big." "It's something we can certainly play with as the days go on," Kirk Minihane said. "I'm not sure how comfortable Michelle is in talking about it."

McPhee was, however, open to talking about it. "I mean, hey," she said to her radio pals, "let's tease away."

The three then went on an anti-gay rampage, using football metaphors to make fun of Aaron's sexuality. The men referred to Aaron as a "tight end on and off the field," adding "then he became a wide receiver." The banter continued with McPhee adding that Aaron kicked "with both feet."

Within twenty-four hours of that radio interview hitting the public airwaves, Aaron would be dead.

Did the interview have anything to do with Aaron's suicide? I don't believe so. But Aaron's sexuality was something that he and Shayanna had to deal with as a family, not something to be joked about by some reporter trying to make headlines. At the center of all of this juicy gossip and judgment is a beautiful, innocent four-year-old girl named Avielle Hernandez who should not have to read about her father's sexual preferences in a vile and disgusting manner because prosecutors were desperate to save a case they never should have brought.

21.

TEARS BEHIND THE GLASS

The day before I was to present closing arguments, I buried myself in the one-bedroom space I had rented at Devonshire Apartments in downtown Boston. We also had a two-bedroom apartment upstairs that George and Linda shared. We called it the retirement home, thanks to George and Linda acting like an old married couple. George always did the laundry and the grocery shopping, and once had to take Linda to the emergency room, where he argued valiantly with a nurse about Linda's pain management.

In practice the Devonshire Apartments were more like our bunker. After leaving court each day we would meet in the upstairs apartment around a huge worktable and discuss everything that had transpired during the day, and set up a game plan for the next. For all our planning, we never really knew what each day would bring; often we'd just have to go with the flow.

Preparing for closing arguments is a bit different than making an opening statement. This is when I have to carefully plot out exactly what I want the jury to remember in order to understand our version of what took place. Most prosecutors like to use power points and verbally retrace their key points in the trial. I'm more of a storyteller. I like to use "demonstrative aids" during my closings. These are mainly photos of witnesses, the crime scene, and other exhibits presented in trial. If you blow them up and put them on poster board, jurors more easily remember faces and snippets of testimony. By highlighting dubious testimony and questionable evidence, I draw the road map to reasonable doubt.

So the night before closing, I was locked in my apartment with two interns gathering headshots of witnesses who had testified during trial, and compiling short video clips I wanted to use to highlight the points I wanted to make. Upstairs, George, Linda, and Michelle were working with a few other interns going over motions to be filed attacking certain issues that might come up.

I like to walk the line between being methodical and being impulsive. I need to plan a strategy, but I'm not afraid to include spur of the moment thoughts. I might get an idea about how to attack a piece of evidence or testimony using some weird visual aid, graphic, or recording and then ask my team to make it happen. More often than not they get it done.

No one got much sleep while preparing for closing. I might do all the talking, but it's a team effort. Everything we had went into the production I was planning. Complicating matters was the fact that my back was killing me. The intense back pain was just the latest in the list of ailments that hit me during the trial. Three weeks after I arrived in Boston, I caught the flu. Once that happened my health slid downhill from there.

One day during a sidebar, I could barely stand. I had to squat down to get some relief. Locke looked at me and said, "Go home."

"To Florida?" I said, hoping my prayers had been answered, as I felt I could not take another day of this freezing weather.

Locke ended trial early that day and court was canceled the next day so I could recover. I spent the weekend in bed. Even so, after three months of being seated eight hours a day, my back was killing me by the time closing arguments arrived.

I woke up that morning and spent a good hour rehearsing the bullet points I wanted to hit. I was nervous and excited. It was the final stretch. I put on a blue suit with a white shirt and gray tie and looked in the mirror to give myself a quick pep talk.

"You can do this," I said.

The team gathered in the lobby and we left Devonshire Apartments as prepared as we could be. The doormen, who were starting to recognize us as Aaron's lawyers, offered us a "Good luck today" as we walked out of the building.

Once we arrived at court, I felt anticipation in the air. Maybe it was just me. Michelle would later tell me Aaron whispered to her: "I can't wait to see Jose do his thing."

Judge Locke gave a lengthy instruction to the jury in which he explained that closing arguments are "the attorneys' opportunity to review the evidence with you and argue to you as to what conclusions you should or should not draw from the evidence as you've heard it."

My job as a criminal defense lawyer during my closing statement was to remind the jurors of the journey we'd taken over the past five weeks and show them where there was reasonable doubt. Jurors must know what reasonable doubt is for it to have life. I don't have to prove who is guilty or prove my client's innocence. I have to challenge the evidence. If the evidence is proven true, they can rely on it. If not, then they should discard it. I thought we had done that during the trial.

In Massachusetts the defense goes first during closing arguments. This was unusual for me. Everywhere else I'd practiced, the defense followed the prosecution. I like going second because I can respond to anything the prosecutor says during his closing. Unfortunately, I wouldn't have that tool in my toolbox at this trial. The day started a bit awkwardly. Before beginning, I looked at Judge Locke for his permission to speak by asking: "May it please the court?" Judge Locke had his head down and I guess he didn't hear me. He scribbled notes, leaving me standing and waiting for his acknowledgment. After an uneasy ten seconds of silence, which seemed longer for someone standing with a throbbing back, Judge Locke finally looked up and said, "Yes, sir."

I thanked the jurors for their service and then explained that my task was to make sure I remembered every single thing that related to reasonable doubt. So I opened with our basic premise. "There's absolutely no evidence that Aaron Hernandez committed this crime," I said. "What's scary is how easy it appears to be to get charged with such a serious crime."

I started by placing a collage of photos from Cure Lounge on a large easel so it could be easily seen by the jury. I stressed that Aaron was there for only nine minutes and that there was no evidence of any interaction with Daniel de Abreu, or a spilled drink, which was supposed to be the motive in the case. There was more evidence that Alexander Bradley lied about the whole incident.

I mentioned that only half the video cameras worked. I pointed out that ex-detective Miller Thomas, the head of security for Cure, worked hand in hand with the police. I talked about how the chain of custody to preserve the integrity of evidence was never followed and shouldn't be accepted. I pointed out how the prosecution knew about the photograph Aaron took with Antoine Salvador but didn't bring him to the stand. I even put up a picture of Salvador and mentioned how the prosecution had also ignored Jaime Furtado, who took the picture. I then put up a picture of Furtado. "They didn't speak to anyone who was in the club that night," I told the jury.

I attacked Bradley's deal of a lifetime and how the prosecution had based its whole case on a drug dealer with a reason to lie. Because of the prosecutor's refusal to retract Bradley's deal of a lifetime, I came up with a description I thought painted a good picture of the situation by saying, "He was their three-legged pony and they were going to ride him to the finish line." While I said this, I got a little excited and imitated a jockey whipping his horse, saying, "C'mon, Rocky" as I began to gallop in the courtroom. I don't know what the hell I was thinking. But it felt right at the moment and a couple of jurors could not hold back their laughter.

I held up the picture of Aaron and Salvador and offered: "This is proof that Alexander Bradley is lying, because Bradley said he had been with Aaron the entire time."

I reminded jurors of the video showing Aaron calmly walking out of the bar by himself and not with Bradley escorting him as he claimed. "It's an absolute lie," I said, still holding the picture of Aaron and Salvador in my hands.

I then turned to the credibility of the police and their testimony, suggesting they didn't work hard enough to find the photo because it didn't fit into the story Bradley was trying to sell. The photo offered proof that Aaron didn't have time to get into a beef with anyone and that he was in a cordial mood that night.

One visual I couldn't wait to present was of written quotes taken from the testimony of Detective Paul MacIsaac, who had attempted to defend several obviously untrue statements made by Alexander Bradley. One side of the poster board read: "It's not true, but it's not a lie." The other side read: "Truthful, but inaccurate." I kept flipping those over and over so the phrases could soak into the jury.

"How stupid does he think we are?" I asked the jury, referring to the officer's testimony. "Truthful, but inaccurate? That's what Alexander Bradley is," I said. "This sums up the case in regard to Alexander Bradley."

"C'mon, Rocky." The galloping continued.

I used screenshots of videos to show there was no indication anything had been spilled on Aaron. There were no water stains on his clothing in his photo with Salvador or in video of him leaving Cure, even though everything happened in nine minutes.

"It's all reasonable doubt," I said. "The whole motive is crowded with reasonable doubt."

I used the picture again to attack Bradley's story about what happened when he and Aaron walked to another bar across the street. I put Bradley's photo up and talked about his testimony describing how Aaron was enraged that the Cape Verdean crew had followed them to the second bar even though there was video evidence that they stayed in Cure until it closed.

"It's truthful, but inaccurate," I repeated, flipping the card.

"It's not true, but it's not a lie."

Thirty minutes into my closing statement I had showed that Bradley had lied about the spilled drink and lied about seeing the Cape Verdeans at the second bar. "That's not what you should stand for, accepting lies," I told the jury.

I reminded jurors that Judge Locke had instructed them at the outset to listen with caution and great care. I urged them to use this caution and care when reviewing Bradley's testimony. I knew the prosecution's entire case rested on whether the jury believed Bradley, and I couldn't do enough to discredit him. I detailed all the statements we had disproven. "Those are the lies of Alexander Bradley," I said.

I was feeling good about the way things were going. I could tell the jury was engaged and listening. The painkillers and adrenaline were working on my back. Now it was time to talk more about the police. I played a small clip from the testimony of Boston police sergeant Sean McCarthy, one of the officers on the scene the night of the shooting. He had testified that photos of blood at the crime scene "were a fair and accurate representation of what was there that night." The only problem was he also admitted during testimony that he never saw the particular section of blood photographed. So how could he know whether it was a fair and accurate representation? Why did he not see the blood? I don't know. What's clear is he admitted never seeing the blood.

"That's admitting evidence falsely," I told the jury. "If a sergeant in charge of a crime scene is willing to come here and admit evidence to you that he has no knowledge about and lie to you like that, then everybody is falling into rank. You can't accept that.

That's unacceptable to any citizen accused. And that's the culture of deception throughout this case.

"It started with the scene that night and carried all the way through to the deal with the devil," I said, pointing to a picture of Bradley. "Rocky is going to bring it home for them," I said, keeping my gallop a little more restrained this time.

I saw a few eyebrows raised in the jury when I put up a picture of the second police officer on the scene who was never called, and mentioned the absence of witnesses who had reported they saw a woman or female or someone wearing cornrows or long hair in the shooter's car. To stress the point, I instinctively pointed to Aaron and told him to stand up. This was not planned, but it was an "if it doesn't fit you must acquit" moment and made one of the biggest impressions during the closing.

Aaron wasn't expecting that at all, but he obediently jumped to his feet and stood tall and straight. He had lost weight during the trial, but he looked good in his dark suit and blue dress shirt. Standing there, he looked straight at me wondering what I was about to do or say. "That's not this guy. That's not Aaron Hernandez," I said. "He doesn't have long cornrows. He doesn't look like a female by any stretch of imagination. Even if you squint as hard as they want you to you're not going to get cornrows from him."

All eyes were on Aaron as he sat down next to Sully, who rubbed his back as if to say "well done."

For a man already convicted of murder and serving life without parole, Aaron seemed to connect with the jury. He would smile, make his defense team laugh at times, and was respectful to the judge and the prosecution.

My team would tell me later that they could see the prosecution starting to squirm. They knew the jury was paying attention to what I was saying. Michelle said she could see Pat with his face down, looking anxious; especially when the video of Detective MacIsaac was played saying Bradley was "truthful, but inaccurate."

The head of the district attorney's office was in the courtroom and so were all the major cops in Boston. They were all there waiting to hang Aaron and I was determined to do my best to not let that happen.

I reminded the jury how a forensic scientist concluded that the angle of the shots from the passenger side was completely impossible based on Bradley's testimony. "The science doesn't lie," I said. "The science is the only thing that doesn't have to take the witness stand and choose a side."

I pointed out how Aquilino Freire was covered in blood and initially said he and his friends were in a "gun fight." I also asked why Gerson Lopes and Raychides Sanches left their dying friends at the scene. What were their motives? "Both of these guys ran," I said to the jury. "What did they take with them? Where did they go? Why are they destroying evidence? These are questions we must ask."

Then I put pictures of sixteen individuals on the board, four rows across and four rows down, all of them forensic witnesses for the commonwealth who said there was zero by way of forensic science that connected Aaron Hernandez to the Boston shootings. Zero!

I could simply have said that verbally. But using the headshots of each witness was more dramatic. As I grabbed each picture, I announced: "No DNA, no fingerprints, no gun residue, no computer links, no ballistics, no gun tests." When all the pictures were off the board, I said, "This is what they're left with." I paused while the jury looked at an empty board.

Next I addressed what happened in West Palm Beach, pointing out that Bradley admitted he couldn't account for two of the five days he was down there and refused to explain where he went or what he was doing. I also reminded the jury that the manager of Tootsie's said he gave Alexander Bradley his phone back, countering Bradley's claim that he had left his cell phone there. "He just can't tell you that truth. He's got an incentive and he's lying all over the place," I said about Bradley.

A couple of days earlier Linda had shown me a meme going around social media showing Oprah Winfrey repeatedly pointing to members of her audience with a superimposed caption that read someting like: "The Commonwealth handing out immunity." The meme was a takeoff on one of those episodes where an excited Oprah gives away cars or other expensive gifts to every member of her delighted studio audience.

Over the course of the trial the commonwealth had granted immunity to at least half a dozen witnesses, and the jury knew it. I thought this meme was too good to pass up. The jury, the gallery, and even the press got a good laugh when I talked about the commonwealth giving out immunity like it was "candy on Halloween" and that Pat Haggan was the "Oprah Winfrey of immunity."

Pointing at various members of the jury as if they were Oprah's audience I said, "You've got immunity. You've got immunity. Check under your chairs, ladies and gentlemen. You've *all got immunity*!" The truth can sometimes be a very funny thing.

I used more pictures to show that the shell casings in West Palm Beach were found outside of the car; blood spatter and the hat Bradley was wearing were also outside the car, indicating he was shot outside the car, not inside as he had claimed. I talked about how Bradley was missing for about five minutes after he was shot. "He lives by the sword," I said of Bradley. "He's lying to you. He wasn't shot inside of the car. He was shot near the fence. His lies have carried all the way to Florida."

My throat was beginning to burn as I headed toward my conclusion, which was the text message Bradley had sent to his lawyer and later tried to delete. I had put the words in big letters on a board and now placed it front of the jury.

Now u sure once I withdraw this lawsuit that I wont be held on perjury after I tell the court *the truth* about me not recalling anything about who shot me.

Bradley's deleted text had been a bombshell discovery during the case. Here was the prosecution's star witness admitting to perjury, and the fact that his story about Aaron shooting him was totally fabricated. He was telling his lawyer what the truth was in a message never supposed to be seen.

"He thought this message would never see the light of day," I told the jury. "That is your reasonable doubt for the entire case. And this stands as the cherry on top."

I ended with a video compilation of Bradley's testimony, a memorable album of his lies. I referred to him as Rocky. My video presentation began with Bradley confidently saying his memory got better with time followed by snippets where he couldn't recall this, that, or the other. He must have said, "I don't recall or I'm not sure" more than two dozen times. I called it *Rocky's Greatest Hits*.

I wanted to conclude by telling the jury about *reasonable doubt* and what it requires. I called it the highest burden in American legal jurisprudence, and I honestly believe that. But just as I was going to refresh the jury on the definition of reasonable doubt, Judge Locke interrupted me. "Counsel, I will give the instruction."

This was an unexpected admonishment, considering raising reasonable doubt is the whole basis of a defense attorney's argument. Looking back, I was knocked off track for a moment. I think I had a flow going. Everyone was listening to every word as I ripped the commonwealth's case and accused them of ignoring evidence that would have supported Aaron's innocence. I still maintain that Locke is one of the fairest judges I have ever practiced in front of, and I felt he had been fair throughout the trial, but as the trial came to a close I sensed he was trying to offer some support to the commonwealth. I had attacked the work of the Boston police and the prosecution's case. Maybe he was taking it personally.

I couldn't act like I was rattled. Actually, I was pissed. Later on at sidebar I told him that "by not allowing me to argue and explain reasonable doubt, you have single-handedly ensured Mr.

Hernandez's conviction." Those were powerful words, but I meant them and still do to this day; a defense lawyer should never be barred from explaining and arguing reasonable doubt.

Regardless, I forced myself back on track and pointed out the facts that showed Aaron was not guilty of the charges. I then concluded my statements by acknowledging the jury: "I thank you all for your attention and I thank you for your service on behalf of both sides."

Haggan made his closing statement, which was powerful. He pushed the line and began arguing details about the gun connection to Aaron that were not in evidence, and Locke shut him down. Besides that he was flawless. I can't recall seeing a prosecutor give a better closing argument. His delivery was flat-out amazing, and for the first time I actually began to worry about a possible conviction. His closing argument was probably the one reason the jury took so long in their deliberations.

As the jury deliberated I felt good about the way the trial had gone. I thought we had done our best to discredit Bradley and offered plenty of reasonable doubt. Despite all the negativity in the press about Aaron, we really thought it was a slam dunk. As the defense team we had lost our objectivity, but every time we reviewed the case we all said to ourselves, how do they convict him? It's impossible given the facts.

Throughout the trial we had felt the jury was with us every day. We followed their facial expressions closely. They would look at us a certain way, or react to some of the things the prosecution did in ways that led us to believe we were convincing them. Actually, I can't recall ever having a jury that seemed so clearly with us throughout the course of a trial. We did have our concerns about one or two jurors, especially when Judge Locke appointed a white woman named Lindsey Stringer as the foreperson. We viewed her as more pro-commonwealth, but hoped our case was strong enough that it would be only a matter of time before the jury of seven women and five men voted for an acquittal.

You never spike the ball before you get into the end zone, but we felt good about our chances. At least until the jury came back with questions that seemed to indicate they were leaning toward a guilty verdict.

At one point they asked the judge: "If we feel there's enough evidence to convict do we need corroborating evidence? Can we base our conviction solely on an immunized witness?"

"What the hell kind of questions were those?" I said to our team. Everybody was super down after hearing those questions. Aaron was too. I told him: "I'm trying to stay positive. But those are some terrible fucking questions."

After hearing the questions we began rationalizing a possible conviction. We all sat there and agreed that if they convicted Aaron, it was because of Odin Lloyd and not this case. They couldn't get Odin Lloyd out of their minds and there was nothing we could have done to win the case.

Deliberations were entering their sixth day when Friday, April 14, 2017, arrived. It was Easter weekend and our team reasoned that a verdict likely wasn't going to be rendered until the following week. Linda made plans to return to New York and I decided to head back to Miami to see a specialist about my back.

They kept Aaron in a holding cell at the courthouse during deliberations so he could quickly change from his prison clothes into a suit to attend court. When I visited with him on Friday morning, the sixth day of deliberations, I told him: "My back is done. If I don't get to Miami and have someone see this thing—" Before I could finish Aaron said, "No. Please go. Don't be ridiculous. There are plenty of people here."

There was nothing I could have done; we were simply waiting on the decision. I said my goodbyes and gave him a big hug, knowing that if the deliberations continued on to Tuesday, I would return. It was the last time I would see Aaron alive, and I cannot begin to describe the sorrow I feel as I'm writing this.

The verdict came in while I was on the plane. Sully, Linda, George, and Michelle were there with Aaron as he was led into the courtroom by four guards who stood behind him as he stood for the verdict. Judge Locke first opened the manila envelope and looked at its contents. The court clerk then asked the foreperson: "Do you find the defendant not guilty, guilty of murder in the first degree, or guilty of murder in the second degree?"

"Not guilty," was the answer five times on both charges of murdering Daniel de Abreu and Safiro Furtado and for armed assault with intent to murder against Aquilino Freire, Gerson Lopes, and Raychides Sanches. He was found guilty of unlawful gun possession.

Sully held his arm around Aaron as the verdict was read. Aaron first nodded his head, then began to cry. Members of the victims' families slowly walked out of the courtroom as the not-guilty verdicts were filed. The only sounds were of people crying.

Judge Locke then thanked the jury for their "careful attention to the evidence" and disqualified them for jury service for the next three years. He then sentenced Aaron to four to five years for gun possession.

Aaron gave Sully a big, long hug, then Aaron hugged George and then Linda and then Michelle, taking a second to glance toward Shayanna.

Normally, when my clients are acquitted they go home. Aaron was taken back to the holding cell in the bowels of the courthouse. The team was escorted there minutes later to have a moment of celebration with him. When they arrived, Aaron had changed back into his prison clothes and was crying his eyes out. The teenager who hardly shed a tear when his father died, and held in his emotions to mask the pain, was now a grown man bawling like a baby.

Michelle, George, Linda, and Sully could see Aaron, but a glass door kept them from hugging him. Instead, he reached his tattooed hands through an opening in the glass to exchange handshakes and smiles. Michelle would later regret not asking the bailiff to open the door so everyone could embrace. "All we could do was put our hands in through the glass and touch his hands," she said. By then the bailiffs had left them alone and couldn't be called. Touches would have to do.

Aaron kept crying and saying, "Thank you. Thank you." He was so grateful someone had believed him.

Then it was time to go. Linda had made travel plans for New York and had to get to the train station. George and Michelle had to drive her there. After a ten-minute visit it was time to leave.

Aaron still had tears in his eyes when his lawyers left him. "I love you," he said one last time to his team. On the way toward the exit Michelle had a bad intuition amid all of the celebration. She looked at George and said, "I felt so weird and sad leaving him behind like this . . . it was just an off feeling, I couldn't shake it . . ."

22.

WTF?

The South Florida sun felt like a soothing warm blanket wrapped around my skin. I might have been born in New York, but I'm a Florida boy through and through. If there aren't palm trees around, I don't want to be there. My body doesn't do cold and that's all it had been while I was in Boston: bone-chilling cold.

As I walked down Brickell Avenue, a street near my home in Miami, I couldn't help but think of how good life was. Four days earlier, I'd accomplished what many thought couldn't be done by getting Aaron Hernandez acquitted of double-murder charges. Winning a jury verdict against those odds was exhilarating. As I thought about the outcome of the trial, what it meant for Aaron, and what it meant for my practice, I was in such a good mood. It was time to relax and enjoy a well-earned rest. My body needed it.

Once a trial ends, whether it lasts one week, three weeks, or three months, my body and mind have to go through a decompression period. Trying a case is extremely taxing, both physically and mentally. People don't realize the effort that goes into even one full day of court. They figure you put on a suit and talk a little. Far from it. The mental fatigue is unlike anything I can describe. You have all the preparation you've made beforehand, memorizing certain things and listening to witnesses and processing what they're saying with the knowledge you already have. And you're scared shitless; scared that you missed something that could change the course of somebody's life forever. Each day you leave exhausted. Afterward you really need time to get your head straight and get back into the groove of things. Four days after the end of the trial in Boston, I was home in Miami and starting to feel like myself again.

It was April 18, 2017. I was still riding high from the acquittal, but all I wanted to do was sleep without being interrupted. I'd gotten into the habit of putting my cell phone away because people will call at all hours of the night and if I'm really trying to get some sleep, I have to just turn off the phone and put it away. That's what I did. There was no reason I should have been bothered. I'd spoken to everyone I needed to, including Aaron. When I talked with him on what would turn out to be the final night of his life, he was so happy and so excited for the future. We discussed how we would have the resources to really go after an appeal in the Lloyd case; we were going to leave no stone unturned. He was excited because he had seen how committed we were to his cause. "I really feel I've got hope," he said. "I'm going to get out."

After closing my eyes I enjoyed the best sleep I'd had in quite some time and I awoke expecting a relatively quiet day. Then I turned on my cell phone. It was flooded with text messages and missed calls, a lot of them from the 212 area code. Something had happened.

I'd been down this road before. When big news breaks, area code 212 blows up on my telephone. It's media from New York calling.

I clicked on one of the text messages from a good friend to see what was happening. There were three words that sent a chill through my soul: "Aaron committed suicide."

As happy as I'd been the night before, numbness and disbelief impaled me. I couldn't believe what I was reading. As I began to scan my text messages, I realized it was no joke; and then I noticed Shayanna had been calling me since five o'clock in the morning.

After seeing these missed calls I pressed my iPhone to call her back.

"Shay, what's going on?"

"I got a call at three in the morning from the prison," she said, her voice choked with grief and fear. "They said Aaron hanged himself in his cell. They say he committed suicide. I'm on my way to the hospital. I can't believe it. Jose, this can't be happening."

"I'll call Sully and have him meet you there," I said. "I will handle everything, just go be with him. I will catch the next flight back. I'll take care of everything."

Lawyer mode kicked in. My day of relaxation had turned into a day of horror. My mind began racing, trying to think of all the things I needed to do. Time was of the essence. I needed to get back to Boston.

After hanging up with Shayanna I booked the next flight to Boston's Logan airport. It was on JetBlue, leaving from Fort Lauderdale at 10:41 A.M. After the quickest shower of my life, I packed a small bag of clothes. I began calling the team: Sully, Linda, George, and Michelle.

I made a list of what we had to address immediately. We had to make preparations for a second independent autopsy and preserve the integrity of the investigation. That meant filing a notice of preservation for the things in Aaron's cell. If anything of significance was being tested we wanted some of it held back so we could do our own testing. And we needed to establish his estate and issue a press release; something simple and informative, otherwise the press would not stop hounding us and Shayanna.

I called Linda Kenney Baden to discuss not only Aaron's second autopsy, but also the idea that had lingered in the back of our minds for a very long time: like so many other football players, could Aaron have suffered a brain injury that might explain his problems with memory and self-control? If we wanted answers, now was our chance. We'd have to move with lightning speed to preserve Aaron's brain and have it tested for chronic traumatic encephalopathy, or CTE, as it is more widely known.

I felt like the trial was on again. That's how it felt amid the chaos of it all.

It wasn't until the drive to the airport that the reality of his death started to hit me. Aaron had been portrayed in the media as this callous thug who hung around with gangsters, threatened people with guns, and had no respect for his football career or human life. He was nothing like that. Yes, he had his dark side and certain moments he was not proud of. But he was also kind, thoughtful, and the type of person who made you feel like he would do anything for you.

As I drove north on I-95 toward the Fort Lauderdale airport, I couldn't hold back the tears. I couldn't believe he had done this. I had not only lost a client, I had lost a friend.

Harvey Levin from TMZ was the first reporter to actually get hold of me. He started firing off a million questions, but I was still in a fog and all I basically gave him was "I am on it. We are investigating his death, and none of us saw this coming because Aaron was upbeat and happy. Until I know all the facts, I am not buying any of the stories."

Within minutes TMZ posted a story under the headline "It Could Be Murder . . . Lawyer Claims." I never said that, but I suppose he could have interpreted my words that way because I was questioning the validity of the suicide reports. It wasn't a stretch. I had stated the obvious, that I needed all the facts in order to understand what happened, but now rumors were flying that Aaron was murdered.

If anything, the TMZ piece put everyone on notice that we planned to do our own investigation. That's what lawyers do. We question. We investigate for truth. None of the events of the past twenty-four hours made any sense. I've seen some pretty crazy shit done by law enforcement and government officials, and I don't put anything past anyone. Ninety-percent of the time there's something off in any police report, and 20 to 30 percent of the time the report will be flat-out wrong, either intentionally or inadvertently or through negligence. Until we gathered all the evidence and conducted our own independent investigation, I wasn't going to accept anyone's conclusions.

My first priority when I arrived in Boston was to check in on Shayanna and make sure she was okay. One of our interns, Jeon Favors, picked me up at Logan airport and we drove to Shayanna's home in Rhode Island. She and Avielle had left the mansion and put it up for sale after Aaron's conviction in 2015. They were now living in a two-bedroom townhouse near a golf course in North Providence.

When I entered the house and saw Shayanna I gave her a tight hug. Just yesterday we were discussing her coming to Florida to celebrate the victory with some friends, and hoping for a better future. Now Aaron was gone. "How could this happen?" she said. "Why now? Just when it looked like we had some hope he would be coming home."

A few of her friends were with her when I got to her townhouse. The space was much smaller than the mansion she once decorated herself, but the rooms were tastefully decorated and filled with the same pictures of friends and family, pictures of love.

Sully was also there, along with a paralegal. Avielle was with Shayanna's mother, Jodi, at a house nearby. Shayanna was surrounded by good people. She had been estranged from her younger sister Shaneah, Odin Lloyd's girlfriend, and had had virtually no contact with Aaron's family since the first trial. "I don't hear from them even now," Shayanna had said. "I've been doing everything on my own, which is fine. I don't complain. My daughter is healthy and I'm breathing."

Shayanna was surprisingly strong. She was preparing food for the visitors and trying to stay busy. Being a single woman and having been through what she'd been through with Aaron, I can't begin to describe her strength. You can't rattle her. She's a rock. No one would blame her if she was devastated. She talked of her intention to visit Aaron in prison in the coming days. "It was all planned," she said. "It's like he didn't want to say goodbye."

Aaron did say goodbye. He wrote three letters the night he died, letters discovered in his cell and released to us by corrections officials a few days after his death. One, written on ruled paper, was addressed to me. It was dated April 18, 2017.

Jose,

What's up, brotha? Well, I wrote this letter following my acquittal and wanted to voice how I felt and let some people whos[e] music helped me get through hard times, know that it did. Wrong or right—who knows—I just follow my natural instincts and how it guides me. Pros or cons, didn't weigh them, but I'm sure you'll let me know your view. Besides that, I want you to know you have me forever like you never understood and time will reveal that I'm not perfect but my love and loyalty is like you've never seen! I appreciate all your work, time, effort, and never let that slip your mind! In time, you will see how appreciated you are, as well as all the others equally! But never forget I will whoop your ass if you get too crazy . . . haha! But we could grab a drink after. All jokes aside, I hope your son is well and all your loved ones!

I need a favor—If you have any contacts for any artists like Gates, Meek Mill, Ross, Jay, Game . . . etc. I would like to send you letters so you can send to their information or whichever way you think best. I don't want any media really getting into me, trying to just send my love to all the artists who got me through my tough times and sending my respect to a few of the real ones out there. So I think that's the best idea through you. It's something I have to do and

I'd appreciate if you could do that for me, if possible! If not, I'll figure something out. Well, get at me, love ya brother!

Aaron

Nothing in that suggests Aaron was thinking of killing himself. He talks about contacting artists in the future and that if I can't help him, he'll figure something out. It's a sweet letter I'll always cherish. That was the real Aaron.

Love ya too, brother.

Letters to Shayanna and Avielle written in the same notebook on the same night were more ominous.

Avi,

Daddy will never leave you! I'm entering to the timeless realm in which I can enter into any form at any time because everything that could happen or not happened I see all at once! Life is eternal—believe!!! Love, repent, and see me/ yourself in everyone because that's what the truth is! I'll see you all in the heavens awaiting you all with the same love. Never fear me, but love me with all of you! Fear is the only separation between you and I! We are each other— I/you—you/me—there's no need to fear but what you do unto another will come back around!

Power of Now

Conversations with God 1, 2, 3

Home with God

Anuk Ausar "Metu Neter"

The letter addressed to Shayanna would later be shown on national television, including the *Dr. Phil* show.

Shay,

You have always been my soul-mate and I want you to love life and know I'm always with you. I told you what was coming indirectly! I love you so much and know are an angel. We split into two to come change the world! Your characteristic is that of a true angel and the definition of God's love! Tell my story fully but never think anything besides how much I love you. This was the supreme almightys plan, not mine! I love you! Let Avi know how much I love her! Look after Jano and Eddie for me—they are my boys (You're Rich).

    I KNEW I LOVED YOU = SAVAGE GARDEN

The third page of writing sounded like a man who had accepted his fate. It's as if he saw the angel of death at his door. In huge letters he wrote:

NOT MUCH TIME
I'M BEING CALLED!
JOHN 3:16

On the fourth page he added,

I love you all equally! We are all each other! Don't shed one tear for I am with all of you and never wasn't! DO NOT GO BACK TO LIVING WHILE WORSHIPPING FALSE IDOLS in which I warned you about!

Later, Aaron writes what look to be his final words in inch-high letters.

IT'S TIME!!!
The Real Live Forever

On the bottom of the page there is a drawing that resembles a thin rope dangling from a noose.

23.

THE BATTLE
FOR THE BRAIN

Two days after Aaron's suicide, I sat next to Shayanna on the living room couch in her townhouse in Rhode Island. We were still numb, drifting in and out of daydreams, mourning, and conversation. Our discussion took us to the necessary arrangements.

"Shay, because you and Aaron never married, his mother will be asked to make most of the legal decisions regarding his funeral. Have you thought of the funeral?" I asked.

"Yes," she said sternly. "Terri can have whatever she wants. But I do not want him buried in a box. He needs to be free. They won't have him trapped any longer. Jose, I don't care about anything but that. Please make that happen."

"I think that is a conversation you are going to have to have with Terri," I said. "I know you guys haven't spoken much lately. But this is no time to let your differences come in the way of doing what's right for Aaron."

"I completely agree. I'll call her now," she said.

"Wait, there's one more thing, Shay," I told her. "You know I want us to do a second independent autopsy. I just want to make sure you're okay with it."

Boston's Office of the Chief Medical Examiner was obligated to conduct its own autopsy because of the circumstances surrounding Aaron's death. Any death related to injuries, violence, drugs, and even those that occur without explanation normally require an autopsy. We wanted to conduct our own independent autopsy.

"Just promise me one thing, Jose," she asked.

"Anything." I responded.

"Don't leave him," she said. "Aaron hated doctors and surgery, and I don't want him to go through his final experience with a doctor to be alone," she said warmly.

"I won't leave his side," I promised. "Now go call Terri."

The conversation went well, and they agreed on almost everything. A day earlier I had a conversation with D. J. Hernandez, Aaron's older brother who was now speaking on his mother's behalf. DJ was easy to deal with. I expressed how bad it would look in the media if the family began fighting over such simple issues as the funeral. He agreed and did everything he could to keep the peace and ensure things ran smoothly.

Getting Terri Hernandez's signature to turn over Aaron's brain to the Boston University CTE Center was relatively easy as well. Everyone wanted answers and I agreed to keep everyone informed of our progress and give any information as soon as I could. There was a time early on in the case when the defense team kicked around the idea of getting Aaron a CAT scan to see if he suffered from any neurological problems like CTE. It was an interesting discussion. There was really nothing in Aaron's behavior that stood out to suggest he had brain damage. In the end we thought having him tested might send a red flag that we were attempting to use some type of mental health defense or insanity plea, and people would get the wrong impression. We felt all the evidence pointed to innocence, not someone with a deranged mind who couldn't control himself.

I made the call. Hindsight being twenty-twenty, I wonder if not testing him for neurological damage was the right decision. Only an autopsy can definitively diagnose CTE, but given how advanced his case was, surely there were detectable neurological differences? I might not have changed my court strategy, but I might have changed the way I dealt with Aaron.

I put Sully in charge of working out all the funeral arrangements with Shay, while I coordinated Aaron's second autopsy with Linda's husband, famed forensic pathologist Dr. Michael Baden. Baden became a household name during the O. J. Simpson murder trial when he testified on behalf of the defense. His résumé and list of autopsies reads like a who's who in death. His investigative acumen as well as his broad knowledge of medicine and how people die make him the go-to guy for every high-profile case in the country. Fortunately for me and Aaron, he is family, as I am very close to him and Linda and have been for years.

Sully and I picked Baden up at the train station to take him to Faggas Funeral Home in Watertown, Massachusetts, a small neighborhood that's part of the greater Boston area. It was made famous by the shootout that occurred there with the Boston bombing suspects just a few years earlier.

The funeral home was located in a large Victorian-style house and had been run by the same Greek Orthodox family for over fifty years. We could immediately tell the owners were used to being compassionate to family members, and they were very concerned with Aaron's privacy. By the time we arrived, there were already twenty cameras with about fifty reporters parked across the street, waiting to get a shot of Dr. Baden as he entered. They started yelling questions at us from across the street, as if we were planning to stop and chat. They were desperate for anything. "Just a word," one shouted.

Once we entered the funeral home, we were greeted warmly by the funeral director, who took us down to the basement. A skinny stairway led us down to what looked almost like a makeshift triage center where bodies lay in small areas separated by curtains. Aaron was in the largest room toward the back. As we walked in, there was no noticeable smell other than the formaldehyde that cloaked the entire room. Aaron lay inside a white body bag on a stainless-steel table barely large enough to hold him. The tag on the body bag had some numbers on it and clear all-caps read: HERNANDEZ.

I have attended far more autopsies than I wish to count, but for the first time this one was personal. I was about to see a man that just a few days ago I was hugging as I said goodbye before I headed back to Miami. Baden ripped the zipper open quickly as if he were ripping off a Band-Aid to avoid pain, and for the first time I saw Aaron dead. I realized that until I saw him with my own eyes, I almost hadn't believed he was dead. No one said a word until the funeral assistant and Michael took him out of the body bag. After the assistant left the room and closed the curtain so we could have privacy, Sully said the first words: "Oh Aaron, Aaron, Aaron." He spoke softly in a disappointed tone, as if to say, you didn't have to do this.

I on the other hand couldn't find the words to say anything. After all the arguments in the courtroom, during the investigation, and in the media, Aaron had finally left me speechless. I felt a tear roll down my cheek as Michael Baden, the consummate professional, began his outer examination of Aaron's body. I knew that if Aaron had been murdered we wouldn't have to cut him open to see it. Aaron was a fighter. If the guards had done it, they would have needed several men to take him down; he wouldn't have gone quietly. If it had been inmates they would have had to cut him multiple times and we would see it instantly. But Aaron's body showed no sign that he had fought for his life.

The medical examiner had wiped the blood off his forehead where Aaron had written "3:16." The only sign of violence was an overwhelming purple bruise on his neck about four inches long and three inches thick. You can't replicate a bruise like that on a dead body. Aaron had done this to himself. But understanding why he did it remained a mystery.

As I looked over his massive frame, with legs built like tree trunks, he appeared so peaceful; almost like he was just sleeping. You never expect to see someone so young and healthy lying dead. But the paleness of his skin made it clear: he wasn't going to wake up.

My cell phone started to vibrate as Baden began making incisions. I didn't even look at my phone and let the call go to voicemail. It went off again. They have no fucking respect, I thought, assuming it was the media outside calling trying to get a quote. The ringer kept going off until I finally looked at my cell. It was Linda. "Jose, they are keeping the brain!" she yelled over the phone.

"What?" Still not knowing what she was talking about. "The Boston medical examiner's office will not release the brain to Boston University's CTE Center," she said. "We had everything set for them to pick it up today and when they arrived to retrieve the brain, the medical examiner's office changed its mind and refused to release it, saying that it was going to keep Aaron's body for further review."

"What are you talking about? I'm looking at him right now," I said. "He's lying naked right in front of me."

"Jose, they are going to fuck this up," she said. "They are not trained on how to properly prepare a brain for CTE testing. They don't want us to get our answers, so they can just say he was a murderer who committed suicide out of guilt and not because he may have had a severe brain disease."

"Over my dead body," I said quickly, realizing it was a strange thing to say in a funeral home.

My blood began to boil. I don't usually lose my temper in a professional setting but I couldn't hold back. "Let's go!" I told Sully.

Only hearing half of the conversation, he was perplexed but knew something was up. I stormed out of the funeral home and crossed the street through busy traffic as Sully watched from the sidewalk with a look of what the hell is he going to do now? When the media saw me they began filming me skating through oncoming traffic as if they were planning to report: "Breaking news. Justice is served as the devil's advocate is struck by a car in front of Faggas Funeral home. Film at eleven."

When I joined them the media were surprisingly silent. I guess they figured, if he's going to come racing over here, we better catch every word. I told them I would be holding a major press conference in thirty minutes in front of the Boston medical examiner's office, and would be breaking big news. As I crossed back over to the funeral home to join Sully, the cameras kept filming me, just in case I got hit by a car after all. Sully looked at me, tilted his head, asked, "You want to tell me what the fuck you're doing?"

"We are going to go get the rest of Aaron," I said.

"But you promised Shay you wouldn't leave him," Sully reminded me.

I would have to break my promise. In a way, I felt we didn't have all of him so I wasn't really leaving him. One thing was clear. I had one more battle to fight for Aaron: the battle for his brain.

"Do you even know where the medical examiner's office is?" Sully asked as he tumbled into the car with me.

"Fuck if I know. Let's google it," I said.

We arrived about ten minutes late to our own press conference. The Office of the Chief Medical Examiner was located on a busy street in the center of Boston. It almost looked like an office building, not what I was expecting at all. A major crowd had formed as pedestrians wondered why all the media was there. Sully and I needed to weave through the crowd to get to the microphones, and I began by thanking everyone for coming on such short notice. I then went into a tirade for about thirty minutes explaining what the Office of the Chief Medical Examiner had done. I even named the pathologist who told Linda they were not going to release Aaron's brain. I told them how they had agreed the night before to turn over the brain to Boston University but in a sudden change of plan did not. I also informed the media that the examiner's office was not qualified to prepare the brain or even try to test for CTE or any other brain disease.

There was no medical or investigative reason for them to keep Aaron's brain. "Once the medical examiner's office released Aaron's body to his next of kin, they had no authority to keep his brain," I said. "They are illegally holding his brain, and if they do not release it immediately we will file a motion for injunctive relief and sue not only the medical examiner's office but the individuals responsible for this decision in an individual capacity."

We then fielded about fifteen minutes of questions until the final one: "Why do you think the medical examiner's office is doing this highly unusual action?" "Don't ask me, ask them!" I said, pointing at the front door. "You guys have been reporting on this case from day one. Stop taking the guided tour and go in there and ask them the tough questions."

At that moment one of the several onlookers who had their cell phones out to record the whole show yelled, "Yeah, that's bullshit! Let the family have his brain so they can study it!"

Another person yelled, "Yeah, what the hell is wrong with them? He's dead, what more do they want?"

The cameras shifted over to the small group of bystanders who were all riled up. As soon as the cameras switched back over to me I said, "Thank you," ending the conference. Almost instantly, about fifteen reporters turned and stormed into the medical examiner's office. Later someone sent me a picture of the Office of the Chief Medical Examiner's lobby packed with reporters and cameras just moments later. I wish I could have seen the look on the receptionist's face as those reporters started demanding answers. I have never been a big fan of the media, having been attacked personally by them on many occasions. But for that brief moment I loved them. God bless the First Amendment; approximately an hour later the Boston medical examiner's office released Aaron's brain to the Boston University CTE Center.

Using their best efforts to save face, they simultaneously issued a press release announcing the cause of death as suicide, clearly hoping the media would print that instead of the fact they had caved to pressure. How do I know this? They issued a cause of death without having the toxicology results. What if Aaron was poisoned in prison or given a sedative and then a hanging was staged? If they were planning to investigate that angle the medical examiner would have had to send samples to the toxicology lab. This to me was a clear message that this medical examiner's office was more concerned with saving face than with doing its job properly. Looked like this crap was never going to end.

By the time we got back to the funeral home, Dr. Baden was almost done with his autopsy. Aaron was now fully cut open. He began showing us Aaron's vital organs. "His heart was strong as an ox," Dr. Baden said. "I checked all different possibilities, but I cannot make a call on the cause of death until we get the toxicology results back."

He also said, "One interesting thing I might add is that his skull is unusually thin, about half the thickness of the average adult male, so I have to say the possibility of him having CTE has to be significant."

I was puzzled because my understanding was that the skull had little to do with CTE except that this is what the brain hits repeatedly in football. Why would thickness be important?

Did Aaron have CTE? We would have to wait several weeks before we could get an answer to that question. All the while the world wondered, did Aaron Hernandez really kill himself?

AROUND THIS TIME a fellow inmate came out publicly, claiming he and Aaron had an intimate relationship in prison. The convicted felon went on to claim that one of the three letters Aaron wrote was for him. He also claimed that Aaron promised to leave him an expensive watch. Did Aaron have sex with this guy? I don't know.

I can't imagine, given the fact Aaron was kept separate from the other inmates most of his time in prison. That he was a high-profile inmate made the possibility of any extended type of relationship even more unlikely. Do I believe he had any feelings for this guy? Absolutely not.

I had extensive conversations with Aaron about his relationships with many of the people in his life, and if he had any feelings for someone on the inside he would have told me. We had many conversations about what was going on in prison, so I could counsel him on ways to stay out of trouble and warn him of the possibility of jailhouse snitches, since the commonwealth had such a weak case. We were expecting someone would try and get time off their sentence by exploiting the situation, and we were totally on guard. Aaron was incredibly diligent about watching out for people trying to befriend him under these circumstances.

This convicted felon made all these statements through a lawyer, who held a press conference stating that upon release he would "make himself available for interviews." No doubt paid interviews, I thought. A reporter later informed me that this felon had sold his "life story rights." It came as no surprise to me. What did come as a surprise was that more inmates didn't come forward claiming the same thing to make a few bucks.

24.

CHRONIC TRAUMATIC ENCEPHALOPATHY

Four months after Aaron died I got an email from our contact at Boston University's CTE Center informing me that the results on Aaron's brain were ready to be released to the next of kin. We thought it would be best for the legal team to hear the information over a conference call and then I would tell Shay and Aaron's family myself.

Chronic traumatic encephalopathy is the neurodegenerative disease found in people with multiple head injuries. It's the biggest threat to football as we know it. The movie *Concussion* starring Will Smith tells the story of Dr. Bennet Omalu, a forensic neuropathologist credited with identifying CTE in the early 2000s while exploring the death of Mike Webster, the Pittsburgh Steelers' longtime center during their dynasty in the 1970s. Webster, who died at age fifty, displayed erratic behavior before his death, including spontaneous rage, forgetfulness, and other signs of dementia.

Dr. Ann McKee of Boston University, who examined Aaron's brain, is the world's leading researcher on CTE. She is a Packers fan who loves football, and has the largest brain bank of former athletes in the world. Dr. McKee was very cautious in setting up the call with us and insisted there be no recording devices of any kind. I don't blame her. She didn't know me. I would have proceeded the same way if I was her.

I was in a hotel traveling on another case when the call took place, but I don't think there was a single member of the team who didn't want to be on it. Once Sully, George, Linda, Michelle, and I were on the line Dr. McKee quickly got to the point. She explained all the abnormalities of Aaron's brain, and began rambling off a bunch of medical terms I was not familiar with. When she got down to the core of what she wanted to say, she was clear. "Aaron Hernandez had Stage 3 out of the four stages of chronic traumatic encephalopathy," she said. "We almost called it a Stage 4 but ultimately decided to err on the side of being conservative. It was quite frankly the worst case we have seen in anyone of his age."

Before Aaron's diagnosis, researchers had never seen Stage 3 CTE in a brain younger than forty-six years old. First-stage symptoms of CTE include hyperactivity, confusion, disorientation, dizziness, and headaches. Second-stage symptoms progress to memory loss, social instability, impulsive behavior, and poor judgment. The third and fourth stages include progressive dementia, movement disorders, speech impediments, paranoia, depression, and thoughts of suicide.

I was seated on my bed in the hotel room but slid down on the floor. I was overcome with sadness, and most of all guilt. What could I have done differently? Why didn't I have Aaron tested in some manner? As tears fell down my face, I thought of this big kid with a beautiful smile who died way too soon under the worst of conditions.

Although Dr. McKee has tried repeatedly to tell me there is no way a test would have revealed this while he was alive, I just can't forgive myself. I was his lawyer, his friend, his confidant. I was feeling the kind of survivor's guilt many people feel when a loved one or a friend commits suicide. I have no doubt that CTE is what made Aaron commit suicide. Why didn't I foresee this, and prevent it?

THERE IS AN ISSUE I have to address and here is as good a place as any to do it. When we announced the results in September 2017, many in the media leapt to the conclusion that by releasing his results we were saying football turned Aaron into a killer, and therefore his behavior should be excused because he had CTE. First and foremost, we never said any such thing. Second, and probably more important, as I'm sure you know from reading this book, while certainly there were criminals in Aaron's social circle, I am of the opinion that Aaron was not a killer.

Still, the possible link between CTE and criminality must be considered. Dr. Omalu is not shy about stating his belief that CTE has a direct link to symptoms of erratic and impulsive behavior that could possibly lead to criminality. He has stated in the past that he would bet the house that O. J. Simpson has CTE, and recently commented that Aaron's alleged erratic behavior could have a direct link to playing football. If Dr. Omalu is correct and football creates this disease, and an individual is sick in the brain, then there is no way a society should hold them responsible for their criminal behavior, because the brain is what makes the body go.

One cannot legally generate the requisite intent needed to commit crimes if their mind does not give them the free will to think about their actions and know the difference between right and wrong at the time of the crime. You can't hold anyone with a serious brain disease responsible for their actions any more than you can a four-year-old child who pulls the trigger of a gun and kills a sibling.

The clever counterargument many people make without thinking is that many people play football, get CTE, and don't kill anyone.

The problem with that position is we don't judge people in groups; we judge them individually. In Aaron's or anyone's case we consider their mental health, the situation, what they were going through, and if there was time for reflection. Any number of variables will differ in each case, which is why we have to judge each case individually and not say, "Well, Johnny didn't do it therefore Billy who was in a similar situation shouldn't have done it either."

We live in a punishment-driven society and want someone to be responsible even when sometimes there is no one to blame. I can't tell you how many times I see a death that was purely accidental yet society wants someone to be held accountable and punished. I guess that makes us feel better about ourselves and the ability to make some sense out of life, which many times can be senseless. But sometimes our desires mask accountability. Like the love people have for football makes us want to turn a blind eye to the fact that it might be causing this serious brain disease.

A boxer becoming punch drunk is easier to understand. Football has become America's national pastime, a Sunday afternoon obsession that has grown into a multibillion-dollar industry. From high school to college to the NFL, football borders on religion in many parts of the country and anything that threatens the sport is met with stern resistance.

You would think the NFL would want to do all it could for the health and safety of its players, but when studies on concussions by independent researchers dating as far back as 1989 suggested a link between football and brain damage, they were either ignored or dispelled by the league. The NFL actually launched a calculated campaign in the mid-1990s to counter the findings of brain researchers like Dr. Omalu and Dr. McKee with its own propaganda that insisted an average of "one concussion occurred on an NFL field every three or four games."

Paul Tagliabue, the NFL commissioner from 1989 to 2006, did a disservice to the NFL and its players by calling the growing discussion about concussions in the mid-1990s a "pack journalism issue."

When the growing controversy wouldn't go away, Tagliabue tried to control the discussion by forming the Mild Traumatic Brain Injury Committee in 1994 to study concussions. What seemed like a good idea on the surface was flawed in its organization. Half of the members were NFL team doctors, who had a vested interest in the league and the teams they worked for. There were two trainers on the committee, a consulting engineer and an equipment manager. There was only *one* neurologist, Ira Casson, and the committee chairman was Elliot Pellman, the New York Jets team physician who specialized in bone and joint disorders. He had also served as Tagliabue's personal physician.

This bogus committee began issuing reports insisting concussions occurred about one every three games and were "minor events" that went away quickly. Flaws in the committee's research were ignored, namely that players often didn't report head injuries and hid their symptoms so as not to limit their playing time. Doctors and trainers often deferred to the wishes of coaches and players. One of these one-sided reports from the league's committee came to the conclusion that repeated concussions were of no real consequence. It also suggested NFL doctors might actually be "overly conservative and cautious" when it came to dealing with concussions. What a joke. Authors Mark Fainaru-Wada and Steve Fainaru concluded in their excellent book *League of Denial* that "NFL Commissioner Paul Tagliabue had created a research arm that exactly mirrored his skepticism about the so-called concussion crisis."

In 2005, Dr. Omalu along with his colleagues at the department of pathology at the University of Pittsburgh targeted the perils of playing football when he published his findings in a paper titled "Chronic Traumatic Encephalopathy in a National Football League Player." It was immediately ridiculed by the league's concussion committee, which demanded a retraction. Amid those cries, Omalu published "Chronic Traumatic Encephalopathy in a National Football League Player: Part II" in 2006 detailing the second reported case of autopsy-confirmed CTE following the death of Terry Long, who killed himself by drinking antifreeze. Long had played alongside Webster with the Steelers.

Instead of being alarmed, the NFL continued churning out its propaganda through its committee, which issued five reports between 2004 and 2005 insisting NFL players got very few concussions and didn't get brain damage from playing football. What's frightening about this is that the NFL's so-called science was offering false assurances and impacting the 3 million kids under age fourteen, the 1.1 million kids in high school, and an estimated 68,000 in college who played tackle football believing repeated blows to the head and concussions were no big deal.

The NFL stayed publicly defiant until the names started to mount of former players found to have CTE following their deaths: Ray Easterling, who played with the Atlanta Falcons in the 1970s; Andre Waters, a defensive back with the Eagles in the late 1980s; Dave Duerson, a star safety with the Chicago Bears and Giants in the late 1980s and early 1990s; Hall of Fame linebacker Junior Seau of the Chargers and Patriots; and John Mackey, the great Colts tight end whose name is on the award Aaron received in college as the best tight end in the nation. They all suffered from CTE.

NFL players, past and present, finally took notice. In 2010, four thousand former NFL players joined in a civil lawsuit against the league, seeking damages for its failure to protect players from concussions. In August 2013, the NFL reached a $765 million settlement with the former players. Their case was validated when in July 2017 the *Journal of the American Medical Association* released an updated study reporting that out of 111 deceased former NFL players who donated their brains for research 110, or 99 percent, had CTE.

"That study out of Boston simply reaffirmed something we have always known: that there is nothing like a safe blow to the head," Omalu told the New York Press Club in August 2017. "If you play football, and if your child plays football, there is a hundred percent risk of exposure. There is nothing like making football safer. That's a misnomer."

Dr. McKee called Aaron's brain "one of the most significant contributions to our work" because of the condition of his brain and the chance to study the disease in someone so young. CTE was largely viewed as a disease that might strike players long after they retired. Aaron was just twenty-two years old when he played his last game of football.

During a medical conference in November 2017 Dr. McKee said, "In this age group, he's clearly at the severe end of the spectrum. There is a concern that we're seeing accelerated disease in young athletes. Whether or not that's because they're playing more aggressively or if they're starting at younger ages, we don't know. But we are seeing ravages of this disease, in this specific example, of a young person."

When Aaron's CTE results were released they made national news for a day or two, but were quickly overshadowed by the opening of the NFL season. Still, with fifty-three men on the active roster of each of its thirty-two teams, more than sixteen hundred players in the NFL went to battle knowing they could already be suffering from CTE at age twenty-two the way Aaron was. Their general response was to ignore it.

"I think it scares some people," New York Giants linebacker Jonathan Casillas said during the 2017 season. "I kind of leave it alone and say, 'Maybe I'll worry about it afterwards.' That's how my mindset is to it. I think if I involve myself and start researching and finding out the ins and outs of it, I think it will scare me away from football."

Casillas said CTE is the "elephant" in every NFL locker room. "It's not even spoken about," he said. "It's a sensitive thing because it's real and people don't really have answers for it. Even the professionals in that business don't have answers for it. We try to get the right helmets in here year after year. But you still have people getting concussions, people still getting knocked out, and people still missing games because of head trauma."

Did I see any symptoms of CTE in Aaron? Yes and no. First of all, I'm not an expert on CTE, or a neurologist or a psychiatrist. Aaron was always smiling, courteous, and aware of circumstances. He was focused and alert throughout our trial and remembered key details about his career and his court cases. But he also had memory lapses and headaches and episodes of paranoia and depression. But then again, don't we all?

Clearly, Aaron suffered from depression. He was never able to shake off the death of his father. Not when he became a star at the University of Florida, and not when he was drafted by the Patriots.

There's no question he was upbeat and optimistic about his future when he was acquitted in the Boston shootings. I spoke to him, Shay spoke to him, and several people close to him all spoke to him in the aftermath and all of us found him in good spirits. That's why it was so shocking to learn he had hanged himself in his jail cell. None of us could understand why. It made more sense after getting the CTE results. I absolutely believe his suicide was a product of CTE.

Suicide and CTE are a diabolical tandem. Waters played defensive back for the Philadelphia Eagles and Arizona Cardinals from 1984 to 1995. He died at age forty-four from a self-inflicted gunshot wound to the head at his Tampa, Florida, home in 2006. Omalu examined Waters's brain tissue and said it had degenerated into that of a ninety-year-old man.

Seau starred for thirteen seasons as a linebacker for the Chargers before being traded to the Dolphins and finishing his career with the Patriots in 2010. The twelve-time Pro Bowl selection was found dead from a self-inflicted gunshot wound to the chest in 2012. He was forty-three.

CTE was also found in the brain of Kosta Karageorge, a football player at Ohio State who died from a self-inflicted gunshot wound in 2014. He was twenty-two.

Adrian Robinson Jr., a defensive lineman who played in the NFL in 2012 and 2013, hanged himself in 2015 at the age of twenty-five. He was later diagnosed with CTE.

Tyler Sash, a former safety with the New York Giants, died from an overdose of pain medication in 2015. His family reported he had suffered bouts of confusion, memory loss, and anger episodes prior to his death at age twenty-seven. He was found to have Stage 2 CTE.

Lawrence Phillips, the troubled running back who played at Nebraska and in the NFL, was found dead, hanging in his cell in January 2016 at Kern Valley State Prison where he was serving a seven-year term for felony assault and awaiting trial for murdering his cellmate. His family contends his criminal behavior and suicide stemmed from CTE.

Dave Duerson left a text message donating his brain for research just before killing himself with a gunshot blast to the chest in 2011. He was fifty years old. His death stunned the NFL community. Duerson graduated with honors from Notre Dame and was a member of the university's board of trustees from 2001 to 2005. The father of four had spent part of his retirement evaluating disability claims by former football players. He also was a businessman and entrepreneur and the NFL's Man of the Year in 1987.

"He was one of the most strong-minded persons I've ever met," said Ottis Anderson, who played with Duerson on the New York Giants 1990 Super Bowl XXV team. "There was nothing about him that showed weakness. When I heard he took his life and left his brain to be studied I wondered what kind of pain he was dealing with to go the route that he went. I can't see it, but obviously that's part of it. That's obviously where the decision-making process becomes cloudy. It's a credit to him to have the smarts to say, 'I'm not going to do it to my head because whatever is going on it's up in my head and I think people can study it and figure it out so my peers can understand this and try to correct it.'"

Though CTE is known to impact decision making and behavior, researchers have been leery to confirm the disease is linked with suicide. "We can't take the pathology and explain the behavior," McKee said during a medical conference in November 2017. "But we can say collectively, in our experience individuals with CTE—and CTE of this severity—have difficulty with impulse control, decision making, inhibition of impulses for aggression, emotional volatility, rage behaviors."

McKee said Aaron had lost brain tissue and there were abnormal, large holes in part of his brain. There were other findings: the hippocampus, which plays a key role in memory, had shrunk; the fornix, which contributes to memory function, had also shrunk; the frontal lobe, responsible for problem solving, impulse control, and social behavior, was pockmarked with tau protein, which builds up in the brain and kills brain cells; the amygdala, which regulates emotions and emotional behavior like fear and anxiety, had been severely impacted; and the temporal lobes, which process sights and sounds, had significant damage.

McKee called the results "very unusual findings in an individual of this age," adding, "We've never seen this in our 468 brains, except individuals some twenty years older."

We'll never know to what degree CTE impacted Aaron's behavior. To suggest it didn't would be ridiculous. He was already experiencing extensive damage and how long he could have continued his NFL career is up for speculation.

The NFL has tried to address head trauma in recent years by changing the rules to prohibit helmet-to-helmet blows and developing a concussion protocol for the identification, diagnosis, and treatment of concussions. A player is placed in the protocol if he exhibits or reports symptoms or signs of a concussion. An athletic trainer, team physician, coach, teammate, or spotter can also remove a player to the sideline where he will undergo the concussion assessment. Every player who enters the protocol must follow a five-step process before being cleared to fully practice or play in an NFL game, and there is no set time frame for return.

The five-step process starts with (1) rest and recovery, then (2) light aerobic exercise, followed by (3) light aerobic exercise combined with strength training. Then there is (4) participation in select football activities, and (5) a return to full football activity. It has given players a false sense of security that the league is handling the CTE issue.

"The concussion protocol is the best it has ever been," Casillas said. "I think the NFL is trying to take the necessary steps to get some relief in that regard. In ten or twenty years, we'll see if what we're doing now are actually the things necessary to prevent it. It's all kind of like experimentation now."

Independent data released by the NFL showed a 13.5 percent increase in diagnosed concussions during the 2016–2017 preseason and regular seasons, jumping from 243 to 281. While that might suggest an increase in concussions, it's really just an increase in identifying concussions previously overlooked. "We're disappointed that the concussion numbers are up," the league's chief medical officer said when the findings were released in January 2018. "It is something which challenges us now to roll up our sleeves and work hard to see that number go down."

That should have been their attitude from the beginning, but football is still missing the point. CTE is caused by repeated blows to the head, not by concussions. Concussions are just symptoms of the bigger picture. Imagine how many blows to the head a football player takes not only in the games but in each and every practice, year after year. The number of hits is astounding and the helmets are not only no help, but they make matters worse. A helmet only protects the head and skull from fractures and contusions. It does not protect the brain. The brain sits in a liquid jellylike substance, freestanding inside the skull. When a player rams his head the brain slams violently up against the inside of the skull; this does not fracture the skull or affect it in any way.

Helmets actually make matters worse by creating a false sense of security: a player thinks he won't get hurt if he rams his head against another player. It just makes the contact stronger, harder, and more violent, thereby affecting the brain much worse than a collision between individuals without helmets.

Furthering the public's confusion about concussions and CTE is the movie *Concussion* I mentioned earlier. So many people confuse CTE with concussions, but the two are not interchangeable.

Casillas said he watched *Concussion* and was disturbed by what he saw and learned. "It kind of scared me away from football," he said.

The easy answer would be to retire prematurely, which some players have done in recent years. But that's a difficult decision when most players in the NFL support not only themselves but their extended families. "At the end of the day it isn't just about me," Casillas said. "I've got a lot of people to take care of. My family is depending on me. When it comes to that it kind of sucks. It's a double-edged sword. This is what I signed up for. Maybe I didn't know about that when I first signed up for it and started playing the game, but I'm here for the long run until my body and mind says, 'We're done.' I'm going to go ahead and keep the same approach and try to do everything right for my body to keep playing the game. But the CTE shit is a scary thing."

Retired players wonder if they're living with a silent killer, while active players wonder if they're risking their mental health every time they take a blow to the helmet.

"If you've played any kind of contact football for any significant period of time, you're going to have some type of CTE," said Anderson, who played fourteen seasons in the NFL and amassed 10,273 yards rushing. "There are different levels that have made behavior different than others. But if you've played, you've got it. It's trauma to the head and when you have trauma to the head for a substantial period of time, nothing good is going to come from it."

Casillas remembers going against Aaron when he was a rookie and the Saints and Patriots held a series of practices together before a preseason game. "He was awesome," Casillas said. "A tremendous player."

Interestingly, Aaron's biggest contribution to the NFL could come in death as researchers attempt to figure out why someone so young had such an advanced stage of the disease. Thank goodness the Boston medical examiner's office wasn't allowed to ruin things by conducting the test itself.

Fortunately, Boston University researchers were able to do what they do. In examining their results, McKee said Aaron had a genetic marker that makes some people vulnerable to certain brain diseases and could have been a factor in how quickly he developed CTE. The condition of his brain at such a young age could lead to future breakthroughs and a better understanding of how CTE damages the mind.

"We're very grateful to the family for making this donation," McKee said. "We're hoping this will advance medical science in a very significant way. This will really accelerate and advance our research going forward."

RECENTLY I WAS in my office working on a Saturday and felt the need to take a lunch break, so I walked to a local middle school not far from my office, picking up a sandwich along the way. I like to watch the Little Leaguers play baseball but today there were no baseball games going on, so I walked over to the football bleachers and stopped to watch a Pop Warner football game. The kids could not have been any older than eleven. This being Miami, all the kids were of color; about 60 percent were Hispanic. There was not a white face to be found on the field.

As I scanned, looking at all the children with zs at the end of their names, it didn't take long to find a Hernandez. "Carlito" was playing running back. As the game went on I could hear two dads talking about one of the kids playing linebacker and referring to him proudly as a "thumper."

After turning to get a look at who was talking this nonsense, I looked back at the field as Carlito was handed the ball on a running play. With no hole up the middle, he bounced outside and was hit by the thumper. I could hear the helmets collide in what the idiots in the stand called a "thump!" Carlito was a little slow to get up and my jaw dropped. His coach began yelling at him to get off the field, for not going hard up the middle. "Stop being so soft," he told the kid.

As he got to the sideline Carlito's father decided to chime in and continue the barrage, telling Carlito: "I'm not raising you to be soft. Next time you take it up the middle and you take it strong. Do you understand me?"

Carlito nodded yes. "All right then," yelled the father while slapping him hard on the helmet to toughen him up just a little bit more. As this was going on I stood up thinking I should say something to Carlito's father, but regrettably I did not. He was not my child.

Florida defines child abuse as follows:

1. Intentional infliction of physical or mental injury upon a child;
2. An intentional act that could reasonably be expected to result in physical or mental injury to a child; or
3. Active encouragement of any person to commit an act that results or could reasonably be expected to result in physical or mental injury to a child.

I can't use the line "I'm no lawyer" because I am, so I'll come right out and say it. Any parent who knowingly allows their child to play tackle football, knowing what we know about CTE, is actively and continuously committing child abuse. Adults who know the risks should be allowed to make that decision; that is their choice. But a child?

After watching Carlito's father, I turned away and threw my sandwich in a nearby trash can. I had lost my appetite.

I thought back to when I came across a video of Aaron on YouTube when as a New England Patriot he was doing community service; he had chosen to work for mental health awareness with Hispanic children. Although I used to tease him, Aaron was very proud of being Hispanic. He felt that mental health problems in the Hispanic community were undersupported and underreported because of our machismo culture. In this video Aaron, never the great public speaker, was explaining to a reporter how "I know firsthand that it's important to speak to someone, whether it's a physiologist or a psychiatrist, to talk about your feelings and what you're going through." Was he expressing the fact that he knew something was not right inside of him? I can only hope that Dr. McKee was right and that in death Aaron can help her research, and perhaps prevent other people from suffering the same fate.

AFTER HIS DEATH we filed a motion through Aaron's appellate lawyers, John and Linda Thompson, to have his murder conviction thrown out. Under Massachusetts law if an inmate dies before he exhausts all his appeals, their conviction gets thrown out. Predictably, Bristol County prosecutors opposed the motion and relied on case law that was completely incorrect. In the end the judge ruled in our favor. It was the right thing to do, as I believe we would have had the conviction overturned anyway due to all the errors committed in Aaron's first trial. I also feel strongly that the Odin Lloyd case could have been won at trial to begin with. After winning the double-murder case I would have continued to be there right by Aaron's side fighting the fight, but because of Aaron's CTE it was not to be.

I don't think football will ever be banned, but at least we can do everything we can to ensure our children don't hurt themselves. I know my son Jose Baez Jr. will never play the game as long as I'm alive. He will never endure the "unnecessary roughness" of tackle football.

ACKNOWLEDGMENTS

To my wife, Janelle, who has shown me what true love really is, and our five amazing kids, Taylor, Sanibel, Chi-Chi, Logan, and Spencer
—*George Willis*

I want to thank my entire trial team family, which included my new law partners, Ronald S. Sullivan, Linda Kenney Baden, George Leontire, and my main woo-man, Michelle Medina. My entire law firm for keeping the ship afloat and giving me the flexibility to do what I do, with a special thanks to Sean Landers, Kurt Hagstrom, and Dayliset Rielo, who are all loyal and unselfish warriors. To my main man, Robert Proctor, and his Harvard interns beginning with my Abercrombie & Fitch model and legal eagle Jeohn Favors, who helped me prepare for my closing arguments until all hours of the night, a man whose name you will all want to remember, who will set the world on fire with his talents. Also Rachna Shah, who was responsible for Rocky's greatest hits, and Colin Doyle and Jake Meiseles. While I know we had many more Harvard interns, especially those who stayed up until all hours of the night working on motions that we filed during trial, please forgive me for not naming all of you as there were far too many people than I could name who were extremely helpful.

To my interns in Florida from St. Thomas School of Law, "The Harvard of the South," Shardy Sanon, Priscilla Perez: God has given you a gift; go make the most of it. To the talented Suiry Rodriguez "*El que no te necesitas . . . Hatuay!*" To our file wizard and Michelle's most trusted intern, Cristina Hernandez, who I leaned on heavily not only during the trial but in writing this book. To our lone intern in Orlando, Alexandra "3T" Tosado, I cannot overstate how important all of these interns were to our victory and their fingerprints are all over it.

To our team of investigators who took on the entire Boston PD and came out on top, led by Jeremiah "Jerwey" Lyons, Mike Gugliotti, and Catheryn Gutierrez. To the incredible and world renowned Dr. Michael Baden, who is as amazing a human being as he is brilliant, and our top shelf Forensic Pathologist Jaime Downs, your wisdom helped in more ways than I can ever thank you. To Frank Weimann, my literary agent, who always takes my calls, listens to my madness, and just makes deals. To my publishing team, Georgina Levitt and Amanda Murray, thank you from the bottom of my heart for believing in me and this story and allowing me to tell it my way. To my mother, Carmen Silva, and children, Christina Baez and Jose Baez Jr., you are my inspiration and world. I love you so much. To the one and only Baeatricia, believe it or not, I could not have done this without you.

Last but not least my collaborator, George Willis: we had our struggles, but in the end we did it.

Thank you all with Peace, Love, and Justice,

—*J. B.*

INDEX

Abreu, Daniel de
  background, 17, 165
  description, 17, 31, 172
  murder of, 23, 25, 26, 27, 30, 32
  murder weapon and, 30
  Neusa (sister) and, 18, 75
  See also murders (Boston, July
    2012)
Addazio, Steve, 150
Aiello, Paige, 20, 21, 53
Alcorn, John ("Chicago")
  background, 30, 58–59
  Diaz-Ramos and, 30, 58–59
Anderson, Kevin, 117, 118
Anderson, Ottis, 252, 255–256
Anderson, Teresa, 204–205
Anthony, Casey trial, 35, 166, 205
Ashton, Jeff, 166, 205
Aten, Paul, 57
Athletes First, 121, 127, 154
Autopsy (HBO show), 35

Baden, Linda Kenney
  background/description, 35
  Hernandez defense and, xii, 35, 66,
    72, 208, 213, 214, 221, 225, 226
  Hernandez second autopsy/CTE
    and, 229–230, 239, 245

Baden, Michael
  background/reputation, 35, 237
  Hernandez second autopsy,
    237–239, 242
Baez, Jose
  back problems, 214, 216, 218, 224
  Florida State University and,
    9–10
  following Boston trial, 227–228
  following Hernandez suicide,
    228–231
  Jose Baez Jr. and, 258
  Puerto Rican heritage, 10
  warm/cold weather and, 227
Baez, Jose as lawyer
  anger towards him/clients
    acquitted, 56
  Cape Verdeans families and, 74
  Casey Anthony trial, 35, 166, 205
  client with tattoos and, 196
  fair trial for defendant and, 74
  informants and, 106–107
  police reports and, 35–36
  racism in jury selection and,
    163–164
  responding to prosecutor opening
    statement and, 166
  understanding client and, 14

Baez, Jose/Hernandez
  brain/CTE and, ix, 236–237, 239–242
  college football and, 9–10
  Hernandez football career and,
    9–10
  last letter, 232–233
  Puerto Rican heritage and, 10, 14
  second autopsy and, 229, 230–231,
    236, 237–239
  See also murders (Boston, July
    2012)
Baez, Jose/Hernandez legal case
  beginnings
  finances and, 11, 126
  Hernandez letter and, 8–9
  lawyers and, 10, 12
  Lloyd murder conviction and, 10–11
  media hype vs. evidence and, 12,
    14–15
  meeting/discussions, 11–15, 145
  See also murders (Boston, July
    2012)
"ballistics" ("tool mark evidence"), 63
Baranowski, Alfred, 143
Batson challenges, 163–164
Belichick, Bill
  description/reputation, 114, 116
  statement on Lloyd's murder,
    118–119
Belichick, Bill/Hernandez
  Boston murder trial and, 191–192
  Hernandez on, 115, 125
  Lloyd murder and, 117, 118–119
  meeting/advice and, 103, 114, 115
  trade request and, 117, 191
Belle Glade, Florida
  NFL football players and, 78, 79
  as "the Muck"/"Muck City," 78–79

  See also Super Bowl celebrations
    (2013)
Benson, Eric J., 115–116
Blake, Mingle, Jr, 87
Bogart, Humphrey, 101
Boston Globe, 116, 124
Boston Herald, 72, 169
Boston Marathon bombings/suspects
  (2013), 26, 237
Boston University CTE Center, ix, 236,
  239, 240–241, 244, 245, 256
Bradley, Alexander ("Sharrod")
  background, 30–31, 92
  Bristol move, 92–93
  connections to Diaz-Ramos, 63
  description, 27, 77, 92, 198–199
  domestic violence/arrest, 104–105,
    108
  drugs/violence, 30–31, 53, 63, 77, 79,
    80, 92–93, 108, 112–113, 173, 199
  fear of, 93–94
  guns and, 31, 61, 62–63, 93, 111,
    112–113
  Jamar and, 63, 93, 108
  Kelly Kay and, 93, 102, 104–105, 108
  life after getting shot, 104–105
  Lloyd murder trial and, 132
  police phoning instead of visiting,
    93–94, 108–109
  as possible rat in past, 108–109
  retribution method, 114
  as "Sharrod the Shooter," 93
  Vevo Lounge shootings/
    consequences, 112–113
  Wilcox and, 32
  See also murders (Boston, July
    2012); Super Bowl celebrations
    (2013)

Bradley, Alexander ("Sharrod")/
    Hernandez relationship
  activities together, 94, 98–99,
    102–103
  Bradley lawsuit and, 104, 114, 202,
    204
  Bradley supplying muscle/
    protection, 99, 101–102
  description, 94, 101
  Hernandez friends not liking
    Bradley, 99
  Hernandez on, 12–13
  marijuana and, 94, 99
  meeting/growing relationship, 94,
    98–99
  protecting family/self from
    Bradley, 103–104, 114, 116, 117,
    134–135
  souring, 33, 77, 103
  See also murders (Boston, July
    2012); Super Bowl celebrations
    (2013)
Bradley, Alexander ("Sharrod")
    murders July 2012
  Cure Lounge and, 19–20, 27–28,
    112
  false statements in testimony
    (summary), 110–111
  Hernandez accusing, 12–13, 30–33
  identification of (Cure Lounge
    videos), 30–31, 90, 111
  if convicted of murders, 108, 109
  immunity given, 31, 108, 109, 110,
    111
  joint venture theory and, 109
  "motive"/spilled drink and, 31,
    46–47, 53, 54, 55, 110–111, 190,
    191, 216, 218

  proffer agreement, 31, 109–110
  release/violence following, 111–113
  testimony and, 31–33, 47, 53, 54
  trial and, 198–205
Brady, Tom
  deflating footballs and, 162
  Hernandez and, 115, 124, 125
Breau, Gerard
  description, 4
  Hernandez suicide and, 4–6
Briggs, Mark, 117
Brooks, DaQuan, 94

Callahan, Gerry, 212
Camper, Tyrone
  murder weapon and, 30, 63, 65
  test firing, 58, 65
  trial testimony and, 65–66
Cardozo School of Law, Yeshiva
    University, New York, 64
Casablanca, 101, 163
Casey Anthony trial, 35, 166, 205
Casillas, Jonathan
  background, 250
  on CTE, 250–251, 254, 255
Casson, Ira, 248
chain of custody, 48–49, 53
child abuse definition (Florida),
    257–258
chronic traumatic encephalopathy.
    See CTE
Cioffi, David, 25
Cirino, Luciano
  actions at crime scene, 24
  crime scene tape and, 69
clear and convincing evidence
    standard, 131
Cochrane, Johnnie, 202

Concussion (movie), 244, 255
concussion protocol, 253–254
Cormier, Derek, 57
Courtney, Tyler, 6, 7
Crawford, Tyrone, 79, 80, 81, 82
criminal justice system
    emotions vs. facts, 170–171
    fair trial for defendant and, 74,
        170–171
    independent/interested witnesses,
        171
    legal standards/jury trials, 130–131
    "marinating a jury," 200, 204
    mocking opponent's arguments
        and, 166
    racism in jury selection, 163–164
    See also informants in criminal
        justice system; *specific
        components*; *specific individuals*
CTE
    boxing and, 247
    child abuse definition, Florida and,
        257–258
    concussion protocol and, 253–254
    concussions and, 254–255
    criminality and, 246–247
    definition/description, 244
    diagnosis/living person and, 246
    football connection and, 246–258,
        259
    football helmets and, 253–255
    football players with (examples),
        244, 249, 250–253
    NFL and, 247–256
    NFL committee/propaganda,
        247–250
    NFL settlement, 249
    Pop Warner football game and,
        256–257, 258

stages/symptoms, 245
suicide and, 249, 251–253
See also specific individuals
CTE/brain and Hernandez
    advancing medical science and, ix,
        256, 258
    announcing results/responses,
        246–247
    Boston University CTE Center, ix,
        236, 239, 240–241, 244, 245, 256
    condition of brain/CTE stage and,
        ix, 245, 253
    defense team/CAT scan and,
        236–237
    family donating brain, 236
    genetic vulnerability and, 256
    McKee and, 245, 246, 250, 253, 256,
        258
    media/Boston medical examiner
        office and, 239–242
    need to preserve brain and, 229–230
    Shay on, ix–x, xi–xii
    skull and, 242
    symptoms and, 251
Cummings, Jeffrey
    affair/relationship with Terri
        Hernandez and, 149, 150, 155
    attack by/prison and, 155
    background, 149
Cummings, Joshua
    investigating video surveillance,
        27, 28
    prosecution/Hernandez, 27, 28, 182,
        183
Cummings-Singleton, Tanya
    Cummings and, 149
    Hernandez and, 30, 32–33, 58, 149,
        159
    Jano/Eddie (children), 159, 234

Singleton and, 30, 58, 59
switching cars with Hernandez, 33
Cure Lounge, Boston
    Cape Verdeans and, 18–21
    See also video from Cure Lounge;
      specific individuals

Dauphinais, Peter
    Hernandez/family and, 30
    murders (July 2012) investigation
      and, 30–31, 90, 111
DeMaria, Rick, 166, 168
Diaz-Ramos, Jailene
    Aaron Hernandez and, 28, 58, 59, 62
    Alcorn John ("Chicago") and, 30,
      58–59
    auto accident, 29, 57–58
    Bradley and, 63
    description/background, 29, 57, 58
    D. J. Hernandez and, 58
    "Flaco" and, 30, 58
    gun/changing story, 29–30, 57–58,
      63
    gun "identification" and, 62
    marijuana and, 63
Dickerson, Ed, 123
DiRenzo, Joseph, 115–116
DNA evidence, 64, 66
Dr. Phil show, 209, 233
drug dealing
    aliases and, 79
    floating and, 99–101
    vouching for people and, 79, 85
Duerson, Dave, 249, 252–253
Dunn, David, 121
Dupuis, Renee, 139–140

Easterling, Ray, 249
exigent circumstances, 75

Fainaru, Steve, 248
Fainaru-Wada, Mark, 248
Favors, Jeon, 176, 231
Fee, Michael K.
    background, 10, 127–128
    Lloyd murder case/Hernandez and,
      10, 127–128, 138, 139
firearms comparisons, 64–66
floating and drug dealing, 99–101
"forensic experts" and imbalance,
    63–64
forensic science, 64–66
Fourth Amendment
    exceptions, 75
    function, 75
Freire, Aquilino ("Delmar")
    background, 16
    description, 16
    as eyewitness/testimony and, 174,
      175
    girlfriend/baby, 17
    hospital/"gunfight" talk, 72–73, 75,
      220
    shootings/injuries and, 23, 24, 25,
      220
    See also murders (Boston, July
      2012)
Furtado, Jamie
    fan/photo with Hernandez and, 54,
      55, 176–177, 216
    position at Cure Lounge, 20
Furtado, Safiro
    background, 17, 165
    description, 17
    murder of, 23, 25, 26, 27, 30, 32, 172
    murder weapon and, 30
    work of, 17
    See also murders (Boston, July
      2012)

Gobin, Donald
  background/description, 21
  Boston shootings and, 21–23, 24
  as witness/trial, 173
Graham, Jimmy, 123
Gresham, Jermaine, 123
Gronkowski, Rob
  draft, 123
  Hernandez relationship, 125
  Patriots and, 117, 123, 124, 125
Gyles, Shawnn, 5–6

Haggan, Patrick
  Bradley and, 92
  Cure/videos, 52
  description, 91, 113
  Hernandez phone records, 29
  position, 90–91
  prosecuting Hernandez, 29, 52,
    91–92, 113, 165, 190, 193, 199,
    200, 204, 207, 211, 219, 221
Hall-Brewster, Arthur
  murders (July 2012) investigation,
    37–38, 51
  videos and, 51
Harrison, Rodney, 124
Harvey, Paul, 200
Hashem, Sherif
  "anonymous" call/origins and,
    28–29, 36, 38–39, 40–43, 49–50,
    51, 57, 59
  "B" or "G" guy and, 38–39, 40, 43, 51
  background, 28, 36, 50
  defense investigation beginnings
    and, 37–44
  information on murders (Boston,
    July 2012), 28–29, 36, 37–44
  Lloyd/murders (2012) connection
    and, 28, 33, 38, 41, 57

meeting with Baez/Sullivan and,
  52–53
videos from Cure Lounge and,
  49–50, 52–53
Hernandez, Aaron
  on Avielle/Shayanna, 3, 159, 207–208
  background/streets and, 85, 89
  bar fight, Florida, 122, 151
  community service, 258
  description, 11, 13–14, 95–96, 258
  family importance and, 159
  father's death and, 96, 150, 151
  floating/drugs and, 99–101
  funeral/funeral home and, 235, 236,
    237
  lapses in memory and, 13
  protection after Bradley, 103–104
  Puerto Rican heritage, 10, 12
  second autopsy and, 236
  shooting, Gainesville, Florida, and,
    152–153
  See also Lloyd, Odin murder and
    Hernandez; murders (Boston,
    July 2012); sexuality/Hernandez
Hernandez, Aaron, childhood
  birth, 147
  brother/competitiveness, 147, 148,
    157
  father relationship/death and, 147,
    148, 149, 150
  high school sports and, 150
  marijuana use beginnings, 150
Hernandez, Aaron, football
  2010 NFL draft/preparation and,
    94, 98, 99, 120–121, 123, 153–154
  2011 Super Bowl and, 10, 102
  back injury (2010) and, 154
  career summary, 9–10
  housing at college and, 95

John Mackey Award, 97, 122, 249
letter/marijuana use and, 120–121
marijuana/benefits and, 94, 95, 97,
  98
NFL Scouting Combine/publishing
  results, 98, 122, 151, 154
nickname at Florida and, 153
promotional photo shoot, Arizona,
  79, 114
skills/strengths at college and,
  94–95, 122–123, 153
Sugar Bowl and, 153
surgery/rehabilitation, California,
  117–118
University of Florida, 9–10, 94–97,
  150–153
See also New England Patriots
Hernandez, Aaron/prison
  depression and, 3
  disciplinary charges, 144
  dreams of freedom, 2, 3
  image/gangs and, 143–144, 145
  migraines/effects, 2–3
  mother relationship/phone
    conversation, 158–159
  nights and, 2, 3
  religion/Bible and, 3–4, 145, 234
  Shayanna phone calls and, 1–2, 3
  signs of brain problems, 145
  tattoos and, 144
  See also Souza-Baranowski
    Correctional Center, Lancaster,
    Massachusetts; specific
    individuals
Hernandez, Aaron/prison suicide
  attempts to save life, 5–7
  Baez/second autopsy and, 229,
    229–231, 236, 237–239
  death time, 7

evening/night description, 4
floor condition and, 5, 6
guard finding/help and, 4–6
handcuffs and, 5
letters written same evening, xii,
  232–234
method, 4–5
transport to hospital, 6–7
Hernandez, Avielle
  birth date, x, 3, 77, 78, 103, 156
  description, 3
  father and, 1, 3, 140, 159, 208, 212,
    233
  visiting father in prison, 1
  See also Jenkins, Shayanna, and
    Avielle
Hernandez, Bienvenido/Josephine
  Garcia, 147
Hernandez, David/wife and children,
  147, 159
Hernandez, Dennis ("the King")
  background/description, 147
  death/funeral, 149
  football and, 147
  marrying Terri, 147
  sons and, 147
  work of, 147
Hernandez, D. J.
  Boston trial and, 157
  brother's funeral and, 236
  childhood, 147, 148
  Diaz-Ramos and, 58
  father's death and, 149
  football and, 147
  "Jonathan" name and, 157
  on mother/brother, 148–149
Hernandez, Valentine, Terri
  affair/remarriage, 149, 150, 155
  arrest/Aaron on, 148–149, 158

Hernandez, Valentine, Terri (*continued*)
  Boston trial and, 157–159
  celebration/son joining Patriots
    and, 155
  conversation with Aaron, 158–159
  Lloyd murder trial and, 156–157
  marrying Dennis/as mother, 147,
    148
  son's funeral/brain and, 235, 236
  work of, 147, 155, 156
Hodgson, Thomas
  description/media and, 140, 141
  Hernandez and, 141–142
  inmates treatment and, 140–141
homosexuality
  gay marriage and Massachusetts,
    206
  See also sexuality/Hernandez

informants in criminal justice system
  Baez/reasons for not using, 106–107
  deal and, 106
  overview, 106
  "rat" term, 108
  "snitch"/"bitch," 107
  Terri Hernandez and, 158
  See also Bradley, Alexander
    ("Sharrod") murders, July 2012
Innocence Project/movement, 64

Jenkins, Shaneah, 10, 26, 128, 231
Jenkins, Shayanna ("Shay")
  description, 78, 132, 208–209,
    231–232
  Jodi (mother), 231
Jenkins, Shayanna ("Shay"), and
  Avielle
  following Hernandez suicide, xii, 231
  Hernandez on, 3, 159, 207–208

Hernandez protecting, 103–104,
  114, 116, 117, 134–135
move following Hernandez
  conviction (2015), 231
Murphy and, 127
Jenkins, Shayanna ("Shay"), and
  Hernandez
  Boston trial and, x, 159, 206, 207,
    208, 211
  CTE/brain and, ix–x, xi–xii
  elementary school and, 154–155
  engagement, x, 77, 156
  following Hernandez suicide, xi,
    229, 231–232
  funeral and, 235
  Hernandez father's death and, 150
  Hernandez funeral/second autopsy
    and, 235, 236, 237
  Hernandez last letter to, xii,
    233–234
  high school activities, 155
  as high school sweethearts, ix, 1,
    155
  Lloyd murder trial and, x, 143, 157
  phone calls/visits (prison), 1–2,
    146
  relationship, 77–78, 132, 143, 154,
    159, 207–208
  sexuality/Hernandez and, xi,
    208–211
  Shay on, ix–xii
Johnson, Chad (Ocho Cinco), 100
joint venture theory, 109, 130–131
Jones, Craig, 37–38, 39
*Journal of the American Medical
  Association*, 249–250

Karageorge, Kosta, 251
Kay, Kelly, 93, 102, 104–105, 108

Kennedy family, 78–79
King, Michael, 115–116
Kirk & Callahan Show, The, 212
Kraft, Robert
  Hernandez letter/marijuana use
    and, 120–121
  on Hernandez release, 119–120,
    121
  position with New England
    Patriots, 119

Lambert, David, 6
Lawton, Nicholas, 5, 6
League of Denial (Fainaru-Wada and
  Fainaru), 248
Lee, Mark
  Baez and, 199–200
  jury selection/racism and, 163–164
  McMaster and, 185, 186–188, 189
  nicknames from McMaster, 187,
    189
  prosecution/Boston trial, 163–164,
    177–178
legal cases of elite athletes
  agents/managers and, 10
  white-collar crime vs. murder and,
    10
  See also Baez, Jose/Hernandez
    legal case beginnings; *specific
    cases*
Leontire, George
  Baez and, 35
  description, 194–195
  following Hernandez suicide, 229
  Hernandez CTE and, 245
  Hernandez defense and, xii, 35, 161,
    194–195, 213, 214, 225, 226
  prosecution's "closeted gay motive"
    and, 194–195

Levin, Harvey, 230
Lewis, Ray, 78
Lloyd, Odin
  body discovery, 138
  marijuana/Hernandez and, 128
  Shaneah (Shayanna's sister) and,
    10, 26, 128, 231
Lloyd, Odin murder and Hernandez
  arrest/jail
  background/timing, 156
  bail and, 139–140
  becoming suspect and, 26, 138
  Bristol County and, 138–139, 140
  description, 104, 105, 115, 118,
    137–138, 156
  Hodgson and, 140–141
  jail life/conflict, 141–142, 144
  lawyers/access and, 139, 140, 141
  media and, 137–139
  presumption of innocence and,
    138–140
Lloyd, Odin murder trial
  Belichick and, 117, 118–119
  Bradley and, 132, 199
  Bradley threatening Hernandez/
    family and, 134–135
  conviction, 10, 11, 142–143
  Fee and, 10, 127–128, 138, 139
  Hernandez/gun and prosecution
    image of, 129, 132–133, 134–136
  Hernandez past and, 152
  joint venture theory and, 109,
    130–131
  motive (prosecution) and,
    131–133
  Terri (Hernandez mother) and,
    156–157
  videos and phone records, 128–130,
    132–133, 134

Lloyd, Odin murder trial appeal/
  Hernandez
  after Hernandez death and, 258
  as automatic, 142–143
  plans/expectations, 228, 258–259
Locke, Judge
  Baez back problems and, 214
  Boston trial and, 161, 162, 164, 175,
    185, 193, 194, 197, 198, 204, 205,
    214, 215–216, 218, 222, 223, 225
  jury and, 218, 222, 223, 225
Long, Terry, 249
Lopes, Gerson
  description, 16
  leaving the crime scene, 24, 71, 72,
    172, 220
  as witness, 172, 173–174
  See also murders (Boston, July
    2012)
Lyons, Jerry
  background, 63
  Bradley information and, 92
  investigator/Baez team and, 63, 92,
    175–176

MacIsaac, Paul
  crime scene/Boston murders and,
    74, 217, 219
  McMaster and, 182–185
Mackey, John, 249
marathon bombings/suspects (Boston
  2013), 26, 237
marijuana
  football and, 97–98
  medical benefits and, 97–98
  See also specific individuals
Mateen, Omar, 112
McCarthy, Sean, 218
McGovern, Bob, 169

McKee, Ann
  background, 245
  CTE and, 245, 246, 247–248, 250,
    252–253
McMaster, Warren
  description/background, 180
  eyewitness/Boston murders,
    180–181
  police and, 181–187
McPhee, Michelle, 212
McPhee, Pernell
  Super Bowl celebrations and, 79
  Thompson and, 79
Medina, Michelle
  Baez and, 167
  Hernandez CTE and, 245
  Hernandez defense and, xii, 157,
    167, 169, 203–204, 205, 214, 219,
    225–226
  Hernandez talking to, 157, 215
  premonition and, 226
mere presence standard, 131
Meyer, Urban and player arrests, 152
Meyer, Urban/Hernandez
  Florida State University, 3, 94, 95,
    96, 150, 151, 152
  marijuana/behavior and, 94, 95, 96,
    98, 151
  religion and, 3, 96, 145, 151
  senior year and, 96, 153–154
  Shelley (Meyer's wife) and, 152
Minihane, Kirk, 212
Moeaki, Tony, 123
Moss, Randy, 124
"Muck City." See Belle Glade, Florida
murders (Boston, July 2012)
  car given to Hernandez and, 29
  car involved and, 21–22, 27, 28, 29,
    30, 31–33, 38, 39

Cure Lounge/Bradley, 19–20, 27–28, 30, 54–55, 57, 177
Cure Lounge/photo with fan, 27, 54–55, 176–178
Hashem's information and, 28–29, 36, 40–43
Hernandez blaming Bradley, 12
Hernandez indictments, 145
overview, 26–33
See also Bradley, Alexander ("Sharrod"), murders (July 2012)
murders (Boston, July 2012) and defense investigation beginnings
Baez/Sullivan at Cure and, 36–40, 44–45
Freire "gunfight" talk and, 72–73, 75, 220
Hashem's story/questions and, 37–44
police reports and, 35–36
team, 34–35
See also Hashem, Sherif; video from Cure Lounge; *specific components*; *specific individuals*
murders (Boston, July 2012) Cape Verdeans
cookout and, 17, 18, 24
Cure Lounge, Boston, 18–21
friends/immigrants activities overview, 16–22
Gobin/Quon and, 21–23, 24
"gunfight" talk and, 72–73, 75, 220
leak on, 25
shooting injuries/deaths, 22–25
See also specific individuals
murders (Boston, July 2012) crime scene
Cape Verdeans leaving, 23–24, 71, 72, 172, 220

clearing/timing, 68
containing the area and, 69–70
crime scene log and, 69
crime tape distance and, 69
crime tape inside BMW, 76
EMS activities and, 25, 70, 73
first cop on scene/priorities and, 68–69
location of murders, 67–68
number of shots and, 69
police report numbers and, 70–71
street sweeper and, 24–25, 71, 180–189
towing car with bodies and, 73–76
murders (Boston, July 2012) police investigation
beginning/method, 27
delay/possible reasons, 26, 54, 74
description overview, 26–33, 36, 39–40
increasing efforts/Hernandez as suspect, 54
joint venture theory and, 109
police not interviewing Cure patrons, 53–55
relying on Bradley and, 90, 92
See also Hashem, Sherif; video from Cure Lounge; *specific individuals*
murders (Boston, July 2012) trial
Baez opening statement/comments on, 168–169
"closeted gay" motive and, 192–195
crime scene, 171
defense excluding testimony and, 175
defense preparation/delivering closing statement, 213–223
evidence of Bradley lying, 179
eyewitnesses and, 171–179

murders (Boston, July 2012) trial
  (*continued*)
  families (Cape Verdeans) and, 146
  family (Hernandez) and, 146–147,
    157–159
  fan/photo with Hernandez and,
    175–178
  Haggan on Bradley/texts on
    shooting, 166–167
  Haggan opening statement,
    165–166
  Hernandez sexuality and, 206, 207,
    211
  Hernandez/W hotel and, 178–179,
    182
  Jennifer (Hernandez cousin), 159
  jury deliberation/verdict, 223–225
  McMaster/street sweeper and,
    180–189
  "marinating a jury," 200, 204
  motive and, 190–191, 192–195, 216
  prosecution closing statement, 223
  reasonable doubt and, 215, 217, 222
  tattoos and, 195–198
  views of Hernandez and, 165
  witnesses after Hernandez named
    suspect, 173–174
  woman in SUV and, 172, 173, 182,
    219
  women pen pal and, 192–193, 209
murders (Boston, July 2012) trial/
  Bradley
  Baez closing statement and,
    216–222
  Baez questioning, 200–204
  clothes and, 199
  guns and, 202–203
  phone evidence/waiving rights and,
    203–205
    proffer letter/truth and, 201–202,
      216–217, 221
    "Rock"/"Rocky" and, 201, 216–217,
      218, 222
    text messages and, 201, 202
murders (Boston, July 2012) trial/jury
  selection
  Abreu's uncle and, 161–162
  cause/cause challenges, 162–164
  data on potential jurors, 161
  "Deflate Gate" and, 162
  hardship requests/eliminations,
    160–162
  Lloyd case information and, 162
  media coverage and, 162
  prosecution questions to potential
    jurors, 164
  questioning each potential juror,
    161–162, 164
murders (Boston, July 2012), weapon
  antique gun/history and, 61–62, 63,
    65–66, 111
  "ballistics" ("tool mark evidence"), 63
  before/after Hernandez as suspect,
    59–60
  Bradley and, 31, 32, 61, 62–63
  bullet/fragments from victims and,
    59–60
  Camper trial testimony, 65–66
  finding the gun and, 60–61
  firearms comparisons, 64–66
  gun type possibilities and, 29, 60
  serial numbers and, 62
  See also Diaz-Ramos, Jailene;
    weapon
Murphy, Brian
  Bradley's threats to Hernandez
    and, 103, 202
  description, 127

Hernandez and, 98, 103, 127
Shayanna/Avielle and, 127
training facility of, 98
Muscle Milk, 79
Myra Kraft Giving Back Fund, 125

Narvaez, Coleen, 6
Neufeld, Peter, 64
New England Patriots
stadium, 115
See also specific individuals
New England Patriots/Hernandez
2012 season/injuries, 78, 117
advice/help to Hernandez, 117, 118
"Boston TE Party," 124
contract/extension, 10, 11, 25, 77,
99, 120–121, 125, 143, 154, 156
Hernandez jersey exchange and, 121
not supporting Hernandez,
118–119, 121, 125–126
number/selling number, 100
releasing Hernandez/money and,
11, 119–120, 121–122, 125–126
rookie season, 123–125
See also specific individuals
New York Daily News, 148, 212
Newsweek, 212

Ocho Cinco (Johnson, Chad), 100
O'Donnell, Thomas
crime scene and, 24–25
description, 189
street sweeper and, 24–25, 71, 181,
188–189
Ojimba, Ugo, 178
Omalu, Bennet
background, 244
CTE and, 244, 246, 247–249, 250,
251

Ortiz, Carlos
Hernandez hiring/protection,
103–104
Lloyd murder night and, 129, 130
PCP and, 133
Oxygen channel, 209–211

Pavia, Edmond, 6
Pellman, Elliot, 248
peremptory challenges, 162
Phelan, Andrew, 166
Phillips, Lawrence, 252
Pierre, Je'rrelle, 80
police
security guards/private
investigators and, 50
*See also specific individuals; specific
legal cases*
Pouncey, Mike/Maurkice, 95, 151, 153
preponderance of the evidence
standard, 131
presumption of innocence, 12,
138–140
probable cause, 39–40
public defenders and forensic
evidence, 63–64
Pulse nightclub shootings, 112
punishment-driven society (U.S.), 247

Quon, Brian
background/description, 21
Boston shootings and, 21–23, 24
as witness/trial, 172–173

racism in jury selection, 163–164
Ramos, Marilyn, 63
Randolph, Leslie, 112
Rankin, Charles W., 128
Real Sports, 152

reasonable doubt standard, 130–131
Riddle, Kevin, 87
Robinson, Adrian, Jr., 251
Rolling Stone magazine, 143
Rumor nightclub, 131–132
Ryder, Kelly, 6

Salvador, Antoine ("Junior")
　　as eyewitness/testimony, 176–178
　　as fan/photo with Hernandez,
　　　175–178, 180, 216, 217
Sanches, Raychides Gomes
　　cell phone/records and, 72
　　description, 16, 72
　　English language/"white boy" and,
　　　172
　　leaving the scene/burning clothes,
　　　23–24, 71–72, 172, 220
　　shootings/injuries and, 23–24
　　as witness/testimony and, 172, 173,
　　　174, 175
　　See also murders (Boston, July
　　　2012)
Sash, Tyler, 252
scene screens, 70
Scheck, Barry, 48, 64
Seau, Junior, 249, 251
sexuality/Hernandez
　　Baez/Shay talk, 208–209
　　fellow inmate claims and, 242–243
　　relationship with man and,
　　　206–207, 209
　　Shay on, xi
　　Shay's interviews and, 209–211
　　shock jocks and, 212
　　trial/prosecution and, 206, 207, 211
　　woman pen pal and, 192–193, 209
shooting, Gainesville, Florida,
　　152–153

Simpson, O.J.
　　CTE and, 246
　　trial, 34, 48, 64, 237
Singleton, Thaddeus ("T.L.")
　　Hernandez floating/drugs and,
　　　100–101
　　relationships to Hernandez/Tanya
　　　Singleton, 30, 58, 59
Smart, Ljune, 63
Smith, Will, 244
Souza-Baranowski Correctional
　　Center, Lancaster,
　　Massachusetts
　　conflict/violence and, 143
　　description/location, 2, 143
　　Hernandez transfer to, 140, 143
　　history/name, 143
　　See also Hernandez, Aaron/prison
Souza, James, 143
Sports Illustrated, 148–149
"standing" legal principle, 75
street sweeper. *See* McMaster,
　　Warren
Stringer, Lindsey, 223
Sullivan, Marc
　　background, 27
　　description, 36
　　murders (July 2012) investigation,
　　　26–28, 30, 47, 49, 51, 57, 74
　　trial and, 60
Sullivan, Ronald S. ("Sully")
　　background, 11, 34–35
　　Baez and, 11, 34–35
　　Boston trial and, xii, 178, 208, 219,
　　　225
　　description, 35
　　following Hernandez suicide, 229
　　Hernandez brain/CTE and, ix,
　　　239–240, 245